Introducing Marketing Research

Paul Baines

Middlesex University Business School

Bal Chansarkar

Middlesex University Business School

JOHN WILEY & SONS, LTD

Other Wiley Editorial Offices

John Wiley & Sons, Inc., 605 Third Avenue,
New York, NY 10158-0012, USA

WILEY-VCH GmbH, Pappelallee 3,
D-69469 Weinheim, Germany

John Wiley & Sons Australia, 33 Park Road, Milton,
Queensland 4064, Australia

John Wiley & Sons (Asia) Pte Ltd, 2 Clementi Loop #02-01,
Jin Xing Distripark, Singapore 129809

John Wiley & Sons (Canada) Ltd, 22 Worcester Road,
Rexdale, Ontario M9W 1L1, Canada

British Library Cataloguing in Publication Data

A catalogue record for this book is available from the British Library

ISBN 0-471-49770-3

Typeset in 10/12pt Palatino by Mathematical Composition Setters Limited, Salisbury, Wiltshire.
Printed and bound in Great Britain by Biddles Ltd, Guildford and King's Lynn.
This book is printed on acid-free paper responsibly manufactured from sustainable forestry,
in which at least two trees are planted for each one used for paper production.

This text is dedicated to my mum, Carole, and dad, George, for their continuous support throughout my life. PB, London

This text is dedicated to my wife, Katy, and daughter, Priya, for their understanding. BC, London

The authors would like to thank Middlesex University Press for permission to condense, copy and publish parts of the course reader entitled *Introduction to Marketing Research*.

Brief Contents

Contents

CONTENTS

CONTENTS

Foreword by Robert M. Worcester

Just over thirty years ago Gordon Graham, then Chairman of McGraw-Hill Book Company, asked me to edit the *Consumer Market Research Handbook*, which in three editions sold nearly twenty thousand copies over more than two decades around the world. Since then, a number of British authors and editors have put together its successors. Now, a very well-balanced, up-to-date, text for students and handbook for practitioners has been compiled by Paul Baines and Bal Chansarkar of Middlesex University Business School with the help of a number of other contributors. This, in my view, gives the book its strength, as specialist colleagues at Middlesex have been enlisted to contribute their expertise in their fields, while the conception, organization, much of the writing and the compiling were carried out by Baines and Chansarkar.

For years I've claimed somewhat facetiously that research is a simple business, all that is required is to ask the right sample the right questions and add up the figures correctly. Of course there's much more to it than that. Behind asking the right questions is a subtle blend of psychology, semantics, languages, and logic. To frame a single question isn't simple; to construct a complex questionnaire is always a huge challenge. Still the best book on the subject of survey and questionnaire design, published originally in 1951 by Princeton University Press and now out of print after more than 20 reprints, is Stanley L. Payne's *The Art of Asking Questions*. I have mentioned his book's title to explain simply what survey research is, as a 'marriage of the art of asking questions and the science of sampling'.

Looking through *Introducing Marketing Research*, I am pleased to see that Baines and Chansarkar's coverage is more comprehensive and instructive than was our own, especially in our first edition. They start with a useful overview of what market research is and how the industry is organized, which we neglected. Their second chapter gets down to how to go about actually doing a market research survey, explaining the market research process of problem definition, deciding the research plan, data collection, data analysis and interpretation, and finally report preparation and presentation. All good stuff, and mostly neglected in the *CMRH*, all 800-plus pages of it, which in the first edition began with a chapter on qualitative research (Chapter 4 in Baines and Chansarkar) and their Chapter 3, on desk research and secondary data collection, didn't make it into the *CMRH* until the second edition.

Chapters on Internet research and B2B research are also useful additions, and the former is playing an increasingly important role in data collection; their warnings of representativeness of the sample obtained using the Internet are salutary, and contrast with the careful approaches outlined in Chapter 7, on sampling.

Another useful feature of the book is a comprehensive glossary. This one is 'bang up to date', with not only the definitions of CAPI and CATI, but CAWI as well.

All in all, this book is a good addition to the texts we now have to choose from on the subject of market research. Both the student who learns from this book, and the practitioner who uses it as a guide, will be well served.

Robert M. Worcester, FMRS
Chairman, MORI
Visiting Professor, LSE

Foreword by David Smith

The market research industry is facing many dramatic changes that are taking it into a new information era. This era is characterized by the need for market researchers to now operate on a much wider marketing information canvas than ever before, and to deploy a wide range of new techniques in order to make sense of the often confused and contradictory signals contained within available marketing data. But as market research edges into this new information era, it remains important for the industry not to lose sight of its traditional roots in the more purist classical, social science-based methodologies. This focus on the fundamentals is important both for young practitioners, who need to know the boundaries of the growing interest in more pragmatic approaches, and is also critical to students being introduced to market research for the first time.

Thus, in this book by Baines and Chansarkar – which provides us with all the information we need to understand the fundamental tenets and principles of professional market research – we have an excellent text for newcomers to market research, particularly students studying the subject as an introductory module or via a single semester course. The book provides, in an extremely well written and clear way, a detailed description and account of how market research works. Each chapter specifies clear learning outcomes and also provides a clear set of references, together with a range of interesting work assignments in order to reinforce the points being made in each chapter.

The first part of the book on research design and methods will provide students with all they need to know about the process of undertaking desk research, qualitative and survey research. Then in Part II of the book – statistical considerations – there are detailed introductions to sampling and statistical testing in market research. In Part III various marketing research contexts or scenarios are reviewed. Thus, we find a chapter on International Marketing Research which will alert the reader to the potential, and also to the pitfalls, of undertaking market research on an international basis. Then, given the growing use of the Internet for marketing research purposes, Chapter 11 discusses the role of the Internet, both as a source of secondary data, and as a basis for conducting on-line surveys. There is also a detailed review of the way in which business-to-business research differs from consumer market research.

So, in sum, Baines and Chansarkar provide an authoritative review of market research: their new book provides a comprehensive framework for students keen to study the basics of market research. From the standpoint of the primary audience of the book – students undertaking an introductory market research course – Baines and Chansarkar have prepared an extremely professional and helpful publication.

Dr David Smith
Chairman, Citigate DVL
Visiting Professor at the University of Hertfordshire Business School

Preface

This textbook emerged as a result of teaching marketing research on undergraduate programmes at Middlesex University Business School. Its unique feature is a balance between statistical and non-statistical aspects of marketing research. We have made special attempts to include actual material from current marketing research consultancy projects with which we have been involved.

We have used a number of the marketing group staff, within the school, who have expertise in their own particular areas. Special thanks must go to Lynn Vos who produced Chapter 3 on desk research and worked hard to make Appendix I as inclusive as possible. Dr Martine Spence contributed much of the material for Chapter 10 despite being incredibly busy. Dr Androulla Michaeloudis contributed some of the material for Chapter 6 on data analysis and basic statistics. We would like to thank Professor Ifan Shepherd for contributing Chapter 11—an important chapter in view of the recent changes in the research market and the current focus of much attention—and Dr Ross Brennan for writing Chapter 12 on business-to-business marketing research. The latter area is often left out of textbooks of this nature, despite its obvious significance. We would also like to thank the many anonymous reviewers for their helpful comments, many of which were incorporated into the final manuscript. Thanks particularly to those reviewers who made specific recommendations on material to be included to improve the text. We would like to thank the team at Wiley, particularly the commissioning editors, Steve Hardman and Sarah Booth, the production editor, Catherine Braund, and the marketing manager, Peter Hudson.

The text has been specially designed to cater for semesterized teaching of marketing research. Each chapter can be regarded as a lecture in its own right. Powerpoint slides have been produced for each chapter in order to aid the lecturer in delivering their lectures. Answers to work assignments are also available to both lecturers and students. In order to access this material, please visit the following website: http://www.wiley.co.uk/baines

The text attempts to cover, in brief, the major components of a marketing research project. As such, this text is a useful guide for practising marketing research managers either as those who commission marketing research projects or as those who conduct them. The text considers distinct marketing research topics, chapter by chapter. Chapter One contains an introduction to the market research industry and attempts to provide the reader with an insight into the different marketing research methods. There is also a brief consideration of marketing research ethics. Chapter Two illustrates the marketing research process and the way in which research projects are designed by using real-life examples. The procedures associated with designing the marketing research project are outlined. There is an attempt within the chapter to illustrate the links between the research objectives, the interviewing methods, question and questionnaire design, the research type and methods undertaken, the sampling method and the data analysis methods used. Thus, this chapter links many of the other chapters. Chapter Three deals with the process of desk research and secondary data collection. Chapter Four explains the different qualitative research methods and in what circumstances they are appropriate. Chapter Five covers the design of surveys and questionnaires. Chapter Six has been written to aid the students' understanding of the basic concepts essential for understanding data and its analysis. Chapter Seven describes different methods of sampling and explains clearly how to select a sample of a given size and in what circumstances. Chapter Eight demonstrates the hypothesis-testing process and explains tests of association such as Chi-square, Spearman's rank correlation and Pearson's product-moment correlation. Chapter Nine explains hypothesis testing as applicable to large and small sample sizes and tests of differences. It specifically introduces the student to Z- and t-tests. Chapter Ten provides readers with an insight into international marketing research and attempts to explain the complexity of conducting research in the international environment. Finally, Chapter Eleven outlines the principles associated with conducting on-line research, comparing the methods used with traditional off-line data collection. Chapter Twelve describes the type of research undertaken in business-to-business markets.

The text is organized into three parts. Part I is designed to provide the reader with an understanding of research methods in marketing research. Part II provides an outline of the important statistical considerations often used in marketing research projects. Finally, Part III is an attempt to provide the context within which marketing research projects are undertaken. It is likely that some readers may not be *au fait* with particular jargon and phrases used in the market research industry. Rather than leaving such terms out, we have written the chapters with these terms in, but have provided a detailed glossary at the end of the text for reference. That way, readers can become acquainted with the language used in the industry.

We suggest that the book will be useful as a core text for undergraduate marketing students studying marketing research. In addition, it will also be a useful introductory text for postgraduate marketing students and those studying for the Diploma of the Market Research Society. It also serves as a useful guide for practising market researchers, or marketing managers commissioning market research. We hope you enjoy the text!

Dr Paul Baines
Dr Bal Chansarkar
Middlesex University Business School
London
October 2001

About the Authors

Dr Paul Baines is Senior Lecturer in Marketing and Director of Business Development at Middlesex University Business School. His primary professional interests lie in researching political marketing and the marketing of other mass consumer services. He has published articles on political marketing in numerous journals including *Qualitative Market Research*, *International Journal of Market Research*, *European Journal of Marketing*, *Marketing Intelligence and Planning*, *Journal of Communication Management* and others. Paul has a PhD in political marketing from Manchester School of Management at UMIST. He has also conducted market research consultancy for a number of large organizations including an aerospace maintenance company, a popular London football club, a sales promotion agency and others. Paul is a Member of the Chartered Institute of Marketing, a Chartered Marketer and a Full Member of the Market Research Society. His principal interests outside work include good wine, conversation, reading, cinema and theatre, and travel.

Dr Bal Chansarkar is Principal Lecturer in Statistics at Middlesex University Business School. Bal has a PhD in statistics from Nagpur University, India. His primary professional interests lie in researching and consulting in the pharmaceutical industry and the healthcare market, particularly in consumer profiling and product–company performance measurement. He has published in the *International Journal of Mathematical Education*, *International Journal of Healthcare Quality Assurance* and the *International Journal of Management*. He has also produced two textbooks on economic planning and multivariate analysis and has been active in developing management programmes in India, Poland and China. Bal is a Full Member of the Market Research Society, the Royal Statistical Society and the Royal Economic Society. He has been a former chair of the Association of Statistics Lecturers in Universities (ASLU). In his previous life, he was a Senior Market Research Executive with Watney–Mann Limited for seven years. Outside work, he enjoys travelling widely.

About the Contributors

Dr Ross Brennan is Principal Lecturer in Marketing, and chairperson of the Marketing Group at Middlesex University Business School. His primary professional interests lie in business-to-business marketing, and he has published papers and articles on business-to-business marketing at international conferences, in professional marketing journals, and in academic journals such as *Industrial Marketing Management* and the *Journal of Marketing Management*. Ross holds a PhD in business-to-business marketing from UMIST (Manchester), is a Member of the Chartered Institute of Marketing, and a Chartered Marketer. Outside of the world of marketing Ross is a keen amateur chess player—a former North London open champion, member of the Hertfordshire county team, and enthusiastic supporter of the Internet Chess Club. When time allows he likes to climb mountains, preferably by the more perilous routes.

Dr Androulla Michaeloudis is Senior Lecturer in Statistics at Middlesex University Business School. She obtained her PhD in medical statistics in 1986 at North East London Polytechnic. She has taught statistics to both 'A' level and degree level standard as well as mathematics and statistics to students on undergraduate and postgraduate degree courses in Engineering, Business Administration, Marketing, Management and Finance. She has supervised statistical projects for undergraduate students working in industry. She has previously worked as a statistical consultant in the Royal Berkshire hospital and participated in research on iron deficiency anaemia. Recent research and publications are based on the linear structural relation of the errors in variables model to student performance in Quantitative Methods courses.

Ifan Shepherd is Professor of GeoBusiness at Middlesex University Business School (MUBS). He is Programme Leader of the MA Electronic Business, and teaches courses in geodemographics, GIS, and on-line consumer behaviour. For the past three years, he has coordinated a School-wide project to develop the use of communication technologies. Research interests include data visualization, computer mapping of social information, and the evaluation of information quality on the Internet. Ifan has been active in educational research for most of his working life, having published widely on this subject including two textbooks. He was awarded the 2001 Royal Geographical Society prize for contributions to research in computer-assisted learning. He is a founding member, former editor and continuing editorial board member of the *Journal of Geography in Higher Education*. For the past four years, Ifan has been critically exploring the conceptualization of key skills based on research funded by a grant from the Department for Education and Employment. He has recently set up the Centre for Transfer Research and Applications (CenTRA) at MUBS to convert this line of research into practical applications. Ifan relaxes in the gym, on the roads and on the pistes!

Dr Martine Spence is currently at the Faculty of Administration, University of Ottawa in Canada as Professeure Adjointe. She was previously a Research Assistant and then Senior Lecturer in Marketing at Middlesex University Business School between 1994 and 2000 where she obtained her PhD in marketing. She has also taught courses in international marketing and management strategy at Concordia University, McGill University and HEC in Canada. Her principal research interests are in intercultural marketing and management, and the internationalization of small business. She has published in the *Journal of International Business Education*, *The International Journal of Public–Private Partnerships* and the *Euromarketing Journal*. In her previous life, she advised small business owners on start-up and international development.

Lynn Vos is Senior Lecturer in Marketing at Middlesex University Business School. Previously she was employed at Kwantlen University College in Vancouver, Canada. Her principal teaching interests include marketing research, Internet marketing, and global marketing. She has co-published a textbook on global marketing. Her consultancy interests are in healthcare and Internet marketing. Previous clients include an Internet-based health service, a professional healthcare association and an overseas arts institute. Her principal interests outside work include the arts, philosophy and international relations.

PART I

Research design and methods

Introduction to Marketing Research **1**

Learning Outcomes

After reading this chapter, you will be able to:

- Understand what marketing research is.
- Appreciate the role marketing research plays in the marketing process.
- Know the major players in the market research industry in the UK.
- Choose who should conduct the marketing research.
- Understand and recognize the importance of ethics and the code of conduct for undertaking marketing research.

Introduction

This chapter begins with a definition of what marketing research is and then looks at the three research designs commonly used in the marketing research process. A brief description of the marketing research industry follows, giving the top marketing research agencies in the UK and the percentage turnover by the market research method. It then discusses who should do the marketing research and the importance of the code of conduct as recommended by the Market Research Society.

What is Marketing Research?

The primary purpose of marketing research is to gather information which will allow your company or organization to make better, more informed decisions. Marketing research is closely linked to the marketing concept as it implies a customer focus, that the customer is central to the activities of the company, and the opinions of the customer are a highly valued and useful aid in decision making.

Researching customer needs through marketing research enables the company to fulfil the requirements of the marketing concept.

The terms marketing research and market research are interchangeable in their scope and coverage of information. This is explicitly brought out by the definitions of the American Marketing Association (AMA) and the UK's Market Research Society (MRS).

According to the American Marketing Association, marketing research is defined as:

> the function which links consumer, customer, and public to the market through information—information used to identify and define marketing opportunities and problems; generate, refine, and evaluate marketing actions; monitor marketing performance; and improve understanding of marketing as a process. Marketing research specifies the information required to address these issues; designs the method for collecting information; manages and implements the data collection process: analyses the results; and communicates the findings and their implications. (*Marketing News*, 1985)

The Market Research Society (in the UK) defines market research as:

> the collection and analysis of data from a sample of individuals or organisations relating to their characteristics, behaviour, attitudes, opinions or possessions. It includes all forms of marketing and social research such as consumer and industrial surveys, psychological investigations, observational and panel studies. (MRS, 1994)

However, marketing research and market research are not interchangeable terms. Market research is sometimes described as consumer/business research whereas marketing research looks into marketing strategy problems and as such is considered to subsume market research. This text covers market research particularly and touches upon aspects of marketing research.

Marketing research covers all aspects of the marketing of goods and services. There are various ways of classifying these aspects into categories according to the activity involved such as product research, price research, pricing research, sales research, customer research, and promotion research (Chisnall, 1992). Product research deals with the design, development, and testing of new products, the viability of existing products and estimating the demand in relation to consumers' future preferences in relation to style, product performance, and competition. Sales research involves a detailed examination of a company's selling activities. This is usually carried out using sales outlets or marketing zones and is analysed over a specified time period to enable direct comparisons over time and also with published data. Customer research usually deals with buyer behaviour—researching the social, economic and psychological influences affecting purchase decisions taken under different situations at the consumer, trade or industrial level. Such research covers the consumers' attitudes and opinions, and impact of different marketing practices that a company may adopt in the market. Pricing research deals with decisions all businesses have to make about the cost to the buyer of their goods and services. It is one of the critical factors affecting business success. It requires a creative and analytical approach to judge the sensitivity of price changes, effectiveness of relative positioning, and to estimate demand in a competitive market. Finally, promotional research is concerned with testing and evaluating the effectiveness of the various methods used in developing and promoting a company's product or services. Marketing research provides decision makers with information that allows the reduction of uncertainty surrounding business decisions.

Designing Marketing Research

There are three major categories of research designs: exploratory, descriptive and causal. Each relate to the role they play in the marketing research process. They specify the procedure for collecting and analysing the data necessary to help to identify a problem, such that it maximizes the difference between the cost of obtaining the information and the expected value of information associated with each level of accuracy.

Exploratory designs involve discovering the general nature of a problem and variables that relate to it. It enables the formulation of relevant hypotheses. These designs generally tend to be of a qualitative nature and use primary techniques such as focus groups, in-depth interviews and observational studies. It also uses secondary data, non-probability (subjective) samples, case analysis and subjective evaluation of the resultant data. Descriptive designs, on the other hand, focus on the accurate description of the variables under consideration and are quantitative in nature. They commonly use questionnaires and surveys and are employed for consumer profile and product usage studies, price and attitude surveys, sales analyses, and media research.

Causal designs try to establish the nature of relationship (or association) between two or more variables under investigation, for example study of price elasticity of demand and measuring advertising effectiveness in terms of sales or attitude changes. There is a need for caution in using such designs, as the direction of the causal link is quite important. For example, in the case of advertising effectiveness it is assumed that advertising causes sales to increase rather than vice versa. Further, the links, though strong, may be spurious (not logical/meaningful) in nature, for example sales being linked to the marital status of the salesforce. However, one can always find some explanation or a logical link between two measurements. Causal designs allow use of control variables or groups to facilitate meaningful comparisons between the outcomes. Watney–Mann Ltd, a brewer, in a study to measure advertising effectiveness of its 'best bitter' which was advertised used the 'mild beer' as a control (a similar product but not advertised). Mild beer (the control—used as one of the independent variables in the regression analysis) was allowed to generally account for the market conditions. It thus eliminated other factors affecting the sales and enabled measurement of the true effect of advertising. Experimentation is widely used in these designs.

The UK Marketing Research Industry

The marketing research industry in the UK is one of the most advanced in the world. It went through a lean period in the early 1990s with continual increases in annual turnover in the later years. In many cases companies turn to the marketing research budget when they are forced to make cost savings. This is not unusual, as marketing expenditure, which does not always show a clear and measurable return, is often the first to be cut when growth begins to slow.

Table 1.1 outlines the top marketing research agencies in the UK according to the Annual Report of the British Market Research Association (BMRA, 2000).

The BMRA, the trade body that represents UK market research companies, was formed in 1998 with the merger of the Association of Market Survey Organizations (AMSO) and the Association of British Market Research Companies (ABMRC). The BMRA experienced a substantial increase in membership during the 1990s, and in 1999, the market research sector was worth at least £1 billion (BMRA, 2000). The membership now includes approximately 80% of the total marketing research industry in the UK. Between them, these companies carried out approximately 9.5 million marketing research interviews in 1999. According to the AMSO, the majority of marketing research interviews in the UK are personal interviews (47.4%) and telephone interviews (40.3%). Although Web/Internet interviews accounted for only 1%, these are increasing at a very fast rate (BMRA, 2000).

The Market Research Society is the professional society for organizational and individual membership in the UK. The society was established in 1947 and is the largest body of its kind in the world today. There are a number of other professional associations and societies in the world of marketing research in the UK. The Industrial

Table 1.1 Top marketing research companies and their world ranking

Market research organization	UK turnover (£ million)	World ranking
1. Taylor Nelson Sofres plc	102	3
2. NOP Research Group Ltd	70	4
3. Research International Ltd	60	1
4. Millward Brown International plc	58	2
5. NFO UK (Infratest Burke Group + MBL Group plc + City Research Group plc)	39	6
6. BMRB International	36	8
7. Ipsos-RSL Ltd	34	12
8. Information Resources	25	n/a
9. Maritz–TRBI Ltd	24	5
10. MORI (Market & Opinion Research International)	21	19

n/a = not available.

Source: BMRA Turnover Summary Year 1999 (BMRA, 2000). Reproduced by permission of the BMRA.

Table 1.2 Total turnover by type of research in the UK

Percentage turnover by market research method	
Type of research	%
Face-to-face interviews	32.9
Telephone interviews	19.5
Discussion groups	8.8
Consumer panels	8.3
Postal/self-completion	8.0
Hall/central location tests	7.7
Retail audits	4.5
In-depth interviews	3.6
Street interviews	2.0
Observation	0.3
Web/Internet interview	0.2
Other methods	4.2
Total	100.0

Source: BMRA (2000). Reproduced by permission of the BMRA.

Market Research Association (IMRA), founded in 1982, and the Association of Qualitative Research Practitioners (AQRP), with an individual membership of over 500, are examples.

The marketing research industry uses different methods—observation, group discussions, personal interviews and surveys—for primary data collection. Table 1.2 shows the percentage of the total turnover generated during 1999 by BMRA members by type of method.

Who Conducts the Marketing Research?

Who should do the marketing research depends on size of the organization and the type of products it handles. Most of the large companies have some kind of marketing department and employ outside market research agencies to conduct research and support on their behalf. Small companies generally either are not involved or resort to *ad hoc* research. Companies with their own departments may consist of perhaps either (1) a small section of, say, two or three executive staff, plus administrative support or (2) a large department which can function as an in-house research department. The large department may have its own fieldforce, telephone and computer facilities and employ its own specialist staff, market researchers, psychologists and statisticians. The function of the executives of such a department would be to evaluate and circulate relevant information (for example, financial and trade press). In addition, they would act as the management's liaison with the sub-contracted research agency. Depending upon their ability and experience they may carry out some functions themselves, (for example, writing the questionnaire and/or the report), while leaving the sampling, fieldwork, coding and data analysis to the agency. They would have responsibility for selecting the agency and controlling the quality of their work, including keeping time schedules. They have to agree the research methodology and budget between the relevant persons in the marketing and market research departments. As such, the work of a large 'in-house' research department is similar to that employed in an external agency.

Which Agency to Select?

Two main advantages of using an agency are that it is relatively cheap compared with carrying out the research in-house and the data is collected independently. The fixed cost of recruiting, training and maintaining a large panel of interviewers and specialist staff is prohibitive unless the organization has a constant stream of research projects. The agency spreads these costs over many clients/projects throughout the year. There is fierce competition between agencies, which helps to keep their charges down to the variable costs of each survey plus a contribution towards fixed costs and profits. The agency will often specialize in a particular technique and become very efficient at performing it. They are also not involved in the emotional or political sense and can be more objective than the client's own staff in the research design and reporting. It is often preferable that the client remains anonymous to retain the objectivity of the study and increase the response rate to the investigation.

The main disadvantages of using an agency are that it cannot achieve the depth of knowledge of the client's problems nor of the product or market, unless it continuously researches the same area. With less day-to-day control there is an increased possibility of poor-quality research being carried out as well as rival organizations learning of the client's plans and research findings. The latter disadvantage is perhaps more apparent than real, since a client's staff may leave and join a rival. In many syndicated surveys (for example, retail audits and omnibus surveys) several rival organizations buy the same data from the agency, so that a cost-effective survey can be carried out. For this data to be useful, it needs to be viewed long term as the surveys indicate both short-term tactical performance and long-term trends.

In order to commission market research, the client can obtain a list of agencies (see The *Market Research Society Yearbook* in the UK) and might receive recommendations from other research buyers, i.e., trade associations, advertising agencies, colleagues, friends, and academic institutions. These are sought to draw up a short-list. Agencies that are then short-listed are asked make a 'presentation' of their services. Usually visits are made to their premises to check the quality of their staff and facilities, perhaps some interviewers are accompanied for several days to assess their quality and training, and previous reports may be read and permission sought to interview, or obtain references from, some of their other clients.

Each agency would be evaluated on its ability to carry out work of acceptable quality at an acceptable price within the stipulated time period. This could depend upon the following evaluations: (1) their staff-specialist technical ability, creativity, experience, length of service-stability, education and training, numbers employed and participation in MRS activities, conferences and published papers; and (2) their facilities, e.g., data processing, in-house editing and coding, group discussion rooms and printing and quality control procedures.

Short-listed agencies are then given a preliminary outline of the client's needs and are asked to put forward proposals on research methodology, timing and costs. One or more is then selected and a brief is agreed between the agency and the client. In the UK, there are agencies which specialize in certain aspects of marketing research (qualitative research and data analysis) and there are a number of freelance consultants who are employed on an *ad hoc* basis (see the *Market Research Society Yearbook*, 2001).

Marketing Research and Ethics

The marketing research industry gathers information about individuals as consumers and this is usually stored on computers. The processing power of these data banks of consumer information is consistently increasing. However, this description is exaggerated, as collection of such information is subject to the Data Protection Act 1998. Many supermarkets now employ customer-loyalty schemes in which, in exchange for their continued custom, supermarkets will provide their customers with loyalty points, which may be cashed. The more money the customer spends, the more points he or she receives. However, the true value of these schemes lies in their massive consumption information-gathering capability. Each time a customer reaches the checkout their purchases are recorded at the till with the aid of a barcode reader and the grocery list is matched with the customer's details when the loyalty card details are entered. The supermarket now has a record of all the customer's weekly groceries conveniently matched with their personal details from their loyalty card. It is a short step from gathering this information to analysing an individual household's consumption patterns over a short period of time and predicting when that household will again require certain basic household products.

Marketing research is based on the cooperation of the individuals or organizations that provide the answers or fill in the questionnaires. In order to maintain this cooperation and the flow of information required by researchers, marketing research should be carried out in an objective, unintrusive and honest manner. The aim of marketing research should be to collect data for the purposes of examining consumer behaviour and attitudes. Marketing research should neither attempt to induce sales of a product nor influence consumer attitudes, or intentions of behaviours. When there is no control as to who collects the information and the purpose for which the information is collected, there is danger of overloading the respondent to fill in too many questionnaires.

The key principles of professional market research—founded on honesty, objectivity, confidentiality and transparency—come from the Code of Conduct drawn up by the Market Research Society in the UK. It is designed to support all those engaged in marketing or social research in maintaining professional standards throughout the industry. Key principles of market research are:

- *Honesty* Respondents must not be misled when asked for their cooperation.
- *Objectivity* The main purpose of the research should be to collect and analyse information. It should not influence the opinions of the participants.
- *Confidentiality* All parties are assured that they will not be identified and the information collected will not be disclosed to anyone else.
- *Transparency* Respondents are informed as to the purpose of the research and the time necessary for collection of the information.

The new Code of Conduct—based on the ESOMAR (European Society for Opinion and Market Research) Code—is binding on all members of the MRS, as is adherence to the principles of the Data Protection Act 1998. The MRS has developed a detailed Code of Conduct, which outlines the main principles of marketing research. The basic aims of this code are that the privacy of the public or respondent be respected, that the information they provide be used only for the research purpose in question, and that the research results be reported honestly and accurately. A copy of the full Code of Conduct is available from the Market Research Society.

General Principles

Research is founded on willing cooperation. It depends upon confidence that it is conducted honestly, objectively and without unwelcome intrusion or harm to respondents. Its purpose is to collect and analyse information, and not directly to create sales nor to influence the opinions of anyone participating in it. In this context telephone interviewing is getting a rather tainted image as it is often confused by the respondents with telephone selling.

The general public and other interested parties will be entitled to complete assurance that no information collected in a research survey, which could be used to identify them, will be disclosed without their agreement. Also, that the information they supply will not be used for purposes other than research and that they will in no way be adversely affected as a result of participation. This has implications for the conduct of the research studies, which need to identify respondents, either for sending reminders to increase the response rate or collecting follow-up information or selecting a sub-sample for further in-depth interviews. Wherever possible, respondents must be informed as to the purpose of the research and the likely length of time necessary for the collection of the information. Further, research findings must always be reported accurately and never used to mislead anyone, in any way. In conducting any marketing research, therefore, researchers have responsibility for themselves, their clients and the respondents from whom the information is being gathered.

Responsibilities to Respondents

Respondents' cooperation is entirely voluntary and their anonymity must be strictly preserved. As mentioned above, they should not be misled when being asked for cooperation. Respondents should be told if observation techniques or recording equipment are used. This sometimes results in respondents refusing to participate in the investigation due to fear of being recognized/identified. If this occurs, they should be allowed to leave the study immediately.

Researchers must take special care when interviewing young children, young people and other potentially vulnerable members of society. The informed consent of the parent or responsible adult must first be obtained for interviews with children—classified as under the age of 16 years. Respondents should be enabled to check, without difficulty, the identity and bona fides of the researcher.

Professional Responsibility of Researchers

When acting in their capacity as researchers, they must not undertake any non-research activities, for example database marketing involving collecting data on individuals which will not be used for sales or promotional activity. Permission from the respondents is usually sought during the investigation when the researcher wishes to use the information collected for further follow-up investigation. Any such non-research activities must always be clearly differentiated from marketing research activities. The Market Research Society's code of conduct requires that members shall ensure that the people (including clients, colleagues and sub-contractors) with whom they work are sufficiently familiar with the Code of Conduct and that the Code is unlikely to be breached through ignorance of its provisions.

Responsibilities to Client

Researchers must not disclose the identity of the client or any confidential information about the latter's business, to any third party, without the client's permission. They must provide the client with all appropriate technical details of any research project carried out for that client. Researchers must ensure that clients are aware of the Code of Conduct and of the need to comply with its requirements.

Thus, researchers are bound to protect the identity of informants. This information must not be revealed without their consent to any person not directly involved in the marketing research project in question. The outcome or results of the research should not be used for any purpose other than those of the research project. No respondent or participant should be embarrassed or adversely affected by participating in the research. Marketing researchers should always carry and show some form of identity card including details of the agency running the research project. The privacy of participants or potential participants must be respected and upheld at all times. The participant must reserve the right to withdraw from the study at any time as they wish. Children under the age of 16 should not be interviewed without the consent of a parent or guardian.

Selling, fundraising or other similar activities should not be presented as marketing research. All marketing research should be honest and objective. The findings of this research should not be used to mislead in any way. Most agencies present data in a relatively unbiased form leaving strategic interpretation to the client or a consulting third party.

The identity of the client for whom the research agency is carrying out the research should remain confidential. The results of such studies should also be confidential unless agreed by the client and agency. The agency should provide detailed accounts of the methods employed to carry out the research project.

Conclusion

Marketing research covers all aspects of the marketing of goods and services. Three categories of research designs—exploratory, descriptive and causal—play an important role in understanding and aiding decisions undertaken during the marketing process. The Market Research Society is the main professional body for members in the UK. The British Market Research Association represents many UK market research companies. The market research industry in UK was worth at least £1 billion in 1999. The top five market research agencies in the UK were: Taylor Nelson Sofres plc, NOP Research Group Ltd, Research International Ltd, Millward Brown International plc and NFO UK. Two interviewing methods (face-to-face and telephone), account for more than half of the total UK turnover. The Market Research Society has developed a Code of Conduct, which is to be adhered to by members. This ensures that members follow the key principles of honesty, objectivity, confidentiality and transparency. Thus, it protects and specifies the responsibility the researchers have towards the respondents (the public) and their clients.

References

British Market Research Association (2000). *AMSO Annual Report*, London: BMRA.

Chisnall P.M. (1992). *Marketing Research* (4th edn), Maidenhead: McGraw-Hill.

Kent R. (1993). *Marketing Research in Action*, London: Routledge.

Marketing News (1985). 'AMA board approves new marketing definitions', 1 March.

Marketing Research Society (2000). *The Research Buyer's Guide*, London: MRS.

Tull D.S. and Hawkins D.I. (1993). *Marketing Research: Measurement and Methods* (6th edn), Englewood Cliffs, NJ: Prentice-Hall.

Work Assignments

1. Your company is a leader holding 40% of the market in clothes for young people between the ages of 18 and 30 years and has been trading for the past ten years. The market share of your company has been declining for the last year. The company is facing increased competition in the market and is proposing to introduce a 'new line of clothes'. It needs information on its competition and

acceptability of the 'new line of clothes' it is developing. Suggest a suitable research design for:

   (i) Collecting information about competition.
  (ii) Deciding the need for the 'new line of clothes' and its acceptability.

2. Plastique Ltd is a medium-sized company in the plastic mouldings business. They compete for a well-defined market segment, within which they have a 20% market share, making them number two in the market after Alpha Plastics plc, which is believed to have a share of 45%. Plastique Ltd relies heavily on this segment, from which they derive 75% of their revenue and around 90% of their profits. Recent attempts to identify profitable opportunities for product or market development have been unsuccessful, leading the managing director to conclude that the company will have to rely on this market for survival and growth for the foreseeable future. In view of this, the MD was very concerned to hear a rumour that Alpha Plastics plc might have developed a new plastic moulding process, which would enable it to improve quality while reducing prices by as much as 15%. She is determined to find out as much as possible about the Alpha Plastics plc development, as quickly as possible, in order to develop a counter-strategy. In her view, the survival of Plastique Ltd probably depends on her ability to obtain and exploit meaningful information quickly. Her job, and those of the 50 other people working for the company, could be at stake.

    She is considering a number of possibilities to obtain the market intelligence that she requires:

   (i) Carry out a detailed search of the plastic mouldings trade press to see whether any information has leaked out of Alpha Plastics plc.
  (ii) Persuade her production supervisor to apply for the job of production manager at Alpha Plastics (currently vacant) and to use the interview and plant visit as an intelligence-gathering opportunity.
 (iii) Speak informally to known customers of Alpha Plastics, and ask them what they know about the new production technique.

Make a judgement on the ethics of the above possibilities and recommend a research design appropriate for this situation.

Marketing Research: Process and Design

2

Introduction

This chapter begins with a consideration of the marketing research process. It goes on to describe the three major categories of research before introducing the reader to concepts of qualitative and quantitative, and primary and secondary, research. Factors affecting the design of research studies are also highlighted. The process of marketing research is highlighted using the real-life example of a London football club for each stage of the process. This chapter aims to provide the reader with an understanding of the process of how research projects are designed. The case study used was, at that time, a Second Division football club (renamed London FC to respect the privacy of the actual organization). The club commissioned a marketing research study to determine current levels of supporter satisfaction, to provide a profile of their supporter base and to provide an understanding of the supporters' relative interest in a variety of commercial services offered by the club. The club was also interested in the supporters' perceptions of its image. This chapter is particularly important since it provides the background knowledge that is necessary for understanding later chapters. The reader is therefore asked to read it particularly carefully.

The Marketing Research Process

In this section the research process is outlined. There are probably as many different models of this process as there are textbooks on marketing research. Although each of the models may vary, there are a number of basic stages that should guide any marketing research project and this process is outlined in Figure 2.1.

The first, and probably the most crucial, stage of the process involves defining the problem, then subsequently setting the information needs of the decision makers. At this stage, the client organization explains the basis of the problem(s) it faces to the market research organization (MRO) or internal company research department. This can range from an unexplained drop in sales units or a lack of market information required to aid the decision to launch a new product or enter a new market. Thus, problem definition does not always imply threats facing the organization. The 'problem' could be that the client organization is having difficulties in determining which markets provide the greatest potential.

Thus, this initial stage allows the organization to assess its current position, to define its information needs and to allow it to make informed decisions about its future. The marketing research process indicated will be further examined by referring to the London Football Club research proposal (see Chapter Appendix).

Stage 1—Problem Definition

The process of commissioning research generally occurs when an organization provides the MRO with a marketing research brief, which is a description of the management problem, often in relatively vague terms. An example might be a

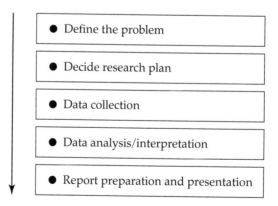

Figure 2.1 The marketing research process

fashion clothes retailer explaining that sales are down in its stores in the northwest region of the UK and that this could be due to the emergence of a new competitor. This problem is shown in Box 2.1. Usually, it is necessary for the marketing researcher to translate the management problem to a marketing research question.

Box 2.1   Example of a management problem

There has been a decline in sales, probably due to the emergence of a competitor with a superior product range.

This description of the problem provides the market researcher with relatively little depth of understanding of the situation in which the fashion clothes retailer finds itself. Thus, it becomes important at this stage for the market researcher to interview the staff commissioning the study and any other relevant personnel who can shed further light on the situation. This should then lead to the development of a marketing research question which may include a number of sub-questions that also need exploring. A possible, very general, marketing research question and a number of more specific sub-questions are shown in Box 2.2.

Box 2.2   Example of a marketing research question

What are the reasons for the recent decline in sales?

1. *Sub-question*: Has disposable income among Fashion Inc.'s customers declined over the last six months?
2. *Sub-question*: Is the new competitor, Phat!Wear, taking customers away from Fashion Inc.?
3. *Sub-question*: Are customers tired/bored of the current product range?

The marketing research question transforms the management problem into a question while trying to remove any assumptions made by the management of the organization. In the example management problem, the management felt that this was related to a new competitor taking away its customers. However, the decline in sales could have occurred for a number of reasons. Some of these reasons, numbered from 1 to 3, are described below and relate to the sub-question of the same number in Box 2.2. Thus, the decline in sales could be due to:

1. Declining customer expenditure, particular to a part of the country, because of recent job losses in a major regional industry (e.g., ship-building in Tyneside, steel in Sheffield).
2. Promotional activity (e.g., sales promotion, advertising) among existing competitors.

3. Changing customer requirements for fashion clothes. This occurred when Levi's™ decided to introduce a new style of jeans (Levi's engineered range) because its target market (the youth bracket) felt that 501s were outdated (and worn by their parents!).

At this stage, the MRO would probably go back to Fashion Inc. and explain the different possibilities for the decline in sales. The fashion firm will then make a judgement on what research sub-questions should be further investigated.

Sometimes, the management problem is clearer. The organization simply needs a customer profile, an industry profile, an understanding of what factors affect the customer's choice of its competitors' products or simply to test advertising concepts and new product concept ideas. Perhaps, the research is required for monitoring and control purposes and so a weekly tracking study is conducted to determine if customers have seen particular advertising campaigns and whether they were effective. Perhaps the organization is a service business and wishes to know current customer satisfaction levels.

The more clearly the commissioning organization defines the management problem, the more likely it is that the MRO will be able to investigate and solve it. Thus, a good market research brief provided to the MRO at the start of the process ensures that the MRO can design market research questions that investigate the management problem properly. Box 2.3 provides an outline for a typical marketing research brief.

Box 2.3 The marketing research brief

The research brief is a formal document prepared by the client organization and submitted to the MRO. In cases where marketing research is carried out in-company, the person in charge of the department that requires the conduct of the research will prepare the proposal for the marketing research manager. The document outlines the management problem. The basic structure and contents of a typical research brief should include the following:

- Background—This should provide a brief introduction giving basic details about the company and its products and/or services.
- The management problem—This should be a clear statement of why the research should be carried out and which business decisions are dependent upon the outcome of the research.
- The marketing research questions—This should be a reasonably detailed list of the information necessary in order to make the decisions outlined above.
- The scope of the research—An indication of the geographical areas to be covered, which industries, type of customer, etc. should be provided. The brief should give an indication of when the information is required and explain why that date is important.
- Tendering procedures—The client organization should outline how MROs are to be selected as a result of the tendering process. Specific information may be required from the MRO, such as CVs from the MRO personnel to be involved in the research

project, contact addresses and important information necessary to evaluate the professionalism of the MRO. The number of copies of the report required and preferences with regard to layout and presentation should also be outlined.

(*Source*: Adapted from BCC, 2001)

Box 2.3 provides an example of how a research proposal is constructed. This provides the client with a basic understanding of how the data will be collected, who will collect the information, when it will be collected by, how much it will cost to collect the data and some understanding of what the data actually means. It is provided as a result of seeing the brief, talking to relevant client personnel and after having conducted relevant desk research (see Chapter 3) on the industry. An example of the research proposal sent to London Football Club by the Centre for European Football Management is presented in the Chapter Appendix.

Stage 1—London FC Example: Define the Problem

In the case of London FC, the management problem was determined by interviewing the marketing manager and the marketing director. Usually, a definition of the problem is sent to the marketing research organization in the form of a formal research brief. This is a one- or two-page document detailing the areas that the organization commissioning the research (client) want the marketing research organization (agency) to explore. In this project, this did not occur. Instead, interviews between the relevant personnel and the agency (i.e., the Centre for European Football Management—CEFM—at Middlesex University) took place over a number of weeks. CEFM then wrote a research proposal that formally outlined the problem from a marketing research perspective, detailing what procedures were necessary to provide the necessary information (Box 2.4).

Box 2.4 A marketing research proposal outline

The research proposal is a formal document prepared by the MRO and submitted to the potential client. In cases where marketing research is carried out in-company, then the person in charge of the research project will prepare the proposal for the marketing manager who then decides whether to fund it. The document outlines the research methods to be used. The basic structure and contents of a typical research proposal should include the following:

- *Executive summary*—a brief summary of the research project including the major outcomes and findings. The executive summary should rarely be more than one page in length. Its purpose is to allow the reader to obtain a summary of the main points of the project without having to read the full report.
- *Background to the research*—an outline of the problem or situation that created the need for the project to be undertaken in the first place and the major issues surrounding this problem. This section should clearly demonstrate the researcher's

understanding of the management problem and any brief that they may have been sent.
- *Research objectives*—a statement outlining the objectives of the research project including the data that the project will generate and how this will be used to address the management problem outlined in the 'background to research' section.
- *Research design*—a clear non-technical description of the research type (e.g., qualitative, quantitative, primary or secondary, or combinations etc.) and techniques that will be adopted to gather the required information. This will include details on data-collection instruments, sampling procedures and analytical techniques.
- *Personnel specification*—the details of the procedures involved in the collection and analysis of the data.
- *Time schedule*—an outline of the time requirements with dates for the various stages to completion and presentation of results.
- *Costs*—this may include a detailed analysis of the costs involved in the project or simply a total cost for the project.

The club wished to find out (1) how it could enhance its revenue from services currently provided to the supporter base and (2) current levels of satisfaction in addition to (3) determining the viability of other potential services. This problem was divided into three broad basic research objectives.

1. To provide the club's management with a stronger understanding of the needs of the three major types of supporters (i.e., season ticket holders, club members and matchday attendees) in relation to the development (i.e., success, stadium, facilities) of the club;
2. To provide the management of London Football Club with a stronger comprehension of the profile and perception of London Football Club within the local community (since it was due to substantially develop its stadium capacity);
3. To provide the management of the club with a deeper understanding of the supporters' needs and desires.

Thus, in the problem-definition stage it is important to break down the management problem into marketing research objectives that are clear and capable of being investigated. This takes place by the development of a research brief by the client and the subsequent production of a proposal by the MRO or internal company research department. This process may be iterative, in that the client may read the proposal and ask for an amended version several times after consideration. At any stage, the client may decide not to proceed with the study.

Stage 2—Decide the Research Plan

This stage involves the consideration of whom to interview (the sample), how to interview them (the interviewing methods), using what procedures (the research methods), when (time) and where (location), and finally why (the research objectives).

Researchers usually start to design their research by considering which type of research category(ies) to employ. This is heavily dependent on the research objectives of the study.

Categories of Research

The research proposal will indicate the type of research approach that will be used to collect the data needed to solve the management problem. There are three basic categories of marketing research projects and the goals and objectives of the researcher and the information required generally determine which type of research is most appropriate for that particular research question. The three basic research types are *exploratory, descriptive* and *causal* and these are further described below.

Exploratory research is carried out to investigate the basic foundations of a research problem and is often undertaken in areas in which the organization or individual has little or no experience. This may involve new product development or entry into a new market or market segment. Exploratory research aids the client organization in understanding its situation before it makes any further decisions regarding its marketing strategy. It typically uses either secondary data collection (see Chapter 3) or qualitative market research methods (see Chapter 4).

The exploratory stage of research is flexible and is usually of a very general nature. It is flexible allowing the researcher to design the research focus around the *outcomes* that the research is generating. Secondary or desk research may play an important role in this type of research. For example, a manufacturing company may be researching the possibility of entering East European markets (e.g., with its range of branded toilet rolls). Instead of having the company's researchers visit the country and conduct their own primary research project, the MRO could conduct a search for relevant data using secondary information sources such as CD-ROMs, library catalogues, Internet sites and publications of international organizations (see Appendix I). Focus groups are particularly useful in investigating consumer behaviour when the client organization has little understanding of why its consumers are behaving the way that they do (see Chapter 4). For example, conducting focus group discussions would be a useful method for a toothpaste manufacturer who wished to determine why some of its consumers brushed their teeth three or more times per day when the average member of the population brushes twice per day.

Exploratory research is geared towards developing insights rather than actually coming to any conclusive findings. The exploratory stage of a research project often aims to generate the questions that will be used to guide later stages. Typically, it is less time-consuming than the other research types. It is also more flexible and allows the researcher to change the focus of their research objectives as the study progresses.

The objective of *descriptive* research is to provide a definitive answer to a marketing research question. This might involve obtaining data in the form of consumer profiles for segmentation or sponsorship purposes, attitude surveys for advertising copy development or sales analysis. Descriptive statistics, derived from the data obtained, summarize the main trends and patterns and are usually characterized by percentages and frequencies. These are discussed further in Chapter 6. Descriptive research often uses advanced statistical methods to measure relationships between variables of interest to the market researcher. For instance, a positioning study might use perceptual mapping methods to determine image constructs. A chocolate-bar manufacturer might use a descriptive marketing research methodology to draw a map of which variables define how the chocolate-bar-eating public view a range of competitors in this sector. Figure 2.2 provides an example of a perceptual map for the US pain reliever market which clearly illustrates how different brands are perceived by consumers. It is a particularly useful method in highlighting gaps in positioning within the market. There is a clear niche for a reasonably priced gentle analgesic.

Image constructs might include expensive–cheap, luxury–economy, or whether the product is hunger-satisfying. Segmentation studies often use advanced statistical methods of classification (e.g., discriminant analysis, cluster analysis, Chi-square automatic interaction detector analysis). Pricing studies might use analysis of variance methods, time-series analysis or multiple regression analysis. A discussion of these and other statistical methods is beyond the scope of this text. The interested reader is referred to Parasuraman (1991) and Malhotra and Birks (2000) for more detailed considerations of these topics.

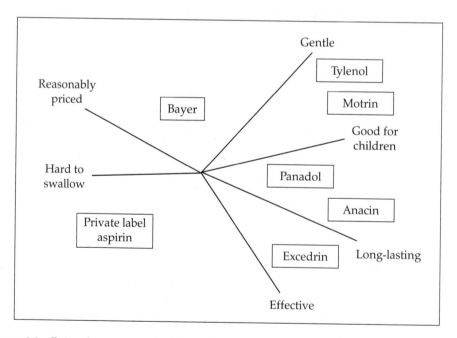

Figure 2.2   Pain reliever perceptual/brand map.

Source: Rice (2001). Reproduced by permission of SurveySite Market Research. http://www.surveysite.com

Causal research typically attempts to explain why things happen. It highlights cause-and-effect relationships and determines the correlation between variables. For example, is there a causal relationship between advertising expenditure and sales revenue? This uses experimental research designs, which attempt to determine whether one or more variables (the independent variables) influence another (dependent) variable. In order to investigate if this is occurring, experimental designs manipulate independent variables to see whether they are having an effect on the dependent variable. This is usually very difficult to detect and requires advanced statistical analysis and experimental research designs. It is difficult to determine if the dependent variable is actually *effected* by the independent variables or whether other variables are having an *affect* (note the difference between affect and effect). For further details on how to design experiments, see Parasuraman (1991).

Although these distinctions between research methods are made in most standard marketing research textbooks, in reality, most marketing research projects will usually adopt a combination of the first two methods. Experimental research is usually more difficult to conduct because of the problems in determining causality. Often, research projects include some form of exploratory stage to obtain a better understanding of the management problem. In later stages, the researcher might collect descriptive data. Occasionally, exploratory research methods are then used afterwards to provide a better understanding of some of the concepts uncovered in the descriptive research.

Qualitative and Quantitative Research Methods

A choice facing the researcher at the outset of a research project is between using qualitative and quantitative research methods, or a combination of both. The client of an MRO, or the in-house marketing research manager, generally has a budget available to finance a variety of studies and he or she will usually have to determine whether it is worth conducting a particular survey or study. This is frequently a subjective decision based on their previous experience of commissioning and conducting research. The choice made usually depends on the circumstances of the research project, its objectives and how much is already known about the management problem from either past research or experience. If there is little pre-understanding of the management problem faced, the researcher may wish to explore the problem further before attempting to research a possible solution. Since every research project is unique, because of its objectives, each can be tackled in different ways, utilizing different techniques and combinations of techniques.

Quantitative research methods (e.g., the ubiquitous survey questionnaire) are designed to elicit responses to predetermined, standardized questions from a large number of respondents. This involves collecting relatively small amounts of information from a large number of people. The responses are then quantified in percentages and descriptive statistics and often statistically analysed (see Chapter 6). Other quantitative research methods include mass observation techniques and experiments. Neither of these relatively less popular methods is covered further within this text.

Qualitative research is quite different from quantitative research. These techniques are often used at the preliminary stages of a research project to identify the basic factors affecting the management problem. The most common forms of qualitative research are focus groups and in-depth interviews. Projective techniques can also be used in both forms. Qualitative research techniques attempt to uncover the underlying motivations behind consumers' opinions, attitudes, perceptions and behaviour. Qualitative methods are unstructured and the researcher will have a number of basic issues guiding the research but not a structured set of questions for each respondent.

Focus groups are small-group discussions generally involving between eight and twelve people, lasting between 1 and 3 hours and are led by a trained moderator who guides the discussion. In-depth interviews are usually one-on-one discussions, often using a broad set of open questions to cover key points of interest, that last around an hour. Projective techniques are often used within focus groups and sometimes within in-depth interviews but may be used as a substitute method for dealing with sensitive topics. These three qualitative methods are covered in greater detail in Chapter 4.

Qualitative techniques generally involve a small number of respondents. The emphasis is on obtaining rich, detailed information from a small group of people rather than short, specific answers from a large number of respondents, as with survey questionnaires. The major characteristics of qualitative and quantitative marketing research techniques are outlined in Table 2.1.

The main advantages of qualitative research lie in its use for uncovering the underlying motivations for people's behaviour, attitudes, opinions and perceptions.

Table 2.1 Characteristics of qualitative and quantitative research methods

Qualitative	Quantitative
To identify and understand underlying motivations, attitudes, opinions, perceptions and behaviours	To generalize the results of a sample to a population
Involves a small number of respondents	Involves a large number of respondents
Rich, in-depth information	Narrowly defined descriptive information
Unstructured questioning approach often using open questions	Structured questioning process often using multiple fixed-response questions
Non-statistical (content) analysis	Descriptive statistics, percentages, proportions, hypothesis tests

Source: Adapted from Baines, Chansarkar and Ryan (1999)

A major disadvantage is that the results derived from this form of research are not generalizable to the wider population of interest and should be used only as a guide. Furthermore, focus groups are particularly reliant on the skill of the moderator in enhancing group members' interaction with each other (group dynamics).

Quantitative research techniques address the issue of representativeness and generalizability by basing the research on large samples of respondents. The researcher establishes the level to which the results will reflect the entire population by choosing the number and type of respondents required (see Chapter 7). A disadvantage of quantitative research is that with such a large number of respondents it is usually difficult to obtain detailed, in-depth information to answer the research questions properly. Often also, because the answers are usually predetermined by the researcher, there is a chance that the respondents are not being allowed to express their true opinion but one that only approximates to it.

Primary and Secondary Research

In deciding the research plan, a distinction also needs to be drawn between whether to collect primary or secondary research data or both. *Primary* research refers to research that has not previously been carried out and involves the collection of data for the specific purpose of a particular project. In contrast, the information available through secondary sources was originally generated using primary research techniques, but probably for different research objectives. *Secondary* research, sometimes referred to as desk research, involves gaining access to the results or outcomes of previous research projects. This is a useful method of research when someone else has carried out a project that provides some of the answers to a client's own management problem since it may be a cheaper and more efficient process of data collection. Desk researchers often make use of internal company reports and documentation and purchase reports from external research agencies (e.g., Mintel). Much secondary research is obtainable free of charge from a local library or the Internet (see Appendix I for a list of secondary data sources).

Most research projects involve a combination of secondary and primary research. Marketing research projects often begin with a desk research phase in which any available and associated information is gathered before the researcher sets about designing his or her primary research data collection instruments. The process of secondary data collection is explored in more detail in Chapter 3. The process of obtaining primary data is covered in more detail throughout this text, particularly in Parts I and II.

Research Design and Methodology

Once the researcher has determined the type of research approach to conduct, and whether it is necessary to collect primary and/or secondary data, a number of other decisions need to be made. These relate to who should be questioned and how (sampling plan and procedures), using what methods (e.g., focus groups or shopping mall intercept surveys), using which types of questions (question and questionnaire design) and how the data should be analysed and interpreted (data analysis). Research methods describe the techniques and procedures that can be adopted in gathering the required information. The methods used may include a survey questionnaire or a series of in-depth interviews. It may involve a researcher observing how consumers behave when they enter the premises of a supermarket, or how long an average shopping trip takes. The observer might record whether consumers shop alone, and if this affects the length of stay or amount of goods purchased. It may involve a panel of consumers who record their weekly purchases or their TV viewing habits over a specified time period. The objective of this section is to introduce the marketing student to the basic choices facing the marketing researcher when deciding which research methods best suit the aims and objectives of a particular research project.

Designing marketing research involves determining how the important research components interrelate. These components concern the research objectives, the sampling method, the interviewing methods, the research type and methods undertaken, the question and questionnaire design, and data analysis. These components impact upon the others. Figure 2.3 illustrates these different components and their interrelationships.

Each of these components is covered in further detail in different chapters of this book. Research type and objectives have been described in this chapter, research methods are considered in a number of chapters, question design, for qualitative research, in Chapter 4, questionnaire and survey design (incorporating interviewing methods) for quantitative research in Chapter 5, sampling methods in Chapter 7 and data analysis in Chapter 4 (qualitative data analysis) and Chapter 6 (quantitative

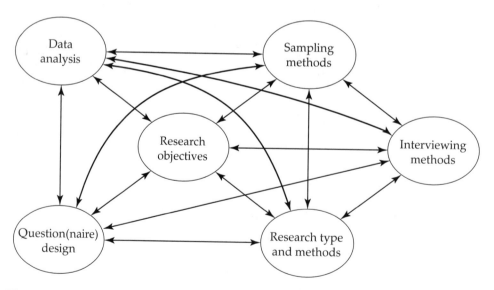

Figure 2.3 The major components of research design

data analysis). Research design involves the process of determining which type of approach to use for a given management problem (e.g., exploratory, descriptive or causal). It then includes determining which techniques are most capable of producing the desired data with the least cost and time expended while maximizing the inherent value of the data. In quantitative research, determining the inherent value ('truth') of the data is determined using methods to measure validity (i.e., does the data collected correctly describe the phenomenon it is attempting to measure?) and reliability (i.e., would the data be replicated in a future study of the same type if conducted again?). These concepts are covered later in this chapter.

Table 2.2 illustrates how the different components of research interrelate. Generally, certain types of research (e.g., exploratory, descriptive, causal) use certain methods and techniques. For instance, exploratory research studies often employ qualitative research methods, using convenient sampling and non-statistical data analysis. Descriptive researchers frequently adopt shopping mall intercept survey interviews using quota sampling and statistical analysis methods. Causal researchers often use an experimental research design using convenience sampling methods and statistical data analysis procedures using variable manipulation of the independent variables (see earlier in this chapter). Table 2.2 shows how the different components affect one another rather than giving an exhaustive description of exactly how all the components interact.

Stage 2—London FC Example: Decide Research Plan

At this stage in our example, the Centre for European Football Management needed to determine how to structure the research in order to collect the necessary data to achieve the marketing research objectives and solve the management problem. Since the objectives required a more detailed understanding of the levels of satisfaction of the supporters, it was necessary to conduct a survey among season ticket holders, club members and matchday attenders. The CEFM decided to question these three types of supporters independently using different survey questionnaires. The first of these study projects, a survey among season ticket holders, is outlined below.

> Project 1—Season Ticket Holders—This would be a quantitative mail survey sending 600 questionnaires to season ticket holders using a systematic random sampling method expecting 60% response. This would yield 360 usable questionnaires and would enable a measure of attitudes and perceptions of this important group with reference to their club.

As can clearly be seen, the study is quantitative and involves the use of a mail survey design with a probabilistic sampling procedure (see Chapter 7). A mail survey procedure was selected because the club holds all season ticket holders' details on a mailing list and, thus, a probability sampling procedure is more likely to ensure that a representative sample can be obtained efficiently.

Table 2.2 Interrelationships between research design components

Research design component	Data analysis	Question(naire) design	Sampling method	Research type and methods	Interviewing methods
Question(naire) design	Certain types of statistical test require data to be in a certain form (e.g., nominal, ordinal, interval or ratio). Content analysis used when data is open-ended				
Sampling method	Size of sample affects likelihood of statistical significance in tests and how sample is drawn also affects how data is interpreted	If sample is drawn from a number of different groups of the population, different questions may be asked of these groups within same research study			
Research type and methods	Qualitative analysis uses content analysis procedures generally while quantitative research uses statistical methods	Qualitative research uses question outlines while quantitative research generally uses questionnaires. Questions are generally more closed for quantitative and open for qualitative research	Sample selected depending on whether research is descriptive, causal or exploratory. Exploratory research generally uses small, convenient samples, descriptive research generally uses large quota, or random samples whilst experiments generally use moderately large samples using both random and convenient samples		

Interviewing methods	Simple rating and ranking scales should be used for telephone research. CATI, CAWI and CAPI facilitate data analysis and input	Different questions should be asked dependent on which interviewing method is to be used. Can ask more questions for personal and mail interviews than when using telephone	Probability sampling methods favour mail and telephone interviewing whereas non-probability sampling methods favour personal interviewing	Generally, qualitative methods use face-to-face methods whereas quantitative methods make use of the telephone and mail data collection instruments.	
Research objectives	Particular types of statistical test might be used for different purposes (e.g., a segmentation study might use multi-dimensional scaling methods)	Questions asked must always contribute directly to the research objectives, i.e., is the question relevant to meeting the information requirements of the research objectives?	This size of the sample and the type of sampling method used affect how confident the researcher can be in the study's findings. Where a high degree of confidence is required, large, random samples should be used	Does the research attempt to obtain rich, in-depth information or more focused, less rich information? If the answer is the former, it is likely that qualitative methods would be used while with the latter, quantitative methods are more useful	If the research requires particular respondents to answer questions a particular method may be more or less appropriate. For instance, questioning new car buyers about their experiences would likely use a mail survey format for one make of car or a personal quota-based sample for multiple manufacturer's makes of cars.

A further study involved measuring the perceptions of the local community with regards to the types of services that they demand from a football club. This study is detailed below.

> Project 4—Local Community—This would be a quantitative survey using a convenience sample to measure the perceptions of the club within the local community. We expect that the response rate will not reach more than 10% and if 1500 questionnaires were sent out, this would yield 150 usable questionnaires.

In this case, the researchers are suggesting the use of a mail survey procedure among the local population by delivering questionnaires door to door. This type of survey uses the convenience sampling method since it is easier and less costly to collect the data.

Another method of research that is exemplified in the London Football Club research example is qualitative. In this case, one of the objectives of the research was to determine supporters' perceptions of the image of the club. This was obtained by implementation of the study detailed below.

> Project 5—Focus group research—This would involve qualitative research using four groups of between 8–12 people. Three groups would comprise males of differing ages (e.g., group 1 has males between 18–34, group 2 has males between ages 35–44, etc.). The fourth group would comprise females. The sample should be selected from new supporters (those having only recently decided to visit London FC). The intention of this research is to provide a deep understanding of the reasons for deciding to support the club. This type of research is invaluable in developing managers' understanding of their customers. You would receive details of what each group had said (including transcripts) and a report outlining the researchers' interpretations of these comments. The members of the group would need to be recruited using announcements during a match and the discussion groups would be held in a comfortable office at the club itself. Refreshments would need to be provided. Similarly, the standard procedure is to give respondents £25 each for around one and a half hours of their time and to cover transport. However, we suggest that you provide each respondent with around this equivalent value (retail price) in merchandise. This would lower costs.

In project 5, it is easier to collect the type of data necessary, that relating to attitudes and perceptions, using focus groups. This is not to say that attitudes and perceptions cannot be investigated using quantitative methods because they can (see Chapter 5). However, in this case, London Football Club's understanding of its supporters' attitudes and perceptions was very limited. Qualitative research allows the organization to build an understanding of these perceptions. The outcomes of this method of research can then be tested on a larger, more representative sample of supporters at a later date. Qualitative research would allow the supporters to discuss their opinions more openly and over a longer period of time.

Stage 3—Data Collection

This stage involves the fieldwork and the collection of the required information or data. It is at this stage that the researchers send out the postal questionnaires, or run the focus group sessions or conduct telephone surveys, depending on the decisions taken in Stage 2 when designing the procedures involved. The procedures undertaken when conducting the fieldwork might relate to how to ask the questions of the respondents—whether this be using the telephone, mail or in person, and how to select an appropriate sample (see Chapter 7). How to precode the answers to a questionnaire (quantitative research) or how to code (*post-hoc*) the answers arising out of open-ended questions (usually associated more with qualitative research) are also issues related to efficient data collection. This stage of the research process relates to the organization of the collection of the data once the research design has been determined. Research methods most commonly associated with quantitative research include the questionnaire survey (see Chapter 5). Observational studies can also be quantitative but are generally considered under qualitative research (see Chapter 4). Focus groups, in-depth interviews and projective techniques are the most frequently used methods in qualitative research studies (see Chapter 4). The Internet environment allows both qualitative and quantitative research to be undertaken (see Chapter 11). Thus, further details relating to data collection are covered in the various chapters outlined after each example in the above sentences since they are environment and context-specific.

Stage 3—London FC Example: Collect the Data

In the London Football Club example it was necessary to outline a few important procedures to the client before the data was collected. Some examples of these procedures included:

- That the questionnaires be precoded (in order to aid in data input).
- The process to be undertaken for the generation of lists of randomly selected supporters for sampling purposes.
- The sending, delivering and receiving procedures for the assembly of the questionnaire, postage-paid envelope, and covering letter and their subsequent postage and, once completed, their return for analysis.
- The process of collection of the replies, which were returned to Middlesex University Business School using a freepost service to increase response rate.
- Projects 1, 2, 3 and 4 (see Chapter Appendix) required that incentives were offered to respondents in order to increase replies and to ensure an adequate response rate.

The data-collection phases of the London Football Club research required that the various people involved in the process of data collection understood a number of different procedures relating to the operationalization of the questionnaire surveys and the subsequent focus group discussions. Procedures for the conduct of the

31

interviews were codified for the interviewers to ensure that a consistent approach was followed. This also occurred with the procedures associated with data input to ensure a consistent approach to data quality and, therefore, that everyone was 'singing from the same hymn sheet'. In other words, the data that is being collected is subsequently capable of comparison.

Stage 4—Data Analysis and Interpretation

This stage of the market research process comprises data input, analysis and interpretation. How the data is input usually depends on the type of data collected (see Chapter 6). For instance, qualitative data (usually alphanumeric, i.e., words and numbers) are typed into word-processed documents as interview transcripts from audio- or video-tape and then entered into computer software applications (e.g., NUDIST—Non-numerical Unstructured Data Indexing, Searching and Theorizing) as rich text files for content analysis. Quantitative data analysis makes use of statistical analysis packages (e.g., SPSS—Statistical Package for the Social Sciences). In these cases, data is usually numeric and is either first entered into spreadsheet packages (e.g., Excel) or directly into the statistical computer application. Once the data has been organized and entered it can then be analysed. Qualitative and quantitative research data are analysed differently. These topics are covered in further detail in Chapter 4 (qualitative research) and Chapter 6 (quantitative research). However, modern data-collection and analysis methods can dramatically reduce the time needed for this stage. For example, computer-aided interviewing techniques allow the researcher to read the questions from a computer screen and directly enter the responses of the respondents. The computer application then analyses the responses instantly. Such methods are commonly associated with quantitative methods of interviewing such as computer-aided telephone interviewing (CATI) and computer-aided personal interviewing (CAPI). More recently the advent of the World Wide Web has created computer-aided Web interviewing techniques (see Chapter 11).

Market research methods are used to aid managerial decision making. It is therefore important that the information obtained is both valid and reliable since significant company resources may be deployed on the basis of such decisions. Validity and reliability are important concepts most frequently used in conjunction with quantitative market research. They aid researchers in understanding the extent to which the data obtained from the study represents reality and 'truth'. Over the last few decades, as qualitative research has increased in importance, the concepts of validity and reliability have been increasingly applied to academic qualitative market research.

Qualitative research methods rely on the extent to which the data generated would be replicated in a repeat study (reliability) and to which the data generated is free from bias (validity). Parasuraman (1991: 441) defines validity as 'a criterion for evaluating measurement scales; it represents the extent to which a scale is a true reflection of the underlying variable or construct it is attempting to measure'. There are various methods that attempt to determine validity. Content validity is the use of the researcher's subjective judgement to determine whether an instrument is really measuring what it is supposed to measure. Thus, a question asked about promotional opportunities does not necessarily measure degree of job satisfaction. Construct validity is another method of determining the validity of the data involving the measurement of the degree of correlation with similar and dissimilar variables.

In qualitative research, construct validity is relatively difficult to measure since the number of variables are limited and unsuited for quantitative analysis because of the smaller sample size. Validity may be determined by sending out transcripts to respondents and/or clients for checking, to ensure that what they have said has not been misrepresented. The data analyst would usually also critically read the data to see whether it fits with their expectations of what they would expect to be said by the respondents. This constitutes a face validity test.

Predictive validity is used to determine the extent to which a variable measures a phenomenon. For example, if a variable measures attitudes (e.g., belief in income tax cuts) and this correlates strongly with actual votes for a political party, attitudes towards income tax cuts can be shown to have a high degree of predictive validity in determining party vote. In qualitative research, such quantification of data is not usually conducted.

Reliability is defined as 'a criterion for evaluating measurement scales; it represents how consistent or stable the ratings generated by a scale are' (Parasuraman, 1991: 443). Reliability is affected by concepts of time, analytical bias and questioning error. Bryman (1989) differentiates between two types of reliability. In order to determine how reliable the data is, researchers might conduct the same research over two or more time periods to determine its consistency. This method is known as the test–retest method and illustrates *external* reliability. Another method used involves dividing the responses into two random sets and testing both sets independently. This would illustrate *internal* reliability. The two different sets of results are then correlated and this method is known as split-half reliability testing. These methods are more suited to testing the reliability of rating scales than data generated from qualitative research procedures.

The results of a quantitative marketing research project are reliable if we conduct a similar research project within a short period and the same or similar results are obtained. For example, if the marketing department of an restaurant chain interviewed 1000 of its customers and discovered that 55% were in favour of a different theme night (e.g., Greek, French, Middle Eastern) every week, then repeated the research project two months later and discovered only 15% of the sample were interested in the weekly theme night, the results of the first study can be said to be unreliable.

In qualitative research, reliability is often achieved by checking that similar statements are made by the range of respondents, across and within the interview transcripts. Thus, interviewees' transcripts (e.g., from either focus groups or in-depth interviews) are checked to assess whether the same respondent (or other respondents) has made the same point several times. This requires detailed analysis and tends to be conducted using computer applications (e.g., NUDIST). Other types of software package can be used but use of this application in qualitative research is relatively common (Weitzman and Miles, 1995). This is considered further in the section on qualitative data analysis in Chapter 4.

While reliability and validity are often considered important concepts in quantitative market research, they are not always regarded as such in qualitative market research. Many practitioners believe that because qualitative data is highly subjective anyway there is no need to measure reliability and validity. Thus, qualitative data, they would argue, is more about generating ideas and formulating hypotheses than testing hypotheses.

Stage 4—London FC Example: Analyse and Interpret the Data

The three sets of completed questionnaires were returned and immediately a team of people was used to enter the data into a spreadsheet software application. The data were analysed using the SPSS descriptive analysis function, which provides frequencies, modes, means, ranges and other basic statistical information (see Chapter 6). In addition, certain data from particular questions was cross-tabulated to determine if there was an association between two different sets of data (see Chapter 8).

The data analysis procedures for all phases of the London Football Club project are detailed below in a sentence explaining how the data would be analysed in the research proposal.

> The intention of the data analysis is to provide insights as to what feelings and issues are of importance and to use the salient points for policy formulation. This analysis will be performed using the statistical package for the social sciences (SPSS) and NUDIST (Non-numerical Unstructured Data Indexing, Searching and Theorizing). Use of these packages will enable us to provide you with a powerful understanding of your supporters.

In the end, NUDIST was not used to analyse the interview transcripts because of a problem in obtaining fully transcribed interviews from the typists involved. In such cases, it is not imperative that a software package be used to analyse the transcripts. The researchers can analyse the interviews either by reading and rereading the interviews transcripts or by listening and re-listening to the tapes. The latter process was used in the above study in the end because it saves time. One should be careful, however, to ensure that all major points mentioned during the interviews are covered and that verbatim quotes are still provided. Usually, this latter procedure is used for qualitative research in market research conducted by practitioners, whereas academic market research tends to use full transcripts.

Stage 5—Report Preparation and Presentation

The final stage of a research project involves the reporting and presentation of the findings of the study. It is vital that the results be presented effectively and free from bias. In many cases, this information is ultimately passed to decision makers who may have had little, if any, involvement with the research study beyond the commissioning stages. Therefore, it is important that the results of the study are presented clearly and according to the needs of the client. Marketing research data has little use unless it can be translated into a format that is meaningful to the manager or client who requested it at the outset of the project. It is not unusual for presentations to be attended by senior people within the commissioning organization (i.e., not just those directly involved in the commissioning of the work but also their bosses). More senior people within the client organization may also read any reports produced. Ultimately, the report (and any handouts from a presentation) is the only physical evidence of the market research service provided to the client firm by the MRO. Thus, reports and presentations should be written with a realization of their strategic nature.

Usually, MROs write their reports using a basic template although the content placed within that template is usually very different for each individual project. This is important to ensure that they adopt a consistent approach when conducting their services. It allows clients to evaluate the quality of the report. It is also important for training purposes since the report may well be written in sections by different people, some of whom might not be familiar with report writing. Further, a basic template allows MROs to project a brand, a style of research approach, which is important in the increasingly competitive market research industry.

The presentation and reporting of findings become even more involved in international studies when decisions arise as to which language to use to communicate the findings, whether to write reports for individual countries, how to translate the results of the study, and a determination of which methods to use. This is covered further in Chapter 10.

Stage 5—London FC Example: Present the Findings

The reporting procedure for the project commissioned by London Football Club is indicated below.

> The Research Centre will provide London Football Club with a report based on the results of the data analysis, complete with implications and recommendations for possible future action. We will also make a presentation to the relevant parties where the opportunity will be provided to further question and dissect the findings.

In total, six reports were eventually produced relating to each of the different projects and a report based on a comparison of the first three projects (which compared answers to a similar questionnaire among the matchday attenders, club members and season ticket holders). Two presentations were conducted and only the marketing manager and the research director attended the first. The second presentation, which involved the presentation of the findings of the focus groups, was held at a London advertising agency and included a number of the club's advisors (on advertising and market research). This was because the findings of this study were to be incorporated into the club's advertising materials. Thus, they wanted to be more sure about what was said by the researchers and the impact that it might/should have on the club's marketing activities.

Conclusion

The marketing research process comprises five stages and these stages of the process are the same in all major types of research. They include problem definition, research plan development, data collection, data analysis and interpretation and the presentation of findings. Usually, if there are problems in the first stage of this process, then these affect all other stages of the process. Thus, it is important for the MRO to properly understand the management problem and formulate appropriate marketing research questions. This process of determining what objectives the research should have arises initially from a research brief provided by the client organization to the MRO and then from a research proposal back to the client organization from the MRO. A dialogue usually ensues between the two organizations until agreement is reached. Research can be characterized as exploratory, descriptive or causal. It is often also classified as either qualitative or quantitative and data generated can be characterized as being either secondary or primary. Research design encompasses determining how the different components of a research project should interrelate. These components include the research objectives, the sampling method, the interviewing methods, the research type and methods, the question or questionnaire design process and, finally, data analysis. Each of these research design components is covered further in later chapters.

References

Baines, P., Chansarkar, B. and Ryan, G. (1999). *Introduction to Marketing Research*, London: Middlesex University Press.

BCC (2001). 'Export zone', http://www.britishchambers.org.uk/exportzone/emrs/mrbrief.htm, British Chambers of Commerce, accessed on 6 October 2001.

Bryman, A. (1989). *Research Methods and Organisation Studies*, London: Unwin Hyman.

Malhotra, N.K. and Birks, D. (2000). *Marketing Research: An Applied Orientation*, European edn, Englewood Cliffs, NJ: Prentice-Hall.

Parasuraman, A. (1991). *Marketing Research* (2nd edn), Wokingham: Addison-Wesley, 280–309.

Rice, M. (2001). 'An introduction to brand/perceptual mapping', http://www.yorku.ca/faculty/academic/mrice/index/docs/brandmap.htm, accessed on 4 October 2001.

Weitzman, E.A. and Miles, M.B. (1995). *A Software Sourcebook: Computer Programs for Qualitative Data Analysis*, Thousand Oaks, CA: Sage.

Work Assignments

1. Given more time and money, how would you modify the London Football Club proposal outlined in the Chapter Appendix in order to explore further the management problem?

2. What are the limitations of the given research designs for each of the projects outlined in the study?
3. Suggest appropriate changes to the proposal in order to reduce the bias arising from the limitations determined in question 2.
4. What type of research (i.e., causal, descriptive or exploratory) should be commissioned in the following contexts? Explain why.

   (a) By a political party that wants to understand why its percentage of the vote has fallen from 45% to 35% within a two-month period.
   (b) By a manufacturing firm wanting to determine whether there is a relationship between its recent expenditure on training and the performance of its salesforce.
   (c) By a toy company that wants to test new ideas for board games.
   (d) By a company wanting information relating to possible competitors, their market share and major suppliers and buyers in a new market.

5. Critically analyse the research design process outlined in Figure 2.1. Point out aspects of the process that you believe might not currently be included. Criticize the sequencing of the process. To help you with this, read the sections related to the London Football Club examples.

Chapter Appendix

Centre for European Football Management

Marketing Research Proposal—London Football Club

Middlesex University Business School

Sukhbinder Barn
Paul Baines
Lecturers in Marketing

Executive Summary

The researchers suggest the use of five distinctive projects, utilizing both qualitative and quantitative research designs, in order to investigate the attitudes of the supporters (season ticket holders holders, club members, matchday attenders) and members of the local community. The researchers intend that the studies be completed within sixteen weeks and the cost is dependent on which studies London Football Club wishes to undertake.

Background

The proposal has been formulated from a number of important issues that were highlighted as a result of discussions with the Marketing Manager and the Marketing Director at London Football Club on Thursday 3 September. This proposal differs significantly from the previous surveys conducted in the sense that the work cannot form part of students' projects (dissertation cycle is from April until November).

Research Objectives

1. A desire for a stronger understanding of all types of supporters' needs in relation to the development of the club to be built upon as a consequence of previous research;
2. Limited comprehension of the profile and perception of London Football Club within the local community;
3. A need for a deeper understanding of the supporters' needs and desires.

From within these three areas there are very specific issues that can be investigated further.

Point (1) Although the previous research provided a strong understanding of the supporters' needs, it was conducted at the end of September 1997. This research would update that understanding and put into context the various significant changes that have occurred at London Football Club since then.

Point (2) illustrates how London Football Club have not involved themselves in any significant research regarding opinion and perceptions. The Research Centre's perspective is that this would prove to be the ideal starting point. It would give the club a solid understanding and profile of the residents within the local community and highlight appropriate strategies for retaining their continual support (e.g., regarding future stadium development).

Point (3) There is a need for a stronger and deeper understanding of the supporters in terms of their opinions and desires regarding developments and possible future product offerings at the club.

Research Design

The centre is proposing five projects, four of which are quantitative and interlinked in the issues that would be addressed while the fifth is qualitative and explores attitudes in more depth. However, should you find the cost prohibitive, the costs for each are detailed separately at the end, thereby, allowing individual projects to be chosen if you so desire.

Project 1—Season Ticket Holders This would be a quantitative mail survey sending 600 questionnaires to season ticket holders using a systematic random sampling method and expecting 60% response. This would yield 360 usable questionnaires (slightly less than last time but still sufficient). This would enable some comparison with previous questionnaire sent out. Would enable a measure of shifts in attitudes and perceptions of this important group with reference to their club.

Project 2—London club members This would be a quantitative mail survey sending questionnaires to every single member (approx. 750)—a census. Currently, the

response rate is unknown, but we estimate the response rate could r/
doesn't, we would send out a second wave of questionnaires to non-resp
increase the rate of response. This group needs to be de-duplicated from all u.
membership databases. This would enable some measure of the success of the
membership scheme and illustrate the perceptions of the members with regard to
any problems or expectations that exist.

Project 3—Match day attenders This would be a quantitative personal interview
survey handing questionnaires to approximately 1500 supporters. Currently, the
response rate is unknown, however, we estimate the response rate could be around
20%. A quota sampling method would be used. We need to determine why this
group has not become season ticket holders and determine whether this is for the
same reasons as in the previous survey. Since there has been a marked increase in
attendance at the ground, there is a need to determine what the reasons are for this
and whether their needs can be catered for.

Project 4—Local community This would be a quantitative survey using a convenience
sample to measure the perceptions of the club within the local community. We
expect that the response rate will not reach more than 10% and if 1500
questionnaires were sent out, this would yield 150 usable questionnaires.

Project 5—Focus group research This would involve qualitative research using four
groups of between 8–12 people. Three groups would comprise males of differing
ages (e.g., group 1 has males between 18–34, group 2 has males between ages
35–44 etc.). The fourth group would comprise females. The sample should be
selected from new supporters (those having only recently decided to visit London
FC). The intention of this research is to provide a deep understanding of the
reasons for deciding to support the club. This type of research is invaluable to
developing managers' understanding of their customers. You would receive
details of what each group had said (including transcripts) and a report stating
what the researchers' interpretations of these comments are. The members of the
group would have to be recruited using announcements during a match and the
discussion groups would be held in a comfortable office at the club itself.
Refreshments would need to be provided. Similarly, the standard procedure is to
give respondents £25 each for around one and a half hours of their time and to
cover transport. However, we suggest that you provide each respondent with
around this equivalent value (retail price) in merchandise. This would lower
costs.

Personnel Specification—Allocation of Tasks

Fieldwork and Data Collection
The questionnaires will be coded and the data entered onto our computers by
students at MUBS who will be paid on an hourly rate. The quality of the data will be

checked by using another set of students to input the data and another set to check the inputted data. The generation of the lists of the randomly selected supporters, the sending and delivering of the post will be done at London FC. However, the replies will be returned to MUBS using a freepost service to increase response rate. Projects 1, 2, 3 and 4 will require the offering of incentives to induce replies and also to ensure an adequate response rate.

Project 5—The focus groups should be conducted at London Football Club and *each* individual respondent will need to be compensated with an incentive. Recruitment for the focus groups should occur using pre-match announcements. A select group of people can then be chosen.

Data Analysis

The intention of the data analysis is to provide insights as to what feelings and issues are of importance and to use the salient points for policy formulation. This analysis will be performed using the statistical package for the social sciences (SPSS) and NUDIST (Non-numerical Unstructured Data Indexing, Searching and Theorizing). Use of these packages will enable us to provide you with a powerful understanding of your supporters.

Reporting

The Centre will provide London FC with a report based on the results of the data analysis, complete with implications and recommendations for possible future action. We will also make a presentation to the relevant parties where the opportunity will be provided to further question and dissect the findings.

Cost and Time Schedules

Costing

Below are the anticipated costs and approximate timing for the individual projects (assuming each was undertaken separately):

Table One Costs for individual projects

Project	Questionnaire design (moderation)*	Data input and analysis (transcription)*	Report and presentation	Total cost
Project 1	£2400	£3200	£900	£6500
Project 2	£2400	£3200	£900	£6500
Project 3	£2400	£3200	£900	£6500
Project 4	£2400	£2400	£900	£5700
Project 5*	£1600	£2700	£900	£5200
Totals	£11200	£14700	£4500	£30400

*Bracketed words relate to focus group project.

Please note that if all projects are undertaken together, then costs will reduce considerably since the questionnaire templates will be similar for projects 1, 2 and 3 and the report writing will be made somewhat easier.

Table Two   Costs for all projects undertaken together

Project	Questionnaire design (moderation)*	Data input and analysis (transcription)*	Report and presentation	Total cost
Project 1	£2400	£3200	£700	£6300
Project 2	£600	£3200	£700	£4500
Project 3	£600	£3200	£700	£4500
Project 4	£2400	£2400	£900	£5700
Project 5	£1600	£2700	£900	£5200
Totals	£7600	£14700	£3900	£26200

If you do not wish to conduct the focus groups, the package becomes Table Three.

Table Three   Costs for all projects undertaken (excluding focus groups)

Project	Questionnaire design	Data input and analysis	Report and presentation	Total cost
Project 1	£2400	£3200	£700	£6300
Project 2	£600	£3200	£700	£4500
Project 3	£600	£3200	£700	£4500
Project 4	£2400	£2400	£900	£5700
Totals	£6000	£12000	£3000	£21000

If you only want projects 1, 2 and 3 (excluding focus groups and local community survey), the breakdown becomes Table Four.

Table Four   Projects 1, 2 and 3 (only) undertaken together

Project	Questionnaire design (moderation)*	Data input and analysis (transcription)*	Report and presentation	Total cost
Project 1	£2400	£3200	£700	£6300
Project 2	£600	£3200	£700	£4500
Project 3	£600	£3200	£700	£4500
Totals	£3600	£9600	£2100	£15300

Please work out other combinations using Table One.

Timing

If the projects are undertaken simultaneously the approximate timing for all projects would be:

Timing	
Data collection	8 weeks (1 week)*
Data analysis	4 weeks
Report writing	4 weeks
Total	16 weeks (9 weeks)*

*Refers to focus group project.

However, since the generation of the lists of supporters to be mailed will be undertaken by yourselves, this significantly affects the timing of the whole project. Similarly, it depends somewhat on the number of projects undertaken. Please note that the generation of lists and sending out the letters to these individual supporters will take a considerable amount of time and labour. We will advise on how you need to go about this to have a reasonable sample. You may need extra labour to cope with this. We may be able to arrange for a placement student to undertake this (but you would have to negotiate terms of employment with our placement office).

Desk Research and Secondary Data Collection 3

Introduction

Desk research is conducted from the office, a computer, or a library using existing sources of information and can serve marketing managers' needs for information on their markets, environments, competitors and customers. It also has a particularly important function in *marketing research* where it is usually the first step in the process. Under certain circumstances and if done thoroughly, desk research will solve the research problem at hand without requiring the more expensive stage of primary data collection.

While *primary* or *field research* involves gathering data for the first time, using such instruments as questionnaires or focus groups, desk research uses *secondary data* gathered from existing *internal* or *external* sources. This chapter will first consider how marketers can make use of desk research. Since secondary data are the mainstay of the desk research project, it is also important to identify key sources and locations of secondary data, to consider how to assess secondary information for accuracy and relevance, and to propose steps in the data-gathering process. The chapter will conclude with a discussion of the skills needed by the desk researcher.

When is Desk Research Useful?

As noted above, desk research can assist marketing managers in gathering the information needed for both regular and planning-related decisions. Five important objectives of desk research are:

- To assist at various stages in the *marketing research process*.
- To monitor the *business environment*.
- To make *forecasts* and estimate the *size of a market*.
- To develop an *understanding of current and potential customers*.
- To investigate *international markets*.

Desk Research, Secondary Data and the Marketing Research Process

Secondary data collection and analysis are important at all stages of the marketing research process. In the *problem definition* and *exploratory stages*, secondary information is particularly useful (see Figure 3.1).

Desk Research in the Marketing Research Process

Consider a large, well-established producer of top brands of consumer breakfast cereals. The company has watched its market share and profitability erode over the past two years. The stock market has responded by placing a lower value on the

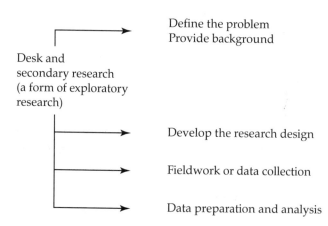

Figure 3.1   Desk research in the marketing research process

company's shares and hence a cycle of slow decline has begun. Management knows that stiff competition and price wars have contributed to the losses, but before making any marketing resource allocation decisions, they want to be certain that all the reasons behind the decline have been uncovered.

In trying to understand the situation and provide background, managers will begin with desk research and consult both *internal* and *external* sources. *Internal data* from accounting, sales, distribution, and customer service records as well as previous company research studies could provide clues as to when retail orders began to decline, the extent of the relationship between price reductions and declining profits, and whether the decline was correlated with promotional spending on key brands.

A wealth of useful information is also available in *external secondary sources*. Business databases and directories can be sourced to identify recent articles, facts and trends about the cereals industry and the competitors. Trade or industry associations will have statistics on general trends in the market as well as studies on how consumer attitudes towards eating breakfast and breakfast cereals is changing. If the company buys regular research from a syndicated service such as AC Nielsen Co., they have already been monitoring market shares, distribution patterns, and the effects of promotions on sales.

In determining the most appropriate *primary research design*, managers will begin with desk research to determine which methodologies and techniques have been used in similar studies. Hundreds of market research reports are published each year and are made commercially available. Given the size of the worldwide cereals industry, it is likely that research companies or syndicated firms have conducted and compiled research reports on a wide range of related issues.

Desk research is usually the first step in determining the population for the study and creating the *sample*. If the cereals company plans to survey retailers then they can make use of customer lists from their *internal database*. If they wish to survey users of breakfast cereals they may purchase a consumer list from one of many list providers.

Finally, desk research can be used in the *data analysis* stage to cross-check the company's primary research findings. Market research is subject to a range of possible errors resulting from weak samples, questionnaire or interviewer bias and poor analysis of findings. Most researchers will compare the approach and findings in their own study with that of similar, already published, studies in order to check for errors and gain additional insights.

Desk Research to Monitor the Environment

All companies must stay abreast of changes in the marketing and business environment. They need an ongoing supply of good information to monitor economic, political, social, consumer and competitor trends.

For example, our cereals company will regularly gather information on *competitor* pricing, promotions, product introductions and retail shelf space. Cereals managers may also want to look at consumer profiles and spending patterns to determine if customers' needs and expectations are changing over time.

Changes in the *economy* may affect both consumer purchase behaviour and the marketing activities of the firm. During recessionary periods, consumers can become more price sensitive and may be more responsive to sales promotions that offer discounts or larger value packs. During times of economic prosperity, cereal companies often face increased costs of ingredients, labour and advertising rates, all of which will place upward pressure on prices to consumers.

Changes in the *social and cultural environment* take place over longer periods of time but can have a very significant impact on a company's fortunes. During the past two decades, the number of families in which both parents are working has increased significantly, while the fastest-growing family unit in the UK is the single-person household. When combined with other factors such as the rising cost of living in major cities and longer working hours, these trends have had a considerable effect on consumer purchases of breakfast cereals. Smaller households purchase fewer cereals and dual-working couples have less time to prepare a sit-down breakfast. As a consequence, cereals manufacturers have introduced new products such as individual serving packs, cereal bars, and other breakfast foods that can be eaten on the run.

Today's modern businesses will have a *management* or *marketing information system (MkIS)* to track and analyse environmental factors that could affect sales, profits and marketing activities. All marketing information systems are made up of tools, techniques, databases, software and hardware that allows data from within the organization and data collected from outside to be stored, manipulated, analysed, and processed in order to provide managers with support for key decisions. While primary research studies are a prime element of any MkIS, most of the data comes from secondary sources collected by desk researchers, sales people, marketers, accountants, IT specialists, and others within the company.

Desk Research in Forecasting and Market Analysis

One of the major functions of an MkIS and secondary information is to help managers make key business decisions such as setting forecasts, measuring market potential, making media choices, establishing sales territories, and setting sales targets. For example, in order to estimate the *total market potential* for cereals in a given area, our company could use the following formula suggested by Kotler (1997):

$$TMP = nqp$$

where TMP = total market potential
           n = number of buyers in the area
           q = quantity purchased in a given period
           p = average price paid per unit

Secondary data can supply some if not all of the data required to make this forecast. The number of cereals buyers and the quantity purchased can be found in market research reports supplied by companies such as Mintel Marketing Intelligence or in estimates of family expenditure produced by the UK government's Office of National Statistics (ONS). Average price per unit could be estimated from data purchased on competitor pricing from syndicated research firms.

Desk Research Used to Understand Customers and Identify Target Markets

Both government agencies and private marketing research firms like Information Resources, Inc. and CACI compile data on consumer buying patterns and habits using a combination of geographic, demographic, and psychographic data. Companies make use of this information to decide where to locate retail outlets, what product combinations to offer, and where to target direct mail promotion. Information from internal customer databases can be supplemented with secondary data from external sources to create an extensive profile of target markets and their buying patterns.

Desk Research to Investigate International Markets

International markets are vital to companies when the national market has become saturated or too competitive, and when opportunities exist to expand revenues. In order to prepare for successful entry into a foreign market, managers need to conduct a significant amount of research into the new environment in which they will be doing business. Information on the economic environment, government attitudes towards foreign business, laws and regulations, availability of infrastructure, competition, distribution systems, and promotional practices can be carried out at home via desk research. A great deal of information on foreign markets is gathered and disseminated by local or national governments who are seeking to expand trade with other countries. Syndicated and independent research companies, like Euromonitor, also gather and sell this kind of information.

Given the range of uses to which secondary data can be put, it has been estimated that 90% of all companies make use of it in their regular decision making as well as in their overall planning framework. In order to obtain the best use of the time and resources needed to conduct desk research, however, it is important to follow a plan.

Steps in the Desk Research Process

A good search plan begins with a clear statement of purpose and a set of objectives before moving on to data collection. Data collection should then begin with the most available, cost-effective information before the researcher moves on to more expensive and harder to access sources. Below is a step-by-step guide that allows the researcher to make the best use of secondary data and desk research.

Steps in the desk research process

1. Begin with a clear definition of research needs, purposes and objectives.
2. Identify any internal data or available syndicated data.

47

3. Talk to experts, professionals, or other interested parties.
4. Make use of a good business library.
5. Use the Internet.
6. Consider relevant government publications or other statistical sources.
7. Contact professional bodies and trade associations.
8. Locate any similar or relevant market research reports.
9. Use on-line databases if available and within the budget.
10. Keep accurate records of your sources; input into a *marketing information system* (MkIS).
11. Assess secondary data for accuracy, cost, and usefulness.

1. Begin with a Clear Idea of Research Needs, Purposes and Objectives

In beginning a desk research project, it is essential to have a clear idea of the key terms for the search and for what purposes the information will be used. For example, if the company is trying to determine whether a primary research study should be done to assess consumer attitudes and purchasing behaviour towards breakfast cereals, the purposes of desk research will be to find any existing information or research studies on these issues, as well as to find background information on the cereals industry, market and competitors. The purposes of the search are to determine whether it is actually necessary to carry out primary research and to provide as much background and insight as possible into the problem.

2. Identify Internal Data or Available Syndicated Data

Internal Data

The research project should begin with the most readily available data. *Internal sources* of secondary data are located within the company. Firms collect information for accounting, marketing, operations, logistics and production purposes, in addition to information on the business environment. Accounting data is often recorded in terms of costs, profits, overall sales, sales by product line and sales by territory. Marketing data can be found in sales records, customer databases, customer inquiries, and complaints. Operations and logistics records may include detailed inventory and distribution summaries.

In an effective management or marketing information system this data can be combined in ways that give decision makers great insights and predictive power. Unfortunately, while many companies have mountains of good data, they do not always make good use of it. Two examples will help to illustrate this point. One of the world's best-known canned goods manufacturers recently introduced a new line of non-dairy beverages for those who cannot or choose not to drink milk. The product range was limited to two flavours of soy-based beverages. While their own research showed that the market segment for non-dairy was growing and offered potential, competitive data indicated that consumers were particularly interested in organic and rice-based products in this category. Consequently, sales of soy-based beverages sold under traditional brand names were not likely to be strong.

A second example of a company that has not made optimum use of the secondary data it gathers is that of a mobile phone service provider that collects information on both customer complaints and on reasons why customers stop using the service. However, the system is not set up to determine whether the customers who complain are those who eventually quit the service. Consequently, there is no way of knowing whether these groups represent the same marketing problem or two different ones.

With the increasing need for good information about customers, competitors and the effectiveness of marketing programmes, and the availability of better technologies for gathering and analysing information, companies are beginning to build more effective internal data systems. *Internal* secondary data still remains the first source of information for the researcher on sales, costs, profitability, competitors and customers.

Syndicated Data

Often, companies will subscribe to a *syndicated research service (SRS)*. An SRS will collect primary data on a range of issues such as sales trends, market and brand shares, competitors' sales, impact of trade promotions on sales, and consumer attitudes. Data is collected from in-store audits and from scanner tapes provided by retailers in a particular industry, in addition to consumer panels.

AC Nielsen, Ltd, one of the world's largest syndicated research companies, has particular expertise in the grocery industry. The company buys or acquires data on sales from thousands of grocery retailers, analyses the data, compiles the figures into easy-to-read formats and sells it back to the same grocers on a weekly or monthly basis. The advantages of syndicated data are that the costs of collecting the information are shared among many users and the data is very up to date. Most major retailers view syndicated data as essential to monitoring sales, competitors and marketing effectiveness.

3. Talk to Experts, Professionals or Other Interested Parties

An often-overlooked source of information are people who are experts in the subject or interested parties.

4. Make Use of a Good Business Library

Public and university business libraries remain an excellent source of secondary data. The reference and business sections of these libraries usually contain all the following:

1. Business bibliographies and reference guides
2. Indexes and abstracts
3. Market research studies
4. Books, periodicals and journals
5. Commercial periodicals and trade journals

6. Major newspapers
7. Company directories, guides and information
8. International market guides and information
9. Major government publications

Begin by looking through the bibliographic indexes for an existing list of publications on the topic. Then make use of indexes, abstracts and directories in published form or on CD-ROM to find the listed publications and other relevant articles and citations on the topic of interest. Having a clearly defined list of key search terms is critical at this stage. Researchers will also review the latest academic and trade publications as well as other sources of data to ensure that they have as complete a picture of the problem or situation as possible. For a discussion of the sources listed above, refer to Appendix I.

Most major libraries are available to the public, but some have visiting restrictions based on time of year, time of week or membership. For advice on which libraries to contact in your search, call the ASLIB (Association of Special Libraries and Information Bureau), London on 0207-903-0000.

Today, an increasing amount of library information is in electronic format. Libraries make use of CD-ROMs, electronic databases and the Internet. Be sure to look for your chosen information in all the available formats.

5. Use the Internet

Anyone with a computer, modem and phone-line can access the Internet, an ever-evolving, often frustrating and seemingly endless source of information, data, anecdotes and interests. There are four major ways to find business and marketing information on the Internet:

(i) Via a designated address
(ii) Through a search engine, directory or portal
(iii) Through sites developed by information providers
(iv) Through a newsgroup or discussion group

(i) Designated Addresses

Most companies have their own Internet site and given a specific URL (Uniform Resource Locator), it is easy to find. While most Internet addresses take the form http://www.company name.com some companies are listed under shorter or adapted versions of the original corporate name or under a different type of address such as:

Those beginning with
http://companyname
http://ww2

and those ending with
.co.uk (for the United Kingdom)
.org
.net
.ac.uk (UK academic institutions)
.gov.uk
.edu (US academic institutions)

Without the specific company URL, try typing the name of the company, such as *Kraft* or *General Mills*, into the browser's search box because some browsers will locate information without the 'www' prefix or the 'com' suffix. Otherwise, try using a search engine (see below) to help locate the company.

Keep in mind that companies may have more than one site on the Web. They may have a corporate site for investors, a site to sell and/or catalogue products, separate sites for each product in the line, and sites that are specifically linked to current off-line advertising campaigns. For example, Kellogg's has a main website at www.kelloggs.com, a UK site at www.kelloggs.co.uk, sites for specific promotions such as the www.2weekchallenge.co.uk that ran in November 2000, and a range of other sites for each individual product and for company and investor news. If searching for competitive information, it pays to look at as many sites and pages as are available.

(ii) Search Engines, Directories and Portals

At the beginning of a new search, researchers might not have any addresses to check and may need to make use of a *search engine* to help find relevant information on their key topic. A search engine is a large directory of information that is accessible via keywords. The six major search engines are www.altavista.com, www.excite.com, www.hotbot.com, www.lycos.com, www.yahoo.com, and www.infoseek.com. There are also hundreds of directories and specialized search engines that may be relevant to the desk research project. A 'portal' is meant to be a search site that specializes in specific information such as health and beauty or travel, but the term has come to be associated with any search engine or directory.

Search engines use their own unique search procedures and techniques so it pays to read their on-line help and searching techniques section in order to get the most out of time on-line. In their book *Search Engines for the World Wide Web* Alfred and Emily Glossbrenner give seven tips for searching the Web for information:

1. *Develop the Web habit*—almost anything researchers are looking for can be found on the Web, if they know how to look and have the patience.
2. *Use the best tool for the job*—begin with the major search engines (listed above), keeping in mind that each uses a slightly different search procedure and each has its strong and weak points. Also make use of Usenet newsgroups and special-purpose engines.
3. *Read the instructions*—read the on-line help and search tips section for *each* search engine before beginning the hunt for information.
4. *Choose unique keywords*—before beginning a search, think about the keywords that are likely to appear in the information being investigated. Start with the more general terms, like sports or business, before moving to more specific terms like athletic footwear or Adidas.
5. *Use multiple search engines and/or metasearch services*—no search engine covers everything so you will need to consult all the major and some minor ones as well

as make use of metasearch engines like Metacrawler (www.metacrawler.com) and Dogpile (www.dogpile.com).

6. *Consider the source*—information on the Net may be biased, inaccurate and/or outdated. (See below for a general discussion on the problems with secondary information.)

7. *Know when to look elsewhere*—never assume that the Internet contains the sum total of human knowledge. Public and private libraries should also be part of the overall information search (see Glossbrenner and Glossbrenner, 1999).

For example, begin a search for information on breakfast cereals via www.findarticles.com by entering the following terms into the search box:

'Kellogg's breakfast cereals'

The search might turn up a link to a site that collects articles specifically on the breakfast cereals industry.

By reading through the titles and abstracts in this list, the researcher can identify specific information on the industry and on competitors as well as finding particular publications that specialize in reporting on the breakfast cereals or packaged goods market.

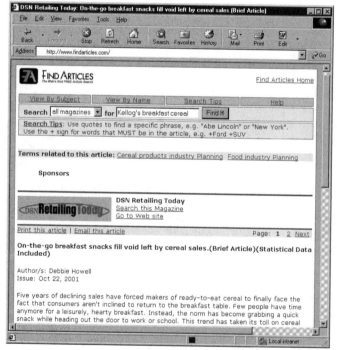

Figure 3.2   Example of a site on the breakfast cereals industry

Source: http://www.findarticles.com, journal article by Debbie Howell from DSN Retailing Today, October 22nd 2001. Copyright © Gale Group.

(iii) Information Provider Sites

In addition to looking at company sites and making use of search engines, researchers use *information provider* sites. These companies compile information in a variety of ways to answer specific business questions and to cover the range of secondary data needs. Companies such as Dialog, FT Profile, FIND/SVP, MAID, and Euromonitor provide information on competitors, industries and markets, consumer trends and buying habits, on legislation and the economy, among other things.

For an insight into the extent of information now available in electronic form, see the two-volume series *Encyclopaedia of Information Systems and Sources* (Detroit: Gale Research Co.) with its list of over 2500 database producers, data sources and on-line vendors; and *On-Line Business Sourcebook* (Headland, Cleveland: Headland Press). Full details of these publications are provided in Appendix I.

There are hundreds of other interesting sources of business information on the Net, some of which are listed in Appendix I.

(iv) Newsgroups and Discussion Groups

The Web has over 80 000 newsgroups on every topic imaginable. Newsgroups or discussion groups are made up of people from all over the world who are sharing their ideas, knowledge, skills, opinions and experiences. They often contain the most up-to-date information on what is happening in an industry or with competitors and current key issues being discussed and debated in the field. One of the best search engines to find relevant newsgroup is Deja News (www.dejanews.com).

6. Government and International Publications

The government is the largest producer of statistics and analyses on the UK population, business and economy. In order to gain an insight into the range of information available, contact or visit the local branch of the Office for National Statistics (ONS).[1]

Two of the many reports published and updated by the ONS are the *Annual Abstract of Statistics*, a regularly updated listing of key statistics on such sectors as housing, population, manufacturing and services; and *Social Trends*, key statistics on social trends and changing expenditure patterns in the UK.

To provide environmental trends in an industry and for insights into consumer behaviour and purchasing patterns the ONS publishes a range of statistics on monthly economic trends, family expenditure patterns, and business prospects, while the European Union Information Service provides updates on legislation affecting industries.

The ONS has Internet access via www.statistics.gov.uk or www.ons.gov.uk. STATBase is an on-line service that provides a comprehensive set of key statistics

---

[1] The London Office of National Statistics (ONS) is located at Room DG18, 1 Drummond Gate, Pimlico, London SW1V 2QQ. Telephone: 0207-533-6262.

drawn from the whole range of official statistics. Note that not all ONS information is free, but a great deal of it is available in libraries. ONS publications are available for purchase from The Stationery Office (TSO).

An excellent source of information on UK companies is Companies House, the official public records organization located in London.[2] Over 1 million companies are registered with Companies House. Registered companies are required to make information such as names of key personnel, share offerings, and profit and loss statements available for public scrutiny. You can contact Companies House on 02920 038 0670 or via their website http://ws1.companieshouse.gov.uk.

An important source of information on national and international markets is the UK government's Department of Trade and Industry (DTI), located in Victoria Street in London.[3] Be sure to phone for an appointment before visiting or make use of their website (www.dti.gov.uk). See also Trade Partners UK at www.tradepartners.gov.uk.

Data and statistics on countries and markets abroad are also produced by non-government and international organizations like the World Bank, the International Monetary Fund (IMF), the United Nations (UN), the Organization for Economic Cooperation and Development (OECD), and International Chambers of Commerce located in all capital cities. Researchers may also contact the British Trade Commissioner's office in the overseas country of interest or the London-based consulate of that country.

7. Professional Bodies and Trade Associations

Most companies will belong to a professional body or trade association and subscribe to a trade journal. For example, brewers will be members of the Brewer's Society and the Export Association, marketers may belong to the Chartered Institute of Marketing and food retailers will subscribe to *The Grocer*. Cereals manufacturers may read reports and findings published by the American Association of Cereal Chemists. Most companies will also be members of their local Chamber of Commerce or, if in a major centre, the International Chamber of Commerce.

Trade and professional associations monitor and report on economic, political and other trends that affect companies in their industry. They may have a library or information service for members, sponsor conferences and trade shows, and offer publications and websites. They will also provide good information on their industry and market, as well as on major companies operating in the sector.

8. Independent Market Research Companies

Independent market research companies conduct major primary and secondary research studies on specific industries (e.g., the car industry), on specific product

---

[2] Companies House is located at 55–71 City Road, London EC1Y 1BB. Five other regional offices exist across the UK.

[3] The Export Market Information Centre (EMIC), Kingsgate House, 66–74 Victoria Street, London SWE1 6SW.

groups as well as on consumer attitudes and buying patterns across a range of product and service categories. They also provide industry forecasts and growth predictions. These reports are usually sold to companies and can be very costly, with prices for individual reports ranging from £300 to £2400. Fortunately, many of these research firms sell to public and university libraries at a significantly reduced rate. The information is then either free to the library user or accessible at a lower on-line research rate. Two very good independent research companies with offerings at local libraries are *Mintel Market Intelligence Service* and *ICC Keynote*, but a more detailed list is provided in Appendix I.

For the most up-to-date list of market research firms across the world, see the *International Directory of Market Research Organizations* produced by the Market Research Society (see Appendix I).

9. Use on-line databases

Online databases are high-speed, computer-assisted information retrieval systems that often include the full text of articles or news stories rather than just summaries or abstracts. These electronic databases are made available to large public libraries but may charge users a fee for time spent on-line. On-line databases will search newspapers, magazines, market research reports, journals, the newswire services, and other publications for information on the topic under research. The researcher can also find up-to-the-minute economic data, political information, company financial reports, and changes in company structure information. Despite the cost, on-line databases are a powerful marketing research tool as they are so comprehensive and offer material that is often more recent than what could be found in printed sources.

10. Keeping Records

Given the potential list of sources that could be accessed for information in the desk research project, it is critical to keep records of the publication, where it was found, article name, author name, and date. When it is not possible to copy an article, keep a brief abstract or description of the information found as well.

As the information gathered accumulates, it is worth using a software package such as Microsoft Access or Lotus Approach as a record-keeping system. The most useful data should also be stored in the company's MkIS.

11. Assessing Secondary Data

Using secondary data to assist in decision making and the desk research component of the marketing research project has many advantages over conducting primary research. Secondary data is readily available, is usually less expensive than a primary research study and is voluminous in output. On the other hand, there can be significant limitations to secondary data when compared with primary data. Among those limitations are accuracy, reliability, relevance, cost, availability and obsolescence.

Accuracy and Reliability of Secondary Information

Raw data is subject to interpretation, analysis, manipulation, and even misuse. As most secondary information sources do not provide the raw data that was used to draw conclusions, you cannot always sure about its accuracy.

A recent study on the market for complementary medicines in the UK will provide a relevant example. Mintel Marketing Intelligence Services commissioned and published a study of this market with information on trends in the market, consumer perceptions, legal issues and key competitors. The report focused on complementary medicines such as homeopathic products, herbs and aromatherapy oils. Mintel reported sales of these preparations at £72 million in 1996, a growth of 41% over five years.

An article published in *The Sunday Times* on alternative and complementary health misinterpreted the data provided by Mintel when it used this £72 million sales figure to describe the size of the *overall* complementary market in the UK. The overall market includes not only medicinal and herbal preparations but also vitamins and supplements and the services provided by practitioners such as acupuncturists, herbalists, homeopaths and aromatherapists. Consequently, the author significantly underestimated total sales—a figure closer to £2 billion annually—in the industry and gave a false impression to the readers of the article.

This example shows that information and, in particular, statistics can often be misinterpreted or reported inaccurately. Therefore, as a researcher, you must always treat secondary information with some scepticism. To be sure they are accurate, try to find the original source for all statistics in reports or articles. The original source should also provide a description of the methodology used to collect the data as well as a description of the sample used and its size.

Inaccuracies in data presentation and interpretation come from author bias, an inadequate sample, poor analysis of findings or simple carelessness. While it is not the only industry fraught with examples of poor secondary information, the complementary and alternative medicine market has its fair share. Vitamin and herbal products are two of the fastest-growing consumer product markets in the UK and manufacturers, retailers, and consumers alike are keen to stay abreast of developments. Because of British and European laws, manufacturers of these products are not allowed to make claims that their product will cure a particular medical condition unless they obtain a product licence, an expensive and time-consuming undertaking. However, retailers in particular health shops often produce their own periodicals and magazines that *do* make claims about the products sold but these claims may be based on studies with poor methodologies and very small samples. For example, a well-known herbal preparation for muscle pain and weakness claimed to be successful with 80% of the patients in the study. The sample size was only 15! When this information is then reported in other articles or finds its way into health websites, for example, confusion and inaccuracy spread.

Relevance

Researchers will also need to consider how *relevant* the secondary information is. Given the vast amount of information available, it is easy to become sidetracked with information that is outside the scope of the study or not relevant to the task at hand. A clear definition of the information needed is thus very important.

Sometimes good information becomes irrelevant because it is defined in terms that are not useful for the research project. For example, if a study reports on 'household consumption' of cereals whereas the required research needs to identify 'individual or per capita consumption' of cereals, if another study cannot be found, the investigator will have to conduct a primary research study.

Furthermore, some research studies do not define the scope of their findings. A 1999 study notes that Kellogg's profits were down 22% over the previous year. It was not clear from the article whether these figures represented global profits or US profits only (Anon., 1999). If the researcher's study was interested in global figures, he or she would not be able to rely on this source of data to draw conclusions about the company's overall financial situation.

Timeliness and Obsolescence

Information can become outdated very quickly. For example, the UK Census is collected only every ten years. Fortunately, some research firms conduct mini-census studies regularly and sell the updated information to users.

Information on consumer buying patterns, competitor activities and market shares can be outdated even before it is published so it is important to use it with caution and as a guide only, especially if planning to make resource allocation decisions based upon it. Always look first for studies published within the past few months, if not the last year. If the first source consulted is dated by more than one or two years, look for something more recent.

Cost

Collecting and disseminating information is increasingly becoming big business. With research reports costing up to £2400 and on-line database vendors charging up to £100 000 in annual fees, some critics feel that good competitive data is now available only to large firms. As more sophisticated digital technology becomes available to the average household, the cost of information may begin to fall. Whatever the direction the information market takes, cost *will* remain a factor. Company managers should view access to good information as a form of competitive advantage that can be valued as part of the company's asset base and therefore be willing to make the investment.

Non-availability

A further problem with secondary information is that it may not be available. Despite finding an abstract or reference to a good source, it is not always possible to get hold of the original publication. It could be out of print, on loan elsewhere, available only to subscribers or not in any accessible libraries.

The problems of availability, accuracy, relevance, and timeliness are increased when the study involves international markets. Not all governments keep accurate records and market research industries in many countries are as yet undeveloped. Primary research and good contacts are even more essential in such countries than at home.

The Mind of the Desk Researcher

Research requires a number of skills as well as a certain disposition. Good researchers are dedicated, resourceful, sceptical, questioning and focused. They are skilled in developing a search plan, finding information, using the tools and resources available and in keeping good records.

In any research project, it is important to begin with the orientation that almost everything required for the project is out there, the researcher just has to find it. This will help to give the researcher an open mind and the perseverance and dedication needed to find all relevant sources. Because of the frequency with which data inaccuracies occur, it is important to remain sceptical about the data and information found. Whenever possible, find the original source of the data quoted, the methodology used, the objectives of the study, when it was collected and the sample size. Cross-check data with other sources.

A good researcher will be resourceful and very familiar with the key sources of information in the field, whether they are indexes, databases, Internet-based, or individual decision makers. Information in other—even non-related—fields should also be consulted for new insights and ideas. When assessing consumer buying patterns, for example, readings in the fields of psychology, sociology and even anthropology can provide the latest thinking on how people, groups and societies behave. To assess consumer buying behaviour in a foreign market, the researcher should also review historical and cultural studies of that country. Trying to consider all relevant sources without facing information overload, however, is a task that requires experience and skill.

Researchers will spend the time necessary to familiarize themselves with the tools and techniques needed to help in the information search. It is also important to keep good records and a proper bibliography of all the identified sources. Over time, the desk researchers will create their own personal marketing and business information system and begin to develop a network of contacts for future searches.

The ability to find and assess information is a critical and a marketable skill. Few people are truly proficient in the search methods and critical thinking skills needed to make good use of business and marketing information. Those that are proficient have developed a significant personal competitive advantage.

Conclusion

Desk research can play an important role in all stages of the marketing research process. Using sources of existing information, marketers can further clarify the problem area and sometimes answer the research question without the need for a primary study. Desk research is also used to define markets, set forecasts, assess the business environment and understand the needs and characteristics of target customers.

Secondary sources are used in the desk research process. Tenacious and creative researchers will familiarize themselves with the wide range of secondary sources that are available, and develop the skills to assess these sources for accuracy and relevance. While desk research using secondary sources is generally less expensive than a primary research study, the information gathered may not be specific enough to the problem or decision area in question. Furthermore, it is rare that data gathered in the desk research process can be generalized to the population under investigation, such as the target market for a new product or the perceptions of current customers about the company's products.

When the research requires such generalizations, then a primary study should be undertaken. Nevertheless, a well-constructed and thorough desk research study will improve the overall design and outcome of the primary study and should remain a starting point and a central component of the marketing research process.

References

Anonymous (1999). 'Kellogg's results fulfil gloomy predictions', *Agra Food News*, 11 February.

Glossbrenner, A. and Glossbrenner, E. (1999). *Search Engines and the World Wide Web*, 2nd edn, Berkeley, CA: Peach Pit Press, 34–38.

Kotler, P. (1997). *Marketing Management: Analysis, Implementation, Planning and Control*, 9th international edn, Englewood Cliffs, NJ: Prentice-Hall International, 135.

Work Assignments

1. Desk research can be used in a number of different marketing decision-making scenarios. Describe three uses of desk research.
2. Explain how desk research can be used in the marketing research process.
3. Consider that you are asked to conduct research into the ice cream market in the UK. You are interested in the size of the market, market shares of key competitors, factors affecting the industry, and target markets for ice cream. Go to the library and identify four appropriate sources of information.
4. Assume you are conducting research for a large breakfast cereal manufacturer. You are planning to develop a range of organic cereals. Using the Internet and the search engines listed in this chapter, collect as much information as you can about the competition and their marketing programmes.
5. Describe the criteria to be used when assessing secondary data.

6. Two critical steps in the secondary information search are beginning with a clear definition of your research needs, and keeping records of your sources in a marketing information system. Explain why these steps are so important.
7. Explain why desk research alone is not usually sufficient to solve a marketing research problem.

Qualitative Research: Data Collection and Analysis

4

Learning Outcomes

After reading this chapter, you will be able to:

- Differentiate between the different data-collection procedures used for the collection of qualitative research data.

- Outline the circumstances in which a particular qualitative data-collection method should be used.

- Organize a focus group, write a moderator's outline, and conduct a group discussion.

- Organize an in-depth interview, write a moderator's outline, and conduct the interview.

- Describe what projective techniques are and in what circumstances they should be used.

- Understand how qualitative data is analysed and why focus group discussions and in-depth interview conversations are taped and transcribed.

Introduction

This chapter seeks to introduce the reader to the field of qualitative market research, to the industry, and to provide an understanding of the nature of qualitative market research. Qualitative market research is defined, its advantages and disadvantages *vis-à-vis* other market research techniques are explored briefly and a discussion of the value of qualitative research, in terms of whether it is valid and reliable, takes place within this chapter. Individual qualitative research techniques are outlined including focus groups, in-depth interviews, projective techniques and observation studies. Focus groups as a market research technique are explored in depth. In most marketing research texts, the nature of qualitative data analysis is left unconsidered. In this chapter, the reader is introduced to some of the more important concepts and techniques in this area. Finally, the text is interspersed with practical examples from consultancy projects undertaken by the author.

The Qualitative Market Research Industry

Qualitative marketing research has become increasingly valued over the last decade or so. It has traditionally been less well regarded than quantitative research as practitioners have argued that it is not objective, its results cannot be generalized and it produces data which can only be interpreted in a very specific context. Qualitative research services are now offered by a number of large agencies. Table 4.1 provides the details of the top ten UK market research organizations offering qualitative research.

Table 4.1 demonstrates clearly that consumer qualitative research is conducted in greater quantities than business-to-business qualitative research by the top ten agencies. Later in this chapter we will discuss which methods are most appropriate for the two different types of sector.

The voice of UK qualitative market research practitioners is the Association for Qualitative Research (AQR) and it had around 1150 individual members in 2001. Many of these members will be research executives from research agencies which specialize in providing qualitative research, although there are a number of agencies providing expertise in both qualitative and quantitative methods. Brand-planning departments within advertising agencies frequently conduct their own qualitative research projects. In addition, companies frequently have their own in-house qualitative research sections within the market research department and some of these individuals will be members of AQR.

Table 4.1   Top ten UK qualitative market research organizations

Rank	Consultancy	Consumer (£m)	Business-to-business (£m)	Total (£m)
1	Maritz-TRBI	8.899	1.203	10.102
2	Research International	—	—	7.852
3	Hauck Research Services	7.214	0.220	7.434
4	Added Value	6.478	0.725	7.203
5	Taylor Nelson Sofres	1.017	6.099	7.116
6	NFO UK	5.454	0.390	5.844
7	Martin Hamblin Group	0.640	3.842	4.483
8	RDSi	—	—	3.740
9	NOP Research Group	2.810	0.703	3.513
10	Insight Medical Research	—	3.174	3.174

Source: Marketing (2000). Adapted from an article in the July 2000 edition of Marketing magazine with the permission of Haymarket Business Publications.

Defining Qualitative Research

Qualitative research adopts a variety of different data-collection methods and techniques and is used in both the consumer and business-to-business sectors. It has been defined slightly differently depending on the author. However, two definitions which broadly agree on the nature of qualitative research, define it as follows:

> A widely used term for research that does not subject research findings to quantification or quantitative analysis (Proctor, 2000: 182).
>
> A form of exploratory research involving small samples and non-structured data collection procedures (Parasuraman, 1991: 251).

In both definitions, the implication is that the research involves small datasets. This has a significant impact upon research design, data collection and analysis. Qualitative market research has a number of distinctive characteristics. These include the fact that it:

- is usually based on small samples or small groups of people
- is not generalizable or representative of larger populations
- seeks to understand consumer behaviour, motivations, opinions and attitudes
- seeks to understand customer and consumer motivations
- produces in-depth data
- uses unstructured data-collection methods
- uses non-statistical data analysis procedures
- requires a high degree of interpretation
- is often used in the exploratory stages of research to set hypotheses
- may be followed by quantitative research to test the generalizability of any findings.

Qualitative research may frequently be conducted with sample sizes smaller than 30 respondents, particularly in business-to-business research. As such, it is not generalizable to larger populations. The objective of this type of research is to understand the nature of consumer and customer behaviour from affective (emotional), cognitive (thought-processing) and conative (motivational) perspectives. Qualitative research more often aims to uncover the emotional and motivational side of behaviour and attitudes. How do consumers feel when they drink ice-cold Coca-Cola on a summer's day? What criteria does a university purchasing team use when buying computer equipment from Compaq?

Qualitative research often uses data-collection procedures that are unstructured. For instance, non-probability methods of sampling are frequently adopted, particularly the convenience sampling method (see Chapter 7). Data analysis procedures used are typically non-statistical although there has been a trend towards more systematic coding of the data collected. Recently, there has been an attempt by research agencies to quantify the qualitative research data where research budgets permit by increasing the sample sizes, using the same data-collection procedures, and analysing the data using computer programs which systematically analyse the qualitative data. A more recent development in this field is data mining, where data is collected and analysed automatically (see Chapter 11). Knowledge management systems also allow large quantities of qualitative data to be analysed and displayed. In both cases, however, it is unlikely that computer systems will replace human interpretation in the near future completely since this would require more advanced systems working using artificially intelligent software.

Such research is often conducted as a preliminary to a larger research study designed to provide the researcher with a better understanding of the background to a particular problem. The qualitative research may allow the researcher to develop a questionnaire, specifically the range of questions and their responses, or to set hypotheses to be tested in a later quantitative study.

Advantages and Disadvantages of Qualitative Research Techniques

Qualitative approaches are frequently used where an exploratory research design is being employed whereas quantitative research designs are used where the research design is conclusive. Malhotra (1996: 89) indicates that exploratory research designs should be used when the objective of the research is to discover new ideas and insights. It is characteristically a flexible and versatile approach to research design and tends to use expert surveys, secondary data-collection methods and qualitative research designs in order to collect the relevant data. Zikmund (1997: 129) argues that when an exploratory research design is employed, the appropriate categories of research design are experience surveys, secondary data analysis, case studies, focus groups, projective techniques and in-depth interviews.

Table 4.2 indicates the advantages and disadvantages of the different qualitative research techniques. The different methods are useful for different circumstances. The experienced qualitative market researcher will know which method to use when. Focus groups are often used to obtain ideas and opinions in consumer research but they do not allow detailed probing of individual respondents. To do this, the researcher would need to use in-depth interviews, but in-depth interviews are costly and time-consuming to conduct and analyse. Focus groups are not so useful obtaining sensitive data (e.g., condom usage among teenagers) although in-depth interviews do allow greater probing of the respondent and a more intimate atmosphere. If the researcher is aiming to uncover such data, the most appropriate method to use is projective techniques, where the respondents are asked questions in such a way that they do not feel that the question they are being asked is directly about them. This will be described further in the section on qualitative research methods. However, if the researcher wants more individual data but does not wish

Table 4.2 Advantages and disadvantages of different qualitative research techniques

Technique	Marketing research type	Advantages	Disadvantages
Focus groups	Primarily used for consumer research	Offers researcher good understanding of the research problem Useful for gaining insights into sample	Difficult to probe individual respondents
In-depth interviews	Primarily used for business-to-business research	Allows detailed exploration of research problem Good technique to use for gaining insights into specific populations	Depends on the skill of the interviewer
Projective techniques	Primarily used for consumer research	Highly useful for obtaining subconscious and sensitive information	High degree of interpretation bias
Case studies	Primarily used for business-to-business research	Entire organizations or entities can be investigated Useful for gaining insights and producing hypotheses for future research	Results are tentative and based on individual cases Highly dependent on the skill of the case investigator
Experience survey	Primarily used for business-to-business research	Helps to formulate research problem and clarify concepts Provides detailed knowledge of area of research interest	Difficulty in contacting and arranging interviews Reliance on few interviews, not generalizable
Secondary data collection	Used for both business-to-business and consumer research	Economical method Helps define background to research	Limited use since circumstances may be very different in current situation
Observation	Primarily used for consumer research	Provides understanding of behaviour Data generalizable	Does not provide an understanding of reasons for behaviour Can be costly

to conduct a quantitative study, probably because the researcher does not have any experience of the research area they are investigating, he or she may opt to conduct a pilot study. This is effectively a small-scale survey that frequently uses an open questioning approach. It is used to pretest the research methodology of a quantitative survey to check its effectiveness.

It may be that the research requires investigation of a specific organization. Perhaps the researcher is a management consultant who has been commissioned to determine why sales revenue has dropped sharply over the past two years. In order to find out why, the management consultant might conduct in-depth interviews, or even focus groups, among a number of employees within the company and obtain detailed records from the firm's management information system, and from outside the industry where these are available. This is known as the case study method. Notice that it mixes the in-depth interviewing technique with internal and external secondary data collection (see Chapter 3). If the researcher wanted to investigate a problem that required considerable expertise on the part of the respondents, he or she might conduct an experience survey. This principally uses in-depth interviews with a sample from a rare population, which is frequently small and difficult to access.

Where the research problem can be solved using existing internal (company) or external (usually market reports, e.g., Mintel, Ovum) records, secondary data collection is usually the method that is used because it is usually cheaper and faster. Finally, where the research problem requires a detailed understanding of human behaviour rather than attitudes, and particularly where it is likely that consumers or customers do not necessarily know how they behave in certain situations, the use of observation studies is advocated. Thus, to determine the demographic make-up of a crowd of fans at a football match, a researcher could organize observers at the gates so that they could record the gender and perceived age of each supporter as they passed by.

Not all the methods that are indicated in Table 4.2 are considered further, since most undergraduate marketing research courses deal with a limited range. The techniques covered in more depth in this chapter include focus groups, in-depth interviews, projective techniques, and observation techniques. Secondary data collection is considered further in Chapter 3.

Qualitative Research Methods

In this section, the most popular techniques used in qualitative research are considered in further detail and the process by which they are conducted is outlined and examples are provided. The methods considered include focus groups, in-depth interviews, projective techniques and observation methods. This is not an exhaustive list of qualitative methodologies and there are many other examples. However, these are the four most used by the market research industry. An understanding of these methods should provide the marketing or market research student or the new qualitative market research executive with a better understanding of the way in which qualitative data is collected and its impact on how the data is analysed.

Focus Groups

Focus groups, or group discussions as they were originally known, are probably the most popular form of qualitative research. Most qualitative research conducted in the UK is based on focus group discussions. Many agencies and clients incorrectly use the terms qualitative research and focus groups synonymously, although this fails to appreciate the range of other methods that are available to the qualitative researcher.

A focus group is an informal discussion conducted with approximately eight to twelve people who are convened by a business or a research agency to discuss some aspect of marketing. They are usually conducted for consumer research purposes. Often, group discussions are conducted with fewer people, usually because of a belief that the group dynamics are improved with slightly fewer people. It is not uncommon to hear of focus groups being conducted with six or seven people. The groups typically last between 1 and 3 hours and are usually conducted in hotel meeting rooms or on agency (or client) premises. Participants are usually financially rewarded for their participation, e.g., £30 for $1\frac{1}{2}$ hours.

Focus groups are often conducted for a variety of different objectives. For instance, they may be convened to discuss:

1. New product concepts, or proposed product changes (e.g., packaging and labelling)
2. Changes in customer tastes and requirements (not necessarily just the consumer but also the business customer)
3. Individual marketing mix issues (e.g., pricing, distribution or service issues)
4. Advertising concepts and copy to determine its receipt among the intended audience
5. Branding issues (e.g., how a new corporate logo or corporate name change will be received).

The membership of a focus group usually depends on the objectives of the research. Thus, a broadcast advertising evaluation study for Tampax[TM] would incorporate menstruating women of different ages possibly with different user requirements. A focus group study designed to determine whether the price of a new football strip is acceptable to a particular club's fans might incorporate a number of different groups depending on supporter loyalty (e.g., season ticket holders, club members and matchday attendees). Typical focus group studies use between four and twelve groups of eight to twelve people and so the sample sizes are relatively small *vis-à-vis* quantitative project samples sizes (see Chapter 7).

Focus groups are usually constructed using similar participants to encourage positive discussion. In this way, the discussion is then focused according to similarities between the respondents. Conversely, the group could incorporate a more diverse membership. Sometimes, the client may be a participant within the group. Often, the issue is whether focus groups should be assembled from current product users or non-users or a mixture of the two, so as to provoke debate between the two factions.

Focus groups usually comprise individuals from the same specific demographic groupings in terms of the age, gender and social class. This is to ensure that group members feel at ease with people of similar characteristics and so are more likely to divulge their opinions.

The group is led by a trained moderator who begins the discussion and attempts to get everyone to participate in honest discussion and debate. The moderator will maintain a certain degree of control throughout the meeting but he or she will usually let the discussion follow any new or interesting paths as they arise. The larger the focus group, the more difficult it is to do this. Box 4.1 provides a brief transcription from an actual focus group conducted to evaluate a sales promotion campaign among students aged between 16 and 24. In this brief snippet of conversation, the moderator is explaining the objectives of the exercise.

Box 4.1   Focus group: introductory conversation

Moderator: 'Let me tell you what this is about. It is a focus group and the general point is to get some idea of what you think about a certain topic. I do not want you to feel you have to hold anything back. Sometimes we may disagree with some of our colleagues here, that is not a problem. Please let us know exactly what you think. This is being recorded for a commercial client. They will not know who you are because when it goes for data analysis purposes you are not individually identified. Thank you for participating. This is a group discussion, you are not talking to me. You are talking to everyone. Can I ask you to introduce yourselves? Tell me your name and what you enjoy doing in your spare time.'

Respondent 1: 'My name is Saj. I enjoy playing football in my spare time and enjoy watching it as well. I enjoy business type newspapers because it helps me with my assignments.'

Respondent 2: 'My name is Stuart. I enjoy drinking, clubbing, just generally socializing really and I seem to spend more time on that than actual academic work.'

DISCUSSION CONTINUES, OTHER GROUP MEMBERS INTRODUCE THEMSELVES

When the discussion begins to move too far from the research objectives, the moderator often intervenes to redirect the debate. However, effective moderation occurs when the discussion takes place between individual group members rather than between the moderator and individual members. In order to achieve this type of discussion, the moderator may have to avoid looking at individual members. Usually, group members then turn to their colleagues in order to explain what they are saying and, hence, avoid embarrassment. This frequently happens in our everyday conversations. If one is talking to a group of friends and the person that we are addressing becomes distracted, we frequently turn to someone else and continue the conversation. Moderators should avoid making judgements about what respondents say since this may stifle further discussion.

Box 4.2 Focus group: beverage sales promotion campaign discussion

Moderator: 'I would like you to think about different promotions you have seen on bottles, cans and so on over the last three or four years. Which is the best promotion you have come across?'

Respondent 1: 'I remember there was a promotion about Pepsi in Italy. The scenario was a beach. There was this beautiful lady and a very nice girl as well. It was a really hot day and everybody was under the shade and you could hear the opening of the can or the bottle.'

Moderator: 'Are you talking about an advert?'

Respondent 1: 'Yes.'

Moderator: 'I don't want you to think about an advert. I don't want you to think about advertising but about sales promotion.'

Respondent 2: 'I remember ring-pulls. If you collected about thirty you got something, I think it was a gold(en) yo-yo.'

Moderator: 'Did anyone take part in that?'

Respondent 3: 'I tried to but it took too long.'

Moderator: 'What was wrong with it?'

Respondent 3: 'You had to buy about thirty cans.'

Respondent 4: 'Yes. Typical.'

DISCUSSION CONTINUES

In Box 4.2, focus group participants are discussing different sales promotion campaigns for a well-known beverage company, recounting examples of previous campaigns that they can remember. In this snippet of conversation, the moderator has to redirect a question because the respondents misunderstood its objective: which was to discuss sales promotion campaigns rather than advertising campaigns. The success of individual focus groups is often heavily dependent on group dynamics. The outcome of the discussion depends on how well the group interacts with each other and whether the moderator can produce an environment where participants feel at ease to divulge their opinions. Pleasant physical surroundings and the provision of refreshments may also encourage respondents to participate. If the respondents feel at ease, they are more likely to start to talk to each other rather than to the moderator.

Box 4.2 provides an example of this occurrence at the end of the conversation, when one respondent explains why they did not participate in a particular sales promotion campaign. Another participant responds providing an interesting understanding into why many young people do not respond to sales promotion campaigns. They find collecting ring-pulls tiresome. Further conversation suggested the notion that young people, particularly students, would be interested in the concept of logging onto a website every time they bought a particular canned beverage (using a password unique to each can) rather than collecting ring-pulls. Such a sales promotion concept would probably be too expensive to administer in such a form but the general concept might provide a way of increasing youth participation in sales promotion campaigns.

The process of designing and conducting focus groups is represented in Figure 4.1. The researcher firsts develops the objectives of the research prior to recruiting focus group members. A moderator is recruited and a moderator's outline is developed at this stage. This is a set of questions that allows the moderator to direct the conversation. Figure 4.2 provides an illustration of a moderator's outline used in a focus group conducted among football supporters of London Football Club.

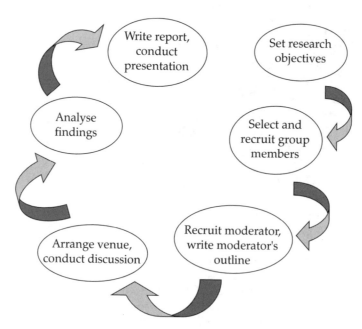

Figure 4.1 The focus group organization process

Question type	Question	Duration (min)
Opening	1. Going around the table, can you tell us your name and what you enjoy doing most when you're not watching football?	5
Introductory	2. What is it about London FC that makes you want to support them?	10
Key	3. We want you to draw a picture of a London FC fan that has been to watch a match and is walking out of the ground. Give the person a name and an age. Tell us what they do for a living. This person that you have drawn is saying something. Draw a speech bubble and let us know what they are saying.	20
	RESPONDENTS HOLD UP PICTURES	
	How are they similar?	
	How are they different?	
Transition	4. When you think of London Football Club and its image, what words come to mind? Take a moment to think about this and then write down 2 or 3 words on a piece of paper.	15
	AFTER A SHORT DELAY SAY:	
	Let's go around the table and I will make a list of these words on the flipchart.	
	If you were to pick one of these words as most appropriately describing London FC, which ONE would it be?	
Key	5. IDENTIFY 6 MOST COMMONLY OCCURRING ITEMS, IDENTIFY 6 ANTONYMS. ASK Q.4.	15
	In what way do these words describe London FC?	
Key	6. If London FC were a person, what kind of person would it be?	15
Key	PROVIDE MEMBERS WITH COPY OF BRAND VALUES	30
	7. Take a few minutes to look over the following words. In what way do you think London FC exhibits these values? What are your first impressions? ENSURE THAT EACH VALUE IS CONSIDERED—TICK BOX—PROBE ON ANSWERS	
	Proactive ☐	
	Stylish ☐	
	Exciting ☐	
	Friendly ☐	
	Accessible ☐	
	Professional ☐	
Ending	8. London FC are trying to improve their gate attendance so that they can afford to enter the Premier League, how can London FC further improve its image among its supporters?	10
Summary	9. Let me summarize the key points of the discussion.	5
	MODERATOR PROVIDES TWO MINUTES ORAL SUMMARY	
	Is that an adequate summary?	

Figure 4.2 Focus groups: moderator's outline

There are some variations in the common or typical focus group discussion. Mini-groups are smaller, usually consisting of four to six members who deal with sensitive or potentially embarrassing issues that may be better suited to more intimate discussion. Some groups may have two moderators, perhaps with different specialisms (e.g., a technical moderator in consumer marketing research may be required to understand buyer behaviour in the private investment market). The client may be involved in moderating the group if the group members are not afraid to speak out in front of him or her and the client has specific knowledge to discuss which is not easily shared with a moderator. On occasion, respondents may be asked to moderate their own groups where the presence of a typical moderator is likely to hinder the group's discussions. For instance, at the end of the semester, during the market research course at the university at which one of the authors lectures, in order to collect student feedback on the design and content of the course, the author organized student-moderated discussion groups. This was important since if the author, or another lecturer, had moderated the groups it is likely that the students would not have been so frank with their opinions.

Consumer panels are focus groups that meet on a frequent basis to discuss their experiences with a particular company or its products. Increasingly, British Premier League football clubs are conducting such panels among their supporters. These discussions typically consider pricing, food-service facilities, ticket availability, and merchandising issues. Local authorities are increasingly conducting citizens panels in order to involve the public in their decision making.

In-depth Interviews

An interview is defined in the *Oxford Handy Dictionary* as: 'meeting of persons for purpose of discussion; oral examination of applicant; conversation between reporter and person whose views he wishes to publish' (Fowler and Fowler, 1986). The word is derived from the French *entrevue* and literally means to see inside. An interview is concerned with gaining insights and determining meaning from an interactional relationship between interviewer and interviewee. There are numerous methods used in in-depth interviews. The most common methods used are laddering, hidden-issue questioning and symbolic analysis. Laddering is a method used whereby questioning proceeds from product characteristics to user characteristics. Hidden-issue questioning attempts to uncover deeply personal opinions and symbolic analysis is a technique used where the symbolic meaning of products or services are determined by asking respondents what they would do if they could no longer use that particular product or service. Another method used in in-depth interviewing is the 'funnel' technique. This is where the discussion is conducted initially at the broadest possible level and slowly narrowed down. In this method, the interviewer has a list of general points that need to be covered.

In in-depth interviews, the communication is between an interviewer and the individual participants. However, there are many differences between an in-depth interview and a traditional survey-based interview conducted in the street. Usually, the in-depth interview lasts for around an hour, whereas, the street survey interview might last between 10 and 30 minutes. Usually, in-depth interviews are conducted in the consumer's home or on business premises and, so, the interview situation is much more comfortable. In-depth interviewers also ask more open-ended questions since the respondents have the time and freedom to provide a deeper response to the questions. The question agenda becomes an interactive production between moderator and respondent as issues are covered which tend to be of more immediate interest to the respondents.

Indirect questioning techniques are often adopted when considering issues with which the respondent may not feel immediately comfortable. This may include dealing with sensitive people (e.g., children) or sensitive topics (e.g., deviant consumer behaviour). This form of questioning is discussed in more detail in the section on projective techniques but projective techniques may be used in either in-depth interviews or focus groups. Indirect questioning may probe the respondents' responses to highly controversial or emotionally charged issues.

The objective of the in-depth interview is to probe the respondent's answers in order to identify underlying reasons and motivations. A prestructured questionnaire is not used as it is in survey research. The interviewer is free to let the respondent explore a number of issues related to the central themes of the questions. The interview normally takes the form of an informal conversation rather than a series of questions and answers. If an interview is semi-structured, the interviewer will usually have a series of topics to cover. If the interview is unstructured, then the respondent has greater freedom to talk about whatever they want to, although the interviewer is still expected to cover certain concepts. The most important considerations for in-depth interviewing are choosing the number and type of respondents and the degree of structure that will form the interview.

Sometimes, the respondents will be experts in the particular area that is being examined (an experience survey). This may involve executives who are experts on the local market for a particular product, for instance, or a number of customers of the company who have experience of the company's operations and services. Both industrial and consumer respondents are usually preselected. They are approached prior to the interview and asked for their participation in the research process. If the research study involves interviews with experts, gaining access to such people is often very difficult. The number of interviews conducted depends on the research objectives and the research funds available. Usually, the required information can be gathered using a small set of interviews. Interviews usually last longer for industrial studies but interviews with consumers are usually between half an hour and an hour.

Figure 4.3 illustrates the process of organizing in-depth interviews. In many ways, the process mirrors that of organizing focus groups. However, because of the greater amount of data generated, the process of editing and transcribing becomes more involved. This impacts upon the writing up of in-depth interview data. Most marketing researchers will attempt to compose a story from the interview transcriptions rather than simply report verbatim comments, as with the analysis of focus group data. Data analysis procedures are covered in more detail in a later section of this chapter.

A further difference is the nature of the data collection. Often, data collection using in-depth interviews requires the interviewer to visit the respondents *in situ* (wherever they are working or living) and so this may impact upon who is eventually selected for interview. Which respondents are eventually recruited and

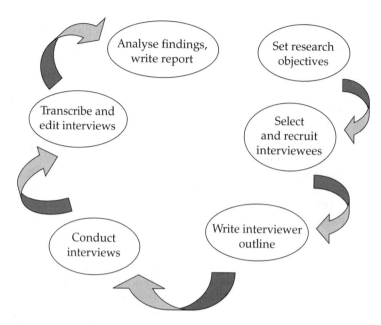

Figure 4.3 The in-depth interview organization process

selected depends on the research objectives and the type of research being conducted, e.g., whether it is business-to-business or consumer marketing research. With in-depth interview studies, the writing of the report and the analysis of findings often take place more or less simultaneously.

Projective Techniques

Projective techniques use indirect forms of questioning, which allow respondents to project their feelings, attitudes and opinions onto a third party. These techniques are most useful when examining issues with which the respondent does not feel at ease. By invoking a third party, often in the form of a cartoon, photograph or illustration, the respondent is asked how the person in the picture would respond, behave or feel in the given situation. This allows respondents to be more open about their feelings. Projective techniques were originally developed for use in clinical psychology. Some psychologists now argue that these methods are being used in commercial contexts for which they were not originally intended or designed. However, marketing seeks to empathize with the customer/consumer whenever that is possible. Thus, techniques aimed at providing the researcher with an understanding of customer/consumer emotions and behaviour should also be relevant in the commercial context.

Projective techniques, when used in marketing research, generally allow respondents to describe their own association with an enterprise or product indirectly, without explicitly stating that the association they have is their own. This technique allows the subjugation of the respondent's superego, ensuring that respondents intervene less with how they really feel, to please the interviewer. The difficulty for the researcher comes in understanding, and interpreting, what the respondent's response really means. There are a number of different projective techniques in use by marketing research organizations.

Word association techniques require the respondent to say the first word that comes to mind when they are exposed to another word (a brand name, a product feature or attribute). Respondents are instructed not to think too hard since it is their immediate response that the interviewer wishes to glean. For example, if a group of consumers are asked to state the first words that come to mind when they see an ice-cold can of Coke, they might say 'refreshing', 'thirst-quenching', 'cool' or even something like 'top beverage'. This method is particularly useful for positioning and branding research.

Completion techniques require the respondent to complete a storyboard or a sentence. The respondent may be presented with a sentence such as 'people who eat at McDonald's are _____ and those eat at Burger King are _____'. This example allows the respondent to consider the two types of person interdependently. Thus, they consider the two types of people and how they think about one particular group affects how they think about the other. Completion techniques may also use a single subject, e.g., 'people who eat at McDonald's are _____'. As well as completing sentences, respondents may be asked to complete paragraphs or even whole stories. Thus, the researcher can structure the extent of the respondent's input. Typically, the greater the degree of input from the respondent, the more difficulty the researcher will have in interpreting the response.

Pictorial construction techniques present a situation to the respondent who may be asked to describe the subjects in the picture, to comment on what is happening and to complete speech or thought bubbles in a diagram. Respondents are asked to construct a story from a variety of pictures provided. The Thematic Apperception Test (TAT) exemplifies the construction technique. Respondents are asked to construct a story based on pictures that are shown to them, thus giving the researcher an indication of their perceptual interpretation of the pictures. This provides the researcher with an indication of the respondents' personality and feelings.

Pictorial construction techniques may often be used in focus groups to get a better idea of how consumers or buyers perceive organizations. In one mini-group of London Football Club supporters conducted by the author, the participants are asked to draw a diagram of a typical London FC supporter with a speech bubble and to explain who they are, what they are saying and what their occupation is. Figure 4.4 provides an indication of what one season ticket holder drew during this exercise. The aim was to see how supporters viewed themselves and their club's fan base. It was felt that if there were to be any strong criticism of the club and its supporters, it would more likely come out in drawings and the supporters' subsequent discussion of these drawings.

Figure 4.4 Pictorial construction example

In *role-playing*, the respondent assumes a particular role and is asked to act it out. They may be asked to impersonate the checkout attendant at a particular supermarket or a retail sales assistant. The researcher hopes that the participant will reveal their attitudes and thoughts through their actions and behaviour when they are placed in different role-playing situations. In this technique, the degree of interpretation required is often considerable, particularly when the respondent acts out aspects of the role with which the observers are not familiar. Asking the respondents what they meant by a particular action enhances interpretation. Respondents often then reveal exactly what they might have previously been less inclined to say.

Observation

In observation studies, the researcher observes the behaviour of consumers. Observational research stems from research in anthropology, which originated as an academic discipline from an examination of the behaviour of people in 'primitive' societies. In this situation, observation was a useful method of understanding the subjects of the study because complex linguistic communication was not possible. Observational methods are also widely used in organizational research to examine how people behave in groups, in teams and as organizational members, particularly for recruitment and selection purposes.

The applications of observation studies are relatively limited in marketing research, although it is extremely useful in collecting behavioural data, as opposed to attitudinal data. This allows marketing researchers to collect data on what people actually do, rather than what they say they will do. With the aid of a video camera, researchers can record when people enter and leave a particular outlet and how they move about within it. This is useful information to have for merchandising purposes. This allows researchers to determine where to place high-profit products in order to maximize sales. For example, research has demonstrated that products placed at eye-level achieve the maximum exposure.

Observational methods are frequently used to understand consumer behaviour in mass transit studies. They can provide a simple understanding of customer demographics, start and end location of travel, price paid (since obtaining a ticket may be by means of self-service) and time taken. Similarly, observational studies would be useful in a theme park in determining the route taken around the park by different groups of people. Thus, if the management of Alton Towers wished to bring more children into the park it might commission a study to observe which rides and attractions children visited most.

In business marketing research, observation studies might investigate how people are using their product. This may help the firm to identify new product formulations. If customers are not using the product correctly, the business may have to change their advertising to demonstrate how to use the product properly. Derivatives of observational methods, where communication is both possible and desired, include accompanied shopping and mystery shopping methods.

In accompanied shopping, a researcher accompanies a customer throughout the purchasing episode. Multiple retailer grocers have frequently used this method in an attempt to understand the thoughts, behaviour and reactions of the respondent during the trip. Participants are contacted in advance and informed of the objectives of the process. Once they agree, participants are usually accompanied on a weekly shopping trip for a specific period of time. The session often begins with an unstructured conversation at the respondent's home about the shopping experience. They are asked how often they visit the supermarket, the transport methods that they use, their weekly expenditure and how that is broken down among different product groupings, and why they choose to shop at a particular supermarket. When accompanying the shopper, the researcher observes the participant's behaviour and the products he or she examines. The method is particularly useful since the interviewer can ask the shopper why he or she did not choose a particular item and why. This provides the researcher with an understanding of the shopper's product preferences. Critics of this method suggest that the very presence of the interviewer alters the behaviour of the participant and produces a different shopping experience than would usually be the case.

One type of research that combines observation methods with a survey-based approach is mystery shopping. This form of research is usually aimed at determining the standard of customer service received by a customer. It allows organizations to measure the service performance of their own (or other organizations') staff. This type of research can be used for either business-to-business or consumer marketing research purposes. High street retail organizations usually commission this type of research although it is increasingly being commissioned by Internet-based organizations who require mystery shoppers to secretly purchase items and fill out website and service-evaluation forms.

Initially, the market research organization has to recruit a panel of mystery shoppers. These are people who are prepared to buy items from preselected retail (or e-retail) organizations and then fill out surveys (usually on-line nowadays) using service-based questions. Examples of these types of comments include:

- Did the member of staff who dealt with your purchase smile?
- Did they make eye contact with you at least twice?
- Did they say please and thank you where appropriate?
- Before leaving the outlet did any member of staff make a friendly parting comment (for example, 'Thanks for calling', 'Hope you enjoyed your meal', etc.)?

The resultant data allows organizations to analyse strengths and weaknesses in their service performance. In turn, this allows them to design and implement appropriate training and internal marketing programmes.

Qualitative Data Analysis

Qualitative market research techniques are analysed in different ways. Some methods require more interpretation than others, e.g., projective techniques versus focus groups. However, text-based market research methods generally use procedures that analyse the content of transcripts. Since this process is more systematic and better documented than the more interpretive methods, this process will be described briefly in this section.

How one interprets and analyses the data associated with the qualitative research process also depends, to a large extent, on the philosophical perspective that one takes. This concerns itself with the extent to which 'reality' can be found in the interview data. For example, a radical positivist perspective would suggest that the interview provides a 'mirror reflection' of the reality that exists in the social world. They suggest that the data produced from an interview can be regarded as free from bias generated from the social setting of the interview. Radical social constructivists suggest that no knowledge about a reality in the social world can be obtained from an interview because the interview is an interactive creation between the interviewer and interview subject. Essentially, the two perspectives could probably be viewed at both ends of a spectrum relating the interview, as a research instrument for gathering truthful data, to the concept of artificiality, on the one hand, and reality, on the other.

Malhotra (1996: 30) argues that some marketing decision makers consider that structured, qualitative data analysis is not particularly important. He states that lengthy analysis might produce boring descriptions instead of insightful conclusions; qualitative research is about imagination and flair; too much analysis can be mechanistic and boring and that many well-known researchers do not conduct any systematic analysis of qualitative data other than to read the transcripts and interpret them while reading. Chisnall (1997: 183) says that 'critics of qualitative research have suggested that some of the "findings" of this method of enquiry are too greatly influenced by the individual analyst's training and background, with resultant subjectivity tending to bias analyses'. It is likely that marketing researchers have not bothered to conduct qualitative analysis to a great extent in the past, due to the fact that they lack the disciplinary tools found in other areas such as the cognate social sciences (Matthews, 1996).

In order to produce a 'story' from the data, NUDIST data analysis software is frequently used although other computer software analysis packages also exist. Generally, however, they use a similar coding methodology. 'QSR NUDIST software is a computer package designed to aid users in the handling of Non-numerical and Unstructured Data in qualitative analysis, by supporting processes of coding data in an Index System, Searching text or searching patterns of coding and Theorizing about the data' (QSR, 1997). This usually requires that interviews are fully transcribed into word document format before being converted into text files in order to facilitate analysis.

Most qualitative research writers agree that composing qualitative research is about storytelling. It is an effort to produce a picture of the world about which one is writing. Researchers can either weave description and interpretation of the data together in one chapter or present them separately. Initially, interviews are first read by the researcher several times and areas of interesting text are highlighted. Each of these paragraphs, lines or words is then 'coded' manually. Each highlighted area is then placed into a free node (a category without connections to other categories) and labelled. For example, a comment from a focus group member in a sales promotion study such as 'Why do they always use can ring-pulls for sales promotions?' could be coded using the term promotion or ring-pulls. This comment might represent a text unit. The analyst then assigns this label. Each text unit could be placed within more than one free node depending on the relevance of the text unit. For example, the sales promotion comment might be placed in both promotion and ring-pulls. Once all those highlighted areas of interest have been placed within the free nodes (coded), these comments are attached to 'umbrella' nodes (fixed nodes) which theoretically (and logically) encompassed them. The text is initially placed into free nodes by a cursory reading of the transcripts and by using the qualitative data analysis software's search text function for the occurrence of certain words.

The NUDIST package allows the researcher to theorize about any linkages that exist between free nodes by determining the relation of text units within and between nodes. Thus, if various text units are coded in two separate nodes, NUDIST is capable of providing the researcher with all those text units that overlap between the two nodes (those text units that are coded in both nodes) or all those text units within the two nodes that do not overlap, and so on. These and other functions allow the researcher to theorize about the relationships between groups of data (nodes).

One such relationship, where text units have been coded in two free nodes, is illustrated in the Venn diagram in Figure 4.5. In this hypothetical case, because the two concepts overlap (with certain text units), it can be argued that they are linked, by those text units that reside in the shaded area. When the data is originally input, the relationship between Concepts 1 and 2 (the text units in the interviews) is unknown. NUDIST allows the researcher to determine where comments have been coded and ascertain the relationship between those coded comments by determining the similarity between the text units.

Another common example of a relationship that often exists between the text units includes one concept subsuming another—see Figure 4.6. In this case, the

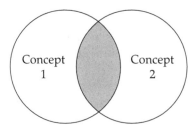

Figure 4.5   Venn diagram illustrating overlapping nodes

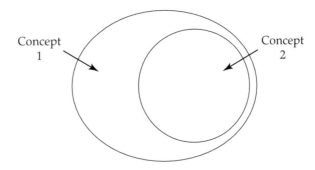

Figure 4.6   Venn diagram illustrating subsuming nodes

software allows the researcher to determine that one concept is linked to another and is a sub-section of it. Thus, Concept 2 forms part of Concept 1.

The data analysis process allows the writer to form an understanding of the linkages between the data. Thus, the data in the overlap area of Figure 4.5 provides the reader with an understanding of how Concepts 1 and 2 are interlinked. For example, if the research study was investigating the reasons for teenage compulsive drinking behaviour using in-depth interviews, Concept 1 might be comments coded under the label 'escapism' and Concept 2 might be comments coded under the label 'parental pressure'. Analysis using NUDIST's index search capabilities provides the analyst with comments that relate to both escapism and parental pressure. This might indicate to the research what aspects of parental pressure lead to a teenager's desire for escapism. In Figure 4.6, Concept 2 is a sub-set of Concept 1. For example, in a business marketing research study investigating the purchase of computers in universities, Concept 1 might be all comments coded under 'purchase criteria' while Concept 2 might specifically be comments related to 'systems specifications'. Thus, 'systems specifications' are a sub-set of 'purchase criteria' because universities would usually buy computers for other reasons, e.g., cost, availability and network capabilities.

Conclusion

Qualitative research is a growing part of the British marketing research industry. It is often used as a preliminary format to inform quantitative marketing research. It uses small samples, unstructured data-collection methods and non-statistical analysis methods. The use of different techniques depends on the circumstances and objectives of the research although in-depth interviews are used more frequently in business marketing research while focus groups, projective techniques and observation methods are employed more in consumer marketing research. Qualitative research collects rich, in-depth data. It is, therefore, more difficult to analyse and requires strong analytical and intepretive skills from the researcher. Frequently, the only way to make sense of such data is to ask the respondents themselves to provide us with an indication of what they mean. Finally, while some market researchers do not care to analyse the qualitative data generated using structured means, it is possible, and desirable, to do so using computer software.

References

Catterall, M. and Maclaran, P. (1995). 'Using a computer to code qualitative data'. In *The Proceedings of the 25th Marketing Education Group Conference*, July, Bradford, UK: Bradford University.

Chisnall, P.M. (1997). *Marketing Research*, 6th edn, London: McGraw-Hill.

Fowler, F.G. and Fowler, H.W. (eds) (1986). *The Oxford Handy Dictionary*, London: Chancellor Press.

Malhotra, N.K. (1996). *Marketing Research: An Applied Orientation*, 2nd edn, London: Prentice-Hall.

Marketing (2000). July, London: Haymarket Business Publications.

Mathews, A. (1996). 'Academic xenophobia and the analysis of focus group data'. In *Proceedings of the 26th Marketing Education Group Conference*, July, Glasgow, Scotland: University of Strathclyde.

Parasuraman, A. (1991). *Marketing Research*, 2nd edn, London: Addison-Wesley.

Proctor, T. (2000). *Essentials of Marketing Research*, London: Financial Times/Prentice-Hall.

QSR (1997). *QSRNUD*IST—Software for Data Analysis, User Guide*, London: Sage Publications.

Zikmund, W.G. (1997). *Exploring Marketing Research*, 6th edn, London: Dryden Press.

Work Assignments

1. Use the template below to design a moderator's outline for a focus group study evaluating five different sales promotion campaigns for a new flavour of crisps. Note that the template asks you to ask questions that are introductory, transitional, key and ending questions. This represents the depth of the concepual flow of the conversation as it goes from general to specific.

Question Type	Question	Duration (min)
Opening	1. Going around the table, can you tell us your name and what you enjoy doing most in your spare time?	5
Introductory	2.	10
Transition	3.	5
Key	SHOW PROMOTIONAL CONCEPT STORYBOARDS IN TURN (**ASK RESPONDENTS TO FILL IN BRIEF QUESTIONNAIRE ON EACH**)	30
	Promotion 1 ☐	
	Promotion 2 ☐	
	Promotion 3 ☐	
	Promotion 4 ☐	
	Promotion 5 ☐	

	What are you first impressions of these promotions? **(PROBE on mechanics and theme for each one, e.g. Would** **you prefer to link up with Vodafone or Cellnet?)**	
Ending	4.	8
Summary	5. Let me summarize the key points of the discussion. MODERATOR PROVIDES ORAL SUMMARY Is that an adequate summary?	2

2. A UK political party wishes to determine the marketing methods that are used by American political consultants when running US presidential campaigns. However, traditionally political parties usually obtain links with supposedly ideological 'sister' parties. Thus, in this case, the UK party can obtain opinions only from one US party's representatives. Assuming that the party can easily arrange the data-collection process, which qualitative market research method should it use?

3. Fictional Bus Company wants to understand the quality of their customer service, the friendliness of the driver, and whether the driver ensures that passengers pay the full fare. What type of research method could be used?

4. Design a topic outline for a study involving in-depth interviews with teenagers about the subject of condom usage.

Survey and Questionnaire Design

5

Learning Outcomes

After reading this chapter, you will be able to:

- Understand how questionnaire design and sample selection are inter-linked.
- Understand how questionnaire design and survey methodology are interlinked.
- Determine which interviewing method is appropriate under what circumstances.
- Outline the questionnaire design process.
- Know what type of questions are most suitable and how to phrase questions in order to obtain the necessary data.
- Critique the design of a survey as well as the format and design of a questionnaire.

Introduction

In this chapter the reader is provided with an understanding of how to design surveys and questionnaires. There is an explanation of how the interviewing method affects the questionnaire design. There follows discussion of the questionnaire design process and its iterative nature. Then the structure and types of questions that are possible are outlined. Rating scales, a type of question structure often used when researching attitudes, are also discussed. Finally, the chapter concludes by explaining the importance of survey and questionnaire design in the wider process of research design. Survey and questionnaire design are operational stages of the research design process (outlined in Chapter 2). The various stages involved in developing, testing and administering a survey questionnaire are outlined.

Respondent Selection and Questionnaire Design

Questions concerning which respondents, and how many, should answer the questionnaire are considered further in Chapter 7. In this section, there is a consideration of how the questionnaire needs to be designed to take into account the nature of the sample. For instance, in a business-to-business marketing research project it might be necessary to use technical jargon that an average person would not understand.

In the Aerospace Maintenance Co. questionnaire (Questionnaire 2) provided at the end of this chapter, when asking respondents which magazine they bought, it is important to ensure that a range of the most popular magazines is included. Since the questionnaire designer often does not have specialist knowledge of every sector they research in, it is important to liaise with the commissioning organization on many aspects of question design. It is also often necessary to conduct secondary research into the nature of the market and its structure. This provides the researchers with an understanding of the context and ensures that they produce a more credible research proposal (see Chapter 2).

It is often necessary to design a couple of questions to determine whether a respondent is eligible to continue answering a particular questionnaire. These are called screening questions (see Box 5.1). In question SQ1 the respondents are asked whether they have answered a questionnaire about football in the last six months. This is to ensure that they have not filled in a previous survey so that they are not sampled more than once in the study.

If questionnaires are designed for specific subcultures (e.g., ethnically diverse populations or young children) it may be necessary to write simpler questions or have questions translated into a different language. The researcher should generally avoid using complex words or jargon when possible.

Box 5.1 Screening questions—London FC supporter survey (street interview)

SQ1   Have you answered a questionnaire about football in the last six months?

☐ Yes—CLOSE INTERVIEW AND THANK RESPONDENT
☐ No—GO TO NEXT QUESTION

SQ2   Which of the following sports are you interested in? (YOU MAY TICK MORE THAN ONE)

☐ Football—IF NOT CODED CLOSE
☐ Cricket
☐ Rugby

☐ Tennis
☐ Hockey
☐ None
☐ Other   PLEASE SPECIFY _____

SQ3   Are you a season ticket holder or a member of London Football Club 2000?

☐ Yes—CLOSE INTERVIEW AND THANK RESPONDENT
☐ No—GO TO NEXT QUESTION

SQ4   Are you interested in going to watch football teams live?

☐ Yes
☐ No—IF CODED CLOSE

Survey Methods: Personal, Telephone and Mail

Questionnaires are designed differently depending on which interviewing method is used. This was established in the previous section. In this section, we consider the impact that survey method has on the design of specific questions. There are general differences in formatting among the questionnaires designed for different survey methods. For example, personal interview questions have to be worded so that both the interviewer and respondent can understand them. In a mail questionnaire, only the respondent needs to understand the question. This usually means that in personal and telephone interviews, messages are usually included in brackets and/or capital letters to indicate to the interviewer that they need to ask the question in a certain way. For example, a multiple fixed-response question may be followed by a message to the interviewer to say 'YOU MAY TICK MORE THAN ONE OPTION' to the respondent. In mail questionnaires, such instructions to the respondent must be very clear since there is no-one there to explain any difficulties in understanding what the questions require. Each of the three main types of interviewing method and their impact upon question design will be considered individually.

Personal Interviews

Personal interview questionnaires are generally administered in a shopping centre (more commonly referred to as a mall intercept) or in the street (street interview) or at the respondents' home (door-to-door interview). This latter option is particularly useful when the researcher is employing a random sampling methodology (see Chapter 2 for further consideration of how sampling and interviewing method are interlinked). The interviewer may also visit business premises or outlets in order to interview various members of an organization if they are conducting business-to-business marketing research (see Chapter 11).

Personal interviewing tends to be time-consuming and expensive. However, this method may be required if the questions are complex and need clarification. The response rate for personally administered questionnaires is higher than for other methods since it is generally more difficult to refuse someone face-to-face. The response rate refers to the number of people who agree to the request to fill out the questionnaire or answer the interviewer's questions. Personally administered questionnaires allow the interviewer to qualify their respondents using screening questions. For example, the interviewer may be required to gather information from a sample of 50 people within various categories (usually defined by age, gender and social grade). The process of satisfying sampling requirements (e.g., quota sampling) is aided because the interviewer can identify who fits the quota criteria visually.

Telephone Questionnaires

Telephone interviewing is quick and relatively inexpensive because respondents can be contacted more quickly, lowering labour costs. The researcher can also reach houses or respondents that may not previously have been accessible, for instance high-security houses and blocks of flats. CATI has revolutionized marketing research recently since data collection and analysis can be combined into one stage. As the information is collected over the phone, the respondents' answers are entered directly onto a computer, which then analyses the responses as they are entered cumulatively. This is particularly useful for data analysis purposes because it allows the researcher to determine whether they have sufficient size of sample for results to be statistically significant.

From a questioning perspective, software packages allow interviewers to automatically rotate sequences of questions in order to ensure that this does not have an impact upon the respondents' responses. In the past, the rotation of questions has been facilitated by printing different versions of the questionnaire or by asking interviewers to rotate questions manually.

Many questions asked in marketing research are of a personal nature. However, many people are unwilling to divulge personal information over the telephone as they cannot see who they are talking to. The simple presence of the interviewer in the personal interview situation may greatly reduce the respondents' unease with answering such questions. Recently, there has been a move by some of the major public opinion polling organizations (i.e., market research for political parties, candidates and media organizations) towards using random sample telephone methods instead of quota sample mall intercept or random cluster sample door-to-door methods. This is probably due to the fact that it is less costly and a larger sample is easier to access.

Many people do not take kindly to being disturbed at home by marketing researchers on the telephone. Telephone research is regarded by many as an invasion of privacy and, whereas many people will stop to answer questions in the street, respondents often refuse to participate in telephone interviews.

Mail Questionnaires

Mail questionnaires are a relatively inexpensive form of administering surveys since the average questionnaire, covering letter, response paid envelope and associated material can usually be sent out for around £1. The major costs are associated with the delivery of the questionnaire, and using second-class post can frequently save significant amounts of money. Box 5.2 illustrates the variable costs associated with a questionnaire interview delivering a package weighing less than 5g (since heavier would incur increased postal charges), including an eight-page interview, and covering letter and a response-paid stamped address envelope for return of the questionnaire to a sample of 2000 households. In the example in Box 5.2, using a first-class stamp adds 10% to the total variable costs, compared with using a second-class stamp. Box 5.2 also shows the difference in variable costs compared with telephone and personal interviews, clearly illustrating the advantage of using the mailed questionnaire. Not only is the respondent prepared to answer more and longer questions but it is also cheaper. The most expensive method is the personal interview, mainly because of the charges associated with deploying and paying interviewers. Although the costs associated with telephone interviews are not too different from the mailed questionnaire, the medium of the telephone is not conducive to lengthy interviews, although it is very useful for obtaining information quickly.

Box 5.2 An example of the variable costs associated with mail/telephone and personal interviews

Components of a mailed questionnaire	Cost (£)
Questionnaire (2000 × 8 × 4.5p—incl. reprographics)	720
Envelopes (2000 × A4 × 2p)	400
Covering letter (2000 × 1 × 4.5p—incl. reprographics)	90
Postal costs (2000 × 2)	800/1040*
Total	2010/2250*

*Costs relates to the price of a second-class (20p) and first-class (26p) stamp in July 2001

Components of a telephone questionnaire	Cost (£)
Questionnaire (500 × 8 × 4.5p—incl. reprographics)	180
Call charges (4.2p per minute*, assume 1/5 calls are personally answered, totalling 2500 calls connected with a further 500 calls of 10 min duration)	315
Interviewer costs (500 @ 10 min/interview, assume 3 interviews/h, hourly rate @ £10/h)	1667
Total	2162

*Cost relates to the charges by British Telecom in September 2001

Components of a personal interview questionnaire	Cost (£)
Questionnaire (500 × 8 × 4.5p—incl. reprographics)	180
Postal charges (25 interviewers, 20 interviews each, 10 interviews posted each time @ £5 per package*)	250
Interviewer costs (£40 pay for 10 completed interviews, 10 interviews per day, 20 minutes per interview £10 expenses per day)	3000
Total	**3430**

*Cost relates to approximate charge by Royal Mail for next-day delivery, $2\frac{1}{2}$ kg package, in September 2001

The cost of employing an interviewer is also avoided, although there are increased labour charges associated with database development, and envelope printing and stuffing. This reduced cost is often the deciding factor for many small companies with a limited marketing research budget. In the UK, the researcher can also obtain a freepost service from the Post Office, which ensures that the postage cost is only incurred for those questionnaires that are subsequently returned. In the above example, using stamps, if the envelope is not returned, the postage charges are incurred nevertheless. However, using stamps (particularly first-class stamps) is thought to have an effect in increasing response rates. Because response rates are generally so low with mail questionnaires, it is important to increase the interest of the respondent in the subject on which they are being interviewed. In the example in Box 5.2, 2000 questionnaires are mailed out but the response rate would probably not be above 5% for the average survey, yielding around 100 questionnaires. The response rate can be increased in a number of ways, some of which are outlined below:

- *Provision of an incentive* This could include an entry to a prize draw or a voucher for returning the questionnaire. With business-to-business surveys offering a copy of the results of the survey this can frequently increase the likelihood of response.
- *Simplistic questionnaire design* This helps to increase response rate, particularly if the questions asked are of a less personal nature and they are made easy to understand and answer.
- *Prenotification of respondents* When the respondents are informed that a survey is taking place before it actually does and where the respondents are given details regarding the reasons for the survey, respondents are far more likely to respond. However, if they are prenotified too early, respondents will also lose interest in the survey. Typically, around a week is good practice.
- *Covering letter* Mail surveys should be accompanied by a covering letter giving details as to why the survey is taking place and what it hopes to achieve (see example in Box 5.3).
- *Third-party sponsorship* Much industrial marketing research benefits when it is conducted by an independent organization. This is because industrial marketing research typically involves competitor monitoring and rival companies would be

unlikely to allow themselves to be interviewed if they knew who was conducting the research. The research conducted for Aerospace Maintenance Co. used this principle to increase response rates for an industrial advertising effectiveness study (see Questionnaire 2 at the end of this chapter).

When using postal questionnaires for industrial marketing research, it is particularly important to increase response rate as much as possible because an industrial firm may rely on a small number of customers for a large volume of business. In such cases, it is important to personalize the questionnaires by addressing them directly to the customer (or decision maker within the firm), imposing deadlines for when it should be sent back, and using express postage (Diamantopoulus and Schlegelmilch, 1996). One advantage of mail questionnaires is that the respondent is free to complete the questionnaire in their own time and in private, although this can often result in the questionnaire not being filled in because respondents forget, thinking they will compete the questionnaires at a later date.

Box 5.3   Standard mail interview covering letter

Date as postmark

[on letterhead]

[Mr A. Nonymous
2 Somewhere Close
Anytown
Somecity
A County]

Dear [Mr Nonymous]

In conjunction with the European Centre for Football Management at Middlesex University Business School, London Football Club are conducting a survey among their supporters in order to understand how they can further improve their service.

We would appreciate it if you would be kind enough to fill in the questionnaire and return it in the postage-paid envelope provided. Everyone who does this will be entered into a prize draw with the opportunity to win signed merchandise if they fill in the address details at the back of the questionnaire.

Please note that your responses to the various questions will not be recorded individually and that all responses will be analysed together in order to ensure your anonymity. Therefore, we would appreciate it if you could provide us with details about your occupation and postcode. These details are not stored either manually or electronically. They are taken so that London FC can determine what their supporter base is and where it is coming from.

> **Please return all replies by [a particular date]**. Many thanks for your cooperation in helping the club understand your needs.
>
> Yours sincerely
>
> [signed with position and organization details below]

Postal questionnaires may prove difficult where the subject being researched is complex or the questions require clarification by the interviewer. In some cases the respondents' replies may also need clarification and this is not possible with mail surveys.

A Summary of Survey Method Selection and Questionnaire Design

Surveys are useful instruments for obtaining a sizeable amount of data from respondents. They are most commonly used in consumer marketing research although they are also employed in business-to-business marketing research (see Chapter 11). Surveys can vary in duration from 10 minutes (e.g., pre-advertising tracking studies) to 30 minutes (e.g., mall tests). In the former example, questions are designed to determine consumers' awareness of the product or service, previous advertising and current attitudes towards the product. In the latter example, there may well be detailed questions on attitudes towards the product or service but there are also likely to be questions on the format and style of the adverts in order to measure advertising effectiveness. This type of procedure is usually called a mall test because it is conducted within a shopping centre (mall in the USA) or area.

However, surveys can be conducted in a variety of different ways. The three main interviewing methods are mail, telephone and personal interviews. More recently, with computer-based technology, researchers are able to use computer-assisted telephone interviewing (CATI), computer-assisted Web interviewing (CAWI), and computer-assisted personal interviewing (CAPI). Each of these methods has an impact upon how the questions are delivered and designed. At this point, it is important to remember that the context (i.e., whether the respondent is at home, shopping or on the Internet) affects how effectively we can communicate with the respondent.

There are a number of factors which will affect the choice of method of administering the questionnaire. In many cases the most important is the cost of the research. In other cases, the information may be required urgently and the time period for the research is extremely limited. Table 5.1 summarizes the most common factors affecting the choice of survey method.

The final decision regarding which interviewing method to use when administering a questionnaire involves an understanding of how factors trade-off against

Table 5.1 Preferred choice of interviewing method by factor

Factor	Preferred interviewing method
Handling complex questions	Personal
Database or list of respondents easily accessible	Mail/telephone
Respondent selection dependent on location	Personal
Data input and analysis time-consuming	CAPI, CATI, CAWI
Collecting large amounts of data	Personal/telephone
When asking sensitive questions	Mail
To obtain data quickly	Telephone/CATI
To increase response rate	Personal
When cost is important	Mail/telephone, CATI/CAWI

each other. For instance, take the example of London Football Club, outlined in Chapter 2. If the club wanted to question its season ticket holders over the facilities and whether supporters would be interested in future services (e.g., credit cards, etc.), they could contact them at the ground when they were at a match. Alternatively, researchers could contact season ticket holders by mail (or possibly even e-mail) since they are likely to hold a database of season ticket holders. So, which one should be chosen? A mailed questionnaire is likely to receive a lower response rate. Response rates for consumer marketing projects generally can typically be around 5–10%. Would the fact that the respondents are supporters make any difference? It would and actually in this survey, which was conducted during the football season, the response rate was around 40% for a mail survey. Table 5.2 provides the reader with an understanding of other factors affecting the decision of which interviewing method to use in the above example.

Generally, there are a number of influencing factors and the researcher must determine the approach that best takes into account the pros and cons for each method with regards to the informational requirements of the study. If the questionnaire required the asking of complex questions, it may be necessary to employ an interviewer and conduct the interview in person, either at the respondent's home (door-to-door survey) or in a shopping centre or street (i.e., street interviewing or mall intercept). There are times when the location of the respondent is a prime factor. For instance, if a supermarket was investigating customer behaviour and attitudes from a geographic and demographic perspective (e.g., geodemographic segmentation), it would be important to interview people within the store's catchment areas. Thus, catching respondents at home is important. Interestingly, all three methods (i.e., mail, personal and telephone) can obtain information from people while they are at home but the personal interview method is the one most likely to obtain the highest response rate. The British Audience Research Bureau (BARB) makes use of door-to-door interviewing when conducting television research to determine programme audience ratings.

Table 5.2 Consideration of factors affecting choice of interviewing method for a football supporter survey

Factor	Application to London FC season ticket holder project	Preferred interviewing method
Handling complex questions	Many questions attitudinal which are more difficult to complete over telephone	Personal/mail
Database or list of respondents easily accessible	Yes, database of addresses in existence, some telephone numbers	Mail
Respondent selection dependent on location	To some extent, although more likely to be dispersed over certain parts of London	Personal/mail
Data input and analysis time-consuming	Yes, but necessary computer equipment not available	Cannot use CAPI, CATI, CAWI
Collecting large amounts of data	Yes	Personal/telephone
When asking sensitive questions	Not necessary	Any method
To obtain data quickly	Not so important	Can use mail
To increase response rate	Important but likely to be higher because of nature of respondent and their support of the club	Personal
When cost is important	Yes, club only just starting to value marketing and research	Mail/telephone

Sensitive questions, such as those related to the purchase of condoms or sanitary towels, may be better answered in private with a postal questionnaire or even qualitative research methods (see Chapter 4). Thus, a better response is obtained to questions on a mail survey because respondents do not feel like they have to provide socially acceptable answers (such answers are affected by response bias). If the researcher has a restricted time schedule in which to obtain the information, telephone interviewing made be the choice of method while budget restrictions may be eased by avoiding personal interviewing. Researchers may adopt computer-assisted methods in order to reduce time taken to input and analyse the data produced. However, this requires considerable up-front investment in expensive equipment. Another important consideration is response rate. There is a need to ensure that sufficient response from the population is obtained in order that the findings are valid, and when a high response is required personal interviews are usually the best medium to use.

The Questionnaire Design Process

The process of designing questionnaires is often long, complex and involved. Many authors suggest that the process is sequential, that stages follow on from one another. While there is some truth to this, in the opinion of the authors, most questionnaire design exercises are iterative with constant movement between the different stages of the process. Proctor (1997) states that questionnaire design encompasses eight different stages as follows:

1. *Identification and specification of the research problem/research objectives* In the first stage, the researcher should consider questions such as 'What is the management problem?' and 'What is the marketing research question?' (see Chapter 2). An example of a marketing problem could be to determine whether a previous advertising campaign had been effective.
2. *Selection of the population to be studied* It is imperative that the researcher determines who the sample will be since particular questions may be more or less appropriate for different populations and for different segments within populations.
3. *Choice of data collection* What interviewing method should the survey make use of? Previous sections of this chapter should have made clear how important a consideration this is on the process of questionnaire design.
4. *Ordering of the topics to be addressed* A questionnaire should be structured such that the questionnaire is logical and should usually proceed from general information (e.g., introductory questions) to specific information (such as respondent demographics). This technique is called laddering.
5. *Establishing the cross-tabulations that will be required* Where a survey is attempting to perform a particular function, and/or identify the relationships between certain variables, it is important to determine whether cross-tabulation is possible between questions and answers. Since different types of cross-tabulation technique are possible, it is important to identify what type of data should be collected. For instance, if the researcher wishes to use the Chi-square statistical test (covered further in Chapter 8), the researcher needs to design questions that obtain categorical (nominal) data. This type of data is best collected using multiple fixed-response questions. Types of data are covered further in Chapter 6. Designing the questionnaire according to which data analysis techniques are going to be used requires answers to be in a specific format. A full discussion of this topic is outside the scope of this book and, interestingly, is seldom covered in other major marketing research texts. An example, might be if a marketing researcher wished to provide a client with information on competitors' product positioning. This might make use of the multi-dimensional scaling statistical technique and, correspondingly, would need respondents to

evaluate competitors' products on a number of different dimensions. Usually, this is achieved by asking respondents rating scale questions.

6. *Deciding how the topics will be covered and how they will be precoded*   This section determines the types of questions that should be used and the relevant coding procedures. Decisions encompass whether or not to use open-ended or closed questions, dichotomous, multiple-fixed response and rating and ranking scale questions.

7. *Questionnaire layout and design of supporting material*   The questionnaire should be presented in such a manner that responding to questions is simplified as far as possible. Prompt cards should also be designed for personal interviews. This allows respondents to view all possible answers to a multiple-response question without forgetting any. Other material may also need to be designed to accompany surveys, such as photos or advertisement stills, etc.

8. *Pretesting of the questionnaire*   Questionnaires should be formally pretested on a small section of the survey population. This helps to ensure that questions are not misunderstood and that the researcher does not assume certain knowledge about the sample. If the researcher has little knowledge of the population, pilot testing the questionnaire may be a more sensible option, where the survey is completed among a small section of the population first and is modified for a larger survey for a later date. This is different from a pretest since it involves larger samples.

This description of the questionnaire design process implies simplicity in sequencing that is not usually apparent in the actual practice of questionnaire design. Some of the stages outlined above leave out or de-emphasize important facets of questionnaire design. Figure 5.1 is an attempt to indicate the different stages of the questionnaire design process and how they interconnect. Some of Proctor's original categories have been recategorized. For instance, the cross-tabulations section has been retitled 'Data analysis' in order to illustrate that the use of specific statistical methodologies impacts upon the questionnaire design process. This fact has seldom been considered in previous marketing research texts. Other sections have been retitled for more effective labelling.

The figure also indicates the linkages between different stages of the process. For instance, Figure 5.1 clearly illustrates the importance of pretesting since it impacts upon all aspects of the questionnaire design process. Similarly, all the processes are two-way in that while data analysis affects question structuring and wording, question structuring and wording affect data analysis. Data analysis also has an effect on the selection of the sample and the selection of the interviewing method (see Chapter 2 for further consideration of this).

Researchers need to check individual questions' relevance against the information needs of the researcher. When information other than that required by the researcher is provided from analysis of the answers to a question, this is known as a surrogate information error. An example might be when a question is asked regarding customer expectations when the data required is customer satisfaction. The researcher also needs to ensure that the question provides the information required in the correct

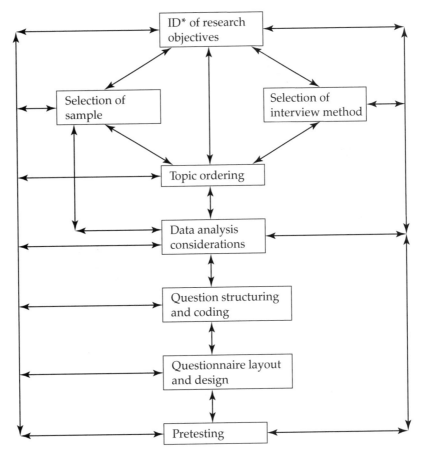

Figure 5.1   A flowchart depicting the iterative questionnaire design process

Note: * Identification.

Source: Adapted by the author, based on Proctor (1997)

format otherwise answers would not be measuring what the researcher intends. This is known as measurement error. The marketing researcher should attempt to design the questionnaire so that errors in the research design are reduced to a minimum.

The researcher should design the questionnaire to ensure that respondents are able to provide relevant responses. Where the respondent cannot answer a particular question, perhaps because the researcher has assumed that the respondent has more knowledge about a particular subject than they actually do, inability error occurs. This would be the case where a man is asked questions regarding what groceries are bought in his household if his wife generally did the shopping. In these cases, the respondent may actually start making up the responses so as not to appear less knowledgeable than they actually are.

The questions should be as unambiguous as possible otherwise, in a personal or telephone interview, the interviewer will have to interpret the questions for the respondents and this may change the meaning and the intentions of the original question design. This is known as questioning error. The answers to particular questions should be clear such that when a respondent or interviewer is filling in a questionnaire the chance of their ticking the wrong category or otherwise providing an inaccurate answer is minimized. This is known as recording error.

Structuring the Questionnaire

There are three basic types of structure in marketing research questionnaires. These range from completely open questions where the respondent is asked a basic set of questions and is totally free to answer in whatever way they wish to more closed questions where the respondent is presented with a limited number of replies. Most questionnaires are a mixture of open and closed questions with the closed questions at the beginning and a number of open questions towards the end of the questionnaire. Placing more specific questions or open questions at the end of the questionnaire ensures that respondents are not demotivated to stop answering the questions since they have already been 'locked in' by the more general preceding questions.

With structured questionnaires, each respondent is asked the same set of questions in the same order. All options have been predetermined by the researcher and the respondent must simply tick or circle the relevant response which best reflects their answer. Structured questions tend to be easier to analyse. The main disadvantage of the structured approach is that the results depend on the predetermined answers closely reflecting the true feelings of the respondents. This is not always the case, particularly where the researcher has limited knowledge of the sample and the context of the research they are conducting. Limiting response variables can deny the respondent the opportunity to adequately report their own particular situation, attitudes and opinions.

In unstructured questionnaires, respondents are asked open-ended questions where the responses are not limited or predetermined. The interviewer is free to change the order in which the questions are asked and may alter the emphasis of the interview depending on the respondents' knowledge or interests. The unstructured questionnaire is most often used in in-depth interviews or during focus group discussions (see Chapter 4). This type of approach is particularly appropriate for studies involving panels of experts and is not generally used in quantitative survey approach.

With semi-structured questionnaires, the questionnaire mixes both closed and open questions. Usually, the closed questions are asked first. This enables the interviewer to establish dialogue and generate the respondent's interest, to 'lock in' respondents. Figure 5.2 illustrates the main types of questionnaire. It is useful to note that questionnaire types can be classified using a continuum since most questionnaires adopt both open and closed questions.

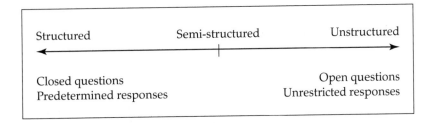

Figure 5.2 Types of questionnaire

Source: Baines, Chansarkar and Ryan (1999)

Types of Questions

There are many different ways to ask the same question. This is dependent on the type of question, the extent of the information sought and how one intends to analyse the data. Questions can be classified as direct and indirect, open and closed, dichotomous and multichotomous, multiple fixed-response, multiple-choice with ranking, and multiple-choice with rating. These categories of questions are considered separately next.

Direct and Indirect Questions

In direct questioning, the respondents are questioned about their own attitude, intentions or behaviour. However, in certain cases where research is focused on unsociable behaviour or potentially embarrassing topics, the interviewer may use a form of indirecting questioning to elicit an appropriate response. In indirect questioning, the respondent tends to be asked about other people's behaviour or opinions or how other people might respond under certain circumstances. Examples of direct questions could include:

'Why do you think you are addicted to shopping?'
'Why did you purchase a Volvo S40?'

Examples of indirect questions, using the same questions as above, could be:

'Why do you think people become addicted to shopping?'
'Why do consumers purchase Volvo S40s?'

Indirect questioning is also undertaken in other forms of marketing research. In qualitative research methods many techniques are employed to discover a subject's true reactions by incorporating a third party or imaginary person. The respondent is asked to describe how this 'other person' would react in various situations (see the projective techniques section in Chapter 4).

Open-ended Questions

Open-ended questions do not have a predetermined set of responses. This allows the respondent to reply using whatever words they wish. An example of this type of question could be: 'Why did you decide to vote for the Green Party in the 1999 European Elections?' Answers to such a question could include a number of possibilities but the respondent, not the interviewer, determines these possibilities. Thus, responses could include the following:

'Because I liked their policies.'
'I agree with their environmental agenda.'
'I know the candidate', etc.

Open-ended questions are generally used when the researcher is not sure of the possible responses to his or her questions or when there are so many possible responses to the question that likely responses are too difficult to predict. It may be that the researcher wants to avoid biasing the answers by producing a set of responses for the respondent to choose among. Open-ended questions usually use what, where, when, how, and why in their structure.

Closed Questions

Closed questions present the respondent with a specific set of possible replies to the question. Box 5.4 provides an example of a closed question.

> ### Box 5.4 Closed question example
> How many times did you watch live matches at London Football Club last season?
>
> | | | | |
> |---|---|---|---|
> | One to five times | ☐ | Six to ten times | ☐ |
> | Eleven to fifteen times | ☐ | More than fifteen times | ☐ |

This type of question is generally used when the researcher is aware of the possible responses to the question Usually, five to seven categories provide the optimal set of responses. Closed questions are much easier to analyse and precode, facilitating data analysis process.

Dichotomous and Multichotomous Questions

A closed question is dichotomous if they are only two possible responses or replies. An example is given in Box 5.5, In this example, the respondent is provided with only two possible answers to the question of whether they (as football supporters) would buy a season ticket if they were allowed to pay for it in instalments.

Box 5.5   Example of a dichotomous question

Q. Would you buy a season ticket if it was possible to pay for it in instalments?

☐   Yes
☐   No

A multichotomous question is one in which the respondent may only choose one response but there are more than two possible answers. Box 5.6 provides an example of this when asking football supporters the last time they attended a football match during the 1998 football season at London Football Club.

Box 5.6   Example of a multichotomous question

Q. When was the last time that you went to see a match at London Football Club?

☐   Within the last month of the current season
☐   Between one and six months of the current season
☐   Within the 96–97 season
☐   Within the 95–96 season
☐   Longer than two seasons ago

In order to ensure that the respondent does not tick more than one answer, which may arise if the question is not designed properly, the question will usually have the instruction 'PLEASE TICK ONE RESPONSE ONLY'.

Multiple Fixed-response Questions

A closed multiple fixed response question (see Figure 5.3) provides the respondent with a predetermined set of responses, allowing them to choose one or more options. In the example, the respondent may identify a number of factors that would affect their purchase of a computer system.

Without providing the respondent with these options, they may not have selected the most appropriate response for them. By listing the key influencing factors, the researcher can obtain a more accurate response.

However, it may be that a number of factors affect the choice of a new computer to different extents.

In Figure 5.3 the question designer includes an 'Other' category to ensure that particularly salient factors can be written in by the interviewer or respondent; depending on the interviewing method used. Notice also that the question suggests that the respondent or interviewer tick all categories that apply. It is important to ensure that only a small number of these types of questions are included in the questionnaire overall. Otherwise, if the respondent feels laboured, in filling

> ### What factor(s) would influence your choice of computer?
>
> *Please tick all responses that apply*
>
> | | |
> |---|---|
> | Memory capability | ☑ |
> | Processing capacity | ☐ |
> | Installed software | ☐ |
> | Installed hardware | ☐ |
> | Brand name | ☐ |
> | Price | ☑ |
> | Warranties and servicing | ☑ |
> | Other, *please explain* | ☐ |

Figure 5.3   A closed multiple fixed-response question

in the questionnaire, they are likely to tick any category simply to fill in the interview. This tends to occur when the questionnaire is too long, or where the respondent is being asked questions on a range of issues, about which they do not know or are not interested.

Multiple-choice with Ranking

Figure 5.4 provides us with an indication of a question where the respondent is asked to provide the researcher with an indication of which factors are more or less important in determining whether or not to purchase groceries on-line.

In this example, the respondent is asked about the factors influencing their purchase of on-line groceries using a ranking question. The use of such questions requires the researcher to provide clear instructions on how to answer the question. In this case, it is important to explain the parameters of the scale, i.e., that 1 is most important and 8 is least important. In the example, the researcher has included an 'Other' category to allow respondents to insert factors that had not previously been considered by the researcher. For some people the downloading speed associated with on-line grocery purchasing is an important factor in the purchase decision.

There are limitations to this question, however. Because it collects ranking (or ordinal data), the researcher cannot determine how much less important downloading speed is compared with the store brand. The ranking scale in the example identifies which factors are more or less important but it does not identify how much more important one factor is when compared with another. For an understanding of different data types, the reader is referred to Chapter 6.

Rank the following factors in order
of their importance to you when
you are purchasing groceries on-line.

1=most important 8=least important

Store brand   [1]
Website format   [2]
Cost delivery   [ ]
Availability of promotions   [ ]
Speed of delivery   [ ]
Replacement of damaged items   [4]
Substitution of items not available   [3]
Other, *please explain*   [5]
Downloading speed

Figure 5.4   Multiple-choice with ranking

Please *rate* each of the following factors out
of 10 in terms of how important they are to
you when purchasing groceries on-line

10=maximum importance
0=no importance

Store brand   [5]
Website format   [7]
Cost delivery   [0]
Availability of promotions   [3]
Speed of delivery   [7]
Replacement of damaged items   [10]
Substitution of items not available   [9]
Other, *please explain*   [7]
Downloading speed

Figure 5.5   Multiple-choice with rating

Multiple-choice with Rating

To measure the difference in importance between two answers in a multiple-choice question, it is necessary to collect interval-type data (see Chapter 6). For this, a rating scale should be used. In the example in Figure 5.5, the respondent is asked to give a score out of ten to indicate how important each factor is when purchasing on-line groceries. Once again, it is important to explain the nature of the rating. Thus, in the example, 0 relates to no importance and 10 to maximum importance.

A rating scale such as that outlined above allows us to measure the importance of each factor. Thus, in the example, to this respondent when deciding which on-line website to connect to for the purchase of groceries, their policy on replacing damaged items is *twice* as important as the store's brand. Perhaps, this was because the delivery person had damaged items on a number of previous occasions and the company had unfairly refused to reimburse the respondent.

Other Considerations in Questionnaire Design

Questionnaires are usually flawed when they are first designed. These flaws are removed through pretesting and reconsideration at each of the different stages outlined in Figure 5.1. However, there are a number of errors common in questionnaire design. These include incorporation of double-barrelled questions, designing sensitive questions insensitively, not including proper instructions to the interviewers, and using different units in the same question.

A double-barrelled question is one where two questions are asked in the same sentence instead of one. This can be a problem because a double-barrelled question can theoretically elicit two responses instead of one. An example of such a question could be:

Are you satisfied with the price and availability of your season ticket at London FC?

In this example the respondent is asked to assess their satisfaction with both the price and availability of their season ticket. This question assumes that the response to one component (e.g., price) will be the same as to the other component (e.g., availability). However, it is entirely feasible that a respondent will be happy with one but not the other.

Another example could be:

How often do you read and purchase *Aerospace Technical Magazine?*

In this example, the question assumes that reading and purchasing of a magazine are the same thing. However, in publishing there is a major difference between circulation and readership. For instance, readership of a Sunday newspaper could include two or three members of a family. However, circulation will only include the one copy purchased. Thus, readership is usually always higher than circulation unless readers are purchasing the magazine for free gifts on the front! In the above example, the trade magazine may be purchased by the office manager for a number of staff. The double-barrelled question above could potentially elicit two different answers: (1) how often the respondent reads the magazine and (2) how often the respondent purchases it. The problem arises where the respondent is provided with only one set of time responses.

Marketing research often deals with sensitive topics, particularly with products associated with personal hygiene and health. Social issues, i.e., contributions to charities and environmental topics are often affected by the respondent's desire to give a 'politically correct' answer. Effectively, this is indirect form of peer pressure, although the pressure is self-directed and imagined. In order to ensure that respondents do answer such questions truthfully, question statements are usually counterbiased. So, a typical question such as 'Are you a member of the New Labour Party?' might be counterbiased by rephrasing it as 'There are 300 000 members currently in the New Labour Party. Are you a member?' In this question, the first part of the question is designed to remove the stigma of being a party member. This first part of the sentence is the counterbiasing statement. Other examples are provided below:

Not all people in the UK believe in God, would you regard yourself as religious?
Not everyone brushes their teeth more than once a day, how often do you brush your teeth?
Not all couples practise safe sex all the time. Have you ever had unprotected sex?

Another problem often found in questionnaire design is when respondents are offered alternatives in a multiple fixed response question that overlap with one another. Box 5.7 provides an example.

Box 5.7 Multiple fixed response question with overlapping units

How many times did you watch live matches at London Football Club last season?

One to five times	☐	Five to ten times	☐
Ten to fifteen times	☐	More than fifteen times	☐

In the example, the reader can see that if a respondent has visited a live match five or ten times, they have two options each time instead of one. Thus, they may either tick the wrong category or tick both categories that apply. This is a common mistake to make.

Questioning on Attitudes

Respondents have different attitudes towards a variety of products. Although psychologists have often discussed the nature of what attitudes are, rating scales can provide an indication depending on the context of the question. Attitudes can often show how consumers feel towards a particular brand name. This may provide a stronger indication of our intention to purchase in the future. Attitudes are related to a person, object, product or service. They arise as a result of learned behaviour and are regarded as relatively enduring. Attitudes are affective. In other words, they arise from emotional understanding and have an impact upon our perception. Since they affect our perception, they also have an impact upon our behaviour.

Thus, measurement of attitudes is imperative in marketing research because it allows researchers to determine the likelihood of future purchasing activity. However, attitudes do not always directly translate into the behaviour they imply. Consider the old adage: 'do as I say, not as I do!' Thus, attitudes are predispositions, which may lead to consistent behaviour. Attitudes are usually measured using a variety of ranking and rating scales. Examples include Likert scales, graphic and verbal rating scales, semantic differential scales and the constant sum scale.

Likert Scales

Likert scales are characterized by statements of agreement or disagreement where the respondent has a choice of five different responses to choose among from 'strongly agree' at one extreme to 'strongly disagree' at the other. The example in Box 5.8 provides the respondent with the opportunity not to express their opinion by picking 'neither agree nor disagree'. However, in questionnaires that are too long this option allows the respondent to speed up the filling in of the questionnaire. When this position is picked in order that the respondent does not have to register their opinion, this is termed 'middle position bias'. Market researchers remove this error by having only an even-numbered scale, thereby removing the middle position.

Box 5.8   An example of a Likert scale question

	Agree strongly	Agree slightly	Neither agree nor disagree	Disagree slightly	Disagree
Chelsea FC are a good team		✓			

Likert scale questions can also be asked in larger numbers if the statements are put together into a battery of questions which usually require tabulating. Table 5.3 provides an example of this type of formatting.

Other scales used include graphic and verbal rating scales and examples of these are shown in Figure 5.6. The graphic scale is particularly useful when the respondent has difficulty in understanding the language that the interviewer is using. This scale is also very useful for interviewing children. The verbal rating scale allows respondents to express their degree of favourability with a particular concept. With both scales, there would be a preceding question, such as 'How do you feel about Vodafone, the mobile telecoms operator, sponsoring Manchester United?'

Semantic Differential Scales

The semantic differential scale provides the respondent with answers to a statement as a series of diametric opposites which can be constructed by using a dictionary of antonyms. The respondent is asked to provide their answer to the question by ticking a box on the scale between the two extremes. The scores are then averaged for each item to construct separate brand profiles. In fact, it can be quite difficult constructing questions using semantic differential scales. It is useful to remember

Table 5.3 Examples of Likert scale questions

	Agree strongly	Agree slightly	Neither agree nor disagree	Disagree slightly	Disagree strongly	Don't know
The London Football Club shop has a limited range of merchandise						
The merchandise sold at the shop is good value for money						
The merchandise sold at the shop is highly priced						
The merchandise at the shop is good quality						

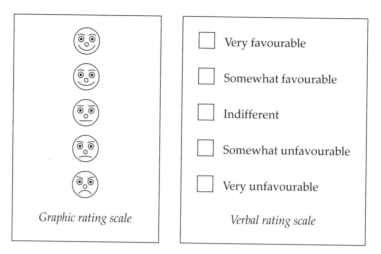

Figure 5.6 Graphic and verbal rating scales

Source: Baines, Chansarkar and Ryan (1999)

that the answers do not have to be bipolar (e.g., friendly—hostile), they can also be monopolar (family-oriented—not family oriented). Box 5.9 provides an example of this type of question. These questions are particularly useful in branding research since the data can be analysed using multi-dimensional scaling statistical techniques to produce maps for product-positioning purposes.

Box 5.9 An example of a semantic differential scale question

Please describe how you feel about London Football Club's image by placing a tick against the appropriate box. Place a tick in the appropriate box on the scale to indicate your strength of opinion.

Progressive	☐	☐	☐	☐	☐	☐	☐	Old-fashioned
Friendly	☐	☐	☐	☐	☐	☐	☐	Hostile
Exciting	☐	☐	☐	☐	☐	☐	☐	Boring
Aggressive	☐	☐	☐	☐	☐	☐	☐	Passive
Family-oriented	☐	☐	☐	☐	☐	☐	☐	Not family-oriented

Constant Sum Scale

In this question, the respondent is asked to divide a quantity between a number of alternatives either evenly between the different responses or in such a way that the researcher can determine the relative difference in importance of the attitude between them. An example would be asking respondents to divide 100 points between four alternatives. Box 5.10 provides an example of a constant sum question. In this example, the interviewer asks respondents to allocate 100 points among five political issues to illustrate how important they are to the interviewer. This type of question is useful because it provides an indication of how much more important one issue is than another. For instance, if the respondent allocates 20 points to health and 10 to tax, they are twice as concerned about health than about tax. Thus, this type of question produces interval data (see Chapter 6).

Box 5.10   Constant sum scale question

We would like you to describe how important you feel certain political issues are in the UK today. To do this, we would like you to divide 100 points into the following five issues. You can give each issue as many points as you like, but the total allocation must not exceed 100. Please write the number in the box provided.

☐ Education
☐ Health
☐ Law and order
☐ Tax
☐ Europe

Coding Questions

Questions are coded in order to facilitate the data input and processing by assigning a numerical code to each possible answer to each question. In the constant sum scale example in Box 5.10, each issue would be numbered as a variable and the actual number allocated would be input into a spreadsheet. A further example of coding with the more common multiple fixed response question is given in Box 5.11.

Box 5.11   Coded question example

How many times did you watch live matches at London Football Club last season?

| One to five times | ☐ 1 | Six to ten times | 2 ☐ |
| Eleven to fifteen times | ☐ 3 | More than sixteen times | 4 ☐ |

Generally, coding occurs by assigning numbers to the different responses for each question and different variable labels to each question. Thus, a spreadsheet is set up and each questionnaire's details are input. Thus, a question such as that illustrated in Box 5.11 has four responses and the variable might be labelled 'matchattend'. All questions are then labelled and coded. Table 5.4 provides the reader with the beginnings of a spreadsheet for data input purposes.

Table 5.4 Beginnings of a spreadsheet for data input

Questionnaire number	Matchattend	Sex	Age
1	1	Etc.	Etc.
2	4	Etc.	Etc.
3	3	Etc.	Etc.
Etc.	Etc.	Etc.	Etc.

Computer-assisted interviewing removes the need for data input since the computer software sorts and analyses the data as it is input. This makes the process much easier. Sometimes codes are assigned to different responses during the design of the questionnaire. This is known as precoding.

Conclusion

Survey design and questionnaire design are complex and iterative processes. Determining whether to use mail, personal or telephone interviewing methods (or their computer-assisted variants) is dependent on a number of factors, including the objectives of the research, sampling considerations and questionnaire design implications. It is important to realize the limitations of the different methods, mainly that personal interviewing is costly, telephone interviewing allows limited respondent contact time and mail interviewing has a low response rate. The questionnaire design process has been depicted as an iterative eight-stage process. Important considerations in this process are that pretesting allows the researcher to understand the limitations associated with the other seven aspects of the design process and that the questionnaire will be more professional if it is designed with sampling, interviewing method and data analysis considerations in mind.

Questionnaires can be structured or unstructured or a mixture of the two. This is usually determined by the quantity of open and closed questions within the questionnaire. There are a variety of different questioning formats, each with their own particular advantages. Since different questions produce different types of data, this has an impact upon how they are statistically analysed. Questions can also be designed to elicit attitudinal information. These questions generally require the respondent to rate or rank something. Common errors in questionnaire design can arise for a number of reasons but are usually removed if the questionnaire is properly pretested. The reader is now referred to the work assignments section of this chapter where three copies of questionnaires are provided for the student to dissect.

References

Baines, P., Chansarkar, B. and Ryan, G. (1999). *Introduction to Marketing Research*, London: Middlesex University Press.

Diamantopoulus. A. and Schlegelmilch. B. (1996). 'Determinants of industrial mail survey response: a survey-on-surveys, analysis of researchers' and managers' views', *Journal of Marketing Management*, **12**, 505–531.

Proctor, M. (1997). *The Essentials of Marketing Research*, London: Pitman Publishing.

Work Assignments

1. The first questionnaire, for London Football Club, was designed to provide the club with an insight into the opinions of local football supporters, regardless of whether they supported London Football Club or a nearby competitor club. The interviews were conducted in the high street by a trained interviewer. In order to ensure that the right sample answered the questionnaire, only those respondents who watched live matches at nearby football stadiums and were not season ticket holders were questioned (since this group was questioned separately).

   (a) Critically assess the questions and the layout of the questionnaire by looking at their design.
   (b) How could the questions be reworded and structured to obtain the same information?
   (c) How would the questions need to be reworded if this survey was conducted by telephone?

2. The second questionnaire, for Aerospace Maintenance Company, was designed to provide the company with an insight into the extent to which the company's trade magazine advertising had impacted upon possible buyers of its services. The interviews were conducted over the telephone by a trained interviewer. Respondents in several different European countries were contacted and questioned.

   (a) Critically assess the questions and the layout of the questionnaire by looking at their design.
   (b) How would the fact that the sample included respondents whose native language was not English affect the design of the questions?
   (c) What kind of information do you think this questionnaire would provide? Do you believe it would help the aerospace organization to determine whether its advertising really had been effective?

3. The third questionnaire, for a political consulting organization, was designed to provide the company with an insight into its competitors' activity in offering political campaign services such as media, research and strategic consultancy. The interviews were e-mailed and respondents were asked to return the handwritten questionnaire, which they needed to print off into hard copy, by fax.

   (a) The questionnaire actually received only a very small response. Why do you think this was?
   (b) Criticize and appraise the types of questions used in this example.

Questionnaire 1: Personal interviews: London Football Club

Questionnaire for local population of London Football Club

Name: _____

Address: _____

_____

_____

_____

Post Code: ☐ ☐ ☐ ☐

For office use only ☐ (5)

Gender:

☐ Male   ☐ Female

For office use only ☐ (5)

Occupation of Head of Household

_____

Circle Relevant Category
☐ ☐ ☐
AB   C1
C2   DE

For office use only ☐ (5)

Age?
☐ Under 16
☐ 17–24
☐ 25–34
☐ 35–44
☐ 45–54
☐ 55+

For office use only ☐ (5)

Marital Status?
☐ Single
☐ Married/Living with partner
☐ Divorced/Separated
☐ Widowed

For office use only ☐ (5)

Q.1   Have you ever been to watch a match at London Football Club?

☐ Yes (PLEASE ANSWER QUESTIONS 2 TO 10)
☐ No (PLEASE ANSWER QUESTIONS 11 TO   )   *For office use only* ☐ (5)

London Football Club Enthusiasts

Q.2   When was the last time that you went to see a match at London Football Club?

☐ Within the last month
☐ Within the last six months
☐ Within the 96–97 season
☐ Within the 95–96 season
☐ Longer than two seasons ago   *For office use only* ☐ (5)

Q.3 For how many seasons have you been coming to watch London Football Club? (PLEASE TICK RELEVANT BOX)

☐ 1   ☐ 2   ☐ 3
☐ 4   ☐ 5–9   ☐ 10+   *For office use only* ☐ (13)

Q.4 How do you travel to watch the matches at London Football Club? (YOU MAY TICK MORE THAN ONE)

☐ Car   ☐ Foot   ☐ Bus   ☐ Tube

For office use only ☐ (6)

Q.5 For what reason have you not purchased a season ticket? (PLEASE TICK THE ONE ANSWER THAT MOST APPLIES TO YOU)

☐ Too expensive (PLEASE GO TO Q.14)
☐ Can't attend every home match (PLEASE GO TO Q.14)
☐ Can't afford it (PLEASE GO TO Q.15)
☐ Other _____

For office use only ☐ (14)

Q.6 Would you buy a season ticket if you could get a refund for matches that you missed?

☐ Yes   (PLEASE GO TO Q.15)
☐ No   (PLEASE GO TO Q.15)   *For office use only* ☐ (15)

Q.7 Would you buy a season ticket if it was possible to pay for it in instalments?

☐ Yes
☐ No   *For office use only* ☐ (16)

Q.8 Please indicate membership of the following:

☐ Riversiders   ☐ Vice Presidents   ☐ None

For office use only ☐ (17)

Q.9 Please indicate, by ticking the appropriate box, how strongly you agree or disagree with the following statements. (PLEASE START FROM TICK)

	Agree strongly	Agree slightly	Neither agree nor disagree	Disagree slightly	Disagree strongly	None	Don't know	Office use only
The London Football Club shop has a limited range of merchandise								___ (31)
The merchandise sold at the shop is good value for money								___ (32)
The merchandise sold at the shop is highly priced								___ (33)
The merchandise at the shop is good quality								___ (44)
I would like to sponsor match balls/players' shirts								___ (35)
I would use the club's rooms for buffets/ weddings/functions if it was possible								___ (36)

Q.10 How loyal a supporter are you of London Football Club? (PLEASE INDICATE GIVING A NUMBER FROM 1 TO 6 WHERE 1 IS VERY LOYAL AND 6 IS NOT AT ALL LOYAL)

VERY   NOT AT ALL

1   2   3   4   5   6

_____   *For office use only* ☐ (21)

London Football Club and Other Football Enthusiasts

Q.11   Which teams have you ever been to see?

☐   Brentford
☐   QPR
☐   Chelsea
☐   Other London Team/s _____
☐   Other Teams _____
☐   None   *For office use only*   ☐ (5)

Q.12   Where would you usually go before a football match?

_____

_____

_____

                                               For office use only   ☐ (7)

Q.13   Where would you usually go after a football match?

_____

_____

_____

                                               For office use only   ☐ (8)

Q.14   What pre-match facilities would you like to see available at football grounds?

_____

_____

_____

                                               For office use only   ☐ (9)

Q.15   What facilities would you like to see available after a football match?

_____

_____

_____

                                               For office use only   ☐ (10)

Q.16 What events, other than football, do you feel should be held at football clubs during both the closed season and non-match days?

_____

_____

_____

For office use only □ (28)

Q.17 Please indicate, by ticking the appropriate box, how strongly you agree or disagree with the following statements. (PLEASE START FROM TICK)

	Agree strongly	Agree slightly	Neither agree nor disagree	Disagree slightly	Disagree strongly	Don't know	*Office use only*
Chelsea FC are a good team							(29)
Brentford FC are a good team							(29)
QPR FC are a good team							(29)
London Football Club are a good team							(29)
I only support teams that are in the Premier division							(29)
I only support teams that are in the first division							(29)
I would never support London Football Club as long as I lived							(29)
London Football Club play an active role in the community							(29)
Brentford FC play an active role in the community							(29)
QPR FC play an active role in the community							(29)
I think that football teams should play an active role in the community							(29)

THANK YOU FOR TAKING THE TIME TO FILL IN THIS QUESTIONNAIRE, PLEASE RETURN IT IN THE PRE-PAID ENVELOPE PROVIDED

Questionnaire 2: Telephone interviews: Aerospace Maintenance Company

Middlesex University Business School

Questionnaire for Aerospace Maintenance Co.—Advertising effectiveness

Name: _____ Company _____ Country _____ Job Title _____	**INTERVIEWER—COMPLETE THIS SECTION AFTER THE INTERVIEW** Call Length (mins.) _____ Call Time (U.K.) ☐ Morning ☐ Afternoon ☐ Evening Number of calls made prior to interview (Write in) _____

Q.1 How often do you read the following publications? (INTERVIEWER—PLEASE READ OUT THE RESPONSE CATEGORIES FIRST FOLLOWED BY EACH PUBLICATION)

Magazine Type	Every Issue	Frequently	Sometimes	Never
Flight				
Aircraft Technology & Maintenance				
Aircraft Economics				
Air Transport World				
Aviation Weekly				
Overhaul & Maintenance				

Q.2 Have you noticed any advertisements in the last twelve months for any of the following companies? (PLEASE READ OUT EACH COMPANY)

Company name	Yes	No
Lufthansa Technik		
S R Technics		
Air France Industries		
British Airways Engineering		
Aerospace Maintenance Co.		
Sabena Technics		
Other (please specify) _____		

Q.3 Which of the following Aerospace Maintenance Companies do you know offer full support for the major commercial types of aircraft? (INTERVIEWER—PLEASE READ OUT AND TICK APPROPRIATE ANSWERS—read out aircraft types from card 1 if respondent has problems)

Company name	Yes	No	B737	DC10	A320	Other (WRITE IN)
Lufthansa Technik						
Aerospace Maintenance Co.						
S R Technics						
Air France Industries						
British Airways Engineering						
ARL						
Sogerma						
Sabena Technics						
Other (please specify) _____						

Q.4   I am now going to ask you the MAIN reason why you are using these companies. Why do you use _____? (READ OUT EACH OF THE COMPANIES MENTIONED IN Q.3 EXCLUDING ARL & SOGERMA)

Lufthansa Technik

_____

S R Technics

_____

Air France Industries

_____

British Airways Engineering

_____

Sabena Technics

_____

Aerospace Maintenance Co.

_____

Q.5   Which of the following attributes do you associate positively or negatively with the following suppliers? (INTERVIEWER—READ OUT THE SUPPLIER FIRST AND RECORD EACH RESPONSE—TICK IF POSITIVE AND CROSS IF NEGATIVE)

Company name	Quality	Experience	Quick turnaround time	Flexibility	Customer satisfaction	Technical enterprise	Reliability	Cost effectiveness	Customized solutions
Lufthansa Technik									
S R Technics									
Aerospace Maintenance Co.									
Air France Industries									
British Airways Engineering									
Sabena Technics									
Other (please specify)									

Q.6 Please give each company a mark out of one hundred in terms of your impression of the company's overall performance for full support and maintenance services—from 1 to 10 where 1 is very poor and 10 is very good.

Aerospace Maintenance Co.   _____
Lufthansa Technik   _____
S R Technics   _____
Air France Industries   _____
British Airways Engineering   _____
Sabena Technics   _____

THANK YOU VERY MUCH FOR YOUR TIME. ARE YOU INTERESTED IN RECEIVING A BRIEF REPORT OF THE RESULTS? (INTERVIEWER—RING RESPONSE AND TAKE ADDRESS)

YES (ASK FOR ADDRESS)

NO (CLOSE INTERVIEW—THANK RESPONDENT)

ADDRESS

_____

_____

_____

_____

_____

THANK YOU, GOODBYE

Questionnaire 3: E-mailed interview: Political Consultancy

Q.1   What is your main area of expertise? (*Please write in 'yes', one option only*)

Media   _____
Research/polling   _____
General   _____
Finance   _____
Other (please write in)   _____

Q.2   What is the current size of your political consulting firm? (*In terms of the number of employees, please write in 'yes'*)

1–5   _____
6–10   _____
11–15   _____
16+   _____

Q.3   How many employees do you have working SOLELY on international campaigns? (*Please write in*)

_____

Q.4   Do you have any offices abroad?

Yes/No   _____

Q.5   Please indicate where your offices are located. (*Please write in*)

_____

_____

Q.6   What are the different areas—major world regions—in which you have operated? (*Please write in 'yes'*)

Western Europe   _____
Central and Eastern Europe   _____
Commonwealth of Independent States   _____
Latin America   _____
Middle East   _____
Asia   _____
Australia/New Zealand   _____
Other (Please write in)   _____

Q.7   Please indicate in the table below, for each major world region, a maximum of THREE countries in which you have operated. The three countries which you choose should be for those countries where you had the most involvement and the names of the three countries should be written in the appropriate cell. Please also indicate in the relevant column, the actual number of campaigns you have been involved in, in each region.

Major world region	Total number of campaigns in which you have been involved	Country 1	Country 2	Country 3
EXAMPLE Western Europe	5	Britain	France	Germany
Western Europe				
Central and Eastern Europe				
CIS				
Latin America				
Middle East				
Asia				
Australasia				
Other (please write in) _____				

Q.8   Please rate the degree of adaptation necessary when using the following US political consulting techniques using a scale from 1–6 where providing an answer towards 1 means that a high degree of adaptation is necessary and providing an answer towards 6 means little adaptation is necessary. Leave blank if you have no experience of a particular technique or do not know.

Direct mail	1–6	_____
Comparative (negative) TV ads	1–6	_____
Telephone canvassing	1–6	_____
Survey-based message formulation	1–6	_____
Opposition research	1–6	_____
Fund-raising via Internet	1–6	_____
Track polling	1–6	_____
Media management	1–6	_____
Focus groups	1–6	_____
Other techniques (please write in)		_____

THANK YOU FOR ANSWERING THIS QUESTIONNAIRE.

BEST WISHES

MARKET RESEARCH CONSULTANCY ORGANIZATION

PART II

Statistical considerations

Basic Statistics and Data Analysis

6

Learning Outcomes

After reading this chapter, you will be able to:

- Understand and use different scales of measurements.
- Choose and calculate measures of location and dispersion.
- Know how to use normal distribution probability tables.
- Draw a scatter diagram.
- Understand the basic concept of standard error used in hypothesis testing.

Introduction

This chapter is designed to provide readers with a basic understanding of the preliminary statistical concepts needed for interpretation of the outcome of any marketing research investigation. It discusses the different scales of measurements and the associated implications for analysis as well as the measures of location and dispersion. Normal distribution, which plays an important role in marketing research analysis due to its use in hypothesis testing, is then introduced. The basic concept necessary for hypothesis testing, standard error of an estimate is then discussed. Finally, the chapter shows how to draw a scatter diagram used in studying the relationship between two variables and serves as a foundation for understanding Chapters 7–9.

The text needs to be used in conjunction with statistical tables for Z, t and Chi-squared distributions, in order to answer this chapter's course work assignments as well as those in in Chapters 7 and 8.

Scales of Measurements

The type of analysis and the statistical technique used depend on the measurement used in the data collection. In this context it is necessary to understand the different scales of measurements. Data can be described according to the level of measurement attained. As shown in Figure 6.1, there are four levels of measurement (Taylor, 1983).

The levels of measurements are arranged in increasing order of flexibility for further analysis. The higher the level of measurement, the greater the flexibility in terms of subsequent statistical analysis. With interval or ratio measurements one can apply a set of analytical techniques known as *parametric statistics*, while with nominal or ordinal measurements less powerful statistical techniques can be used known as *non-parametric statistics* (Siegel, 1956).

A *nominal scale* of measurement is achieved when the observed data is classified into various distinct categories in which no ordering is implied, i.e. classifying individuals according to their nationality, sex, religion, ownership of a particular car, political affiliation, etc. Companies are often classified into three categories according to their turnover as high, medium or low turnover.

An *ordinal scale* of measurement is achieved if data is classified into categories in which ordering is implied, for example:

1. Companies may be ranked according to their turnover. For example, if ten companies are ranked in decreasing order of their turnover, the company with the highest turnover is ranked 1, the company with second highest turnover is ranked 2 and so on until the last company with the least turnover is ranked 10. The differences in ranks do not indicate the actual differences in turnovers. Thus, the difference in the turnover of, say, ranks 2 and 3 is not necessarily the same as the difference in turnover of, say, ranks 5 and 6. Companies with the same turnover are ranked equally.
2. Respondents may be asked to rank the facilities provided by a supermarket in the order of importance they attach when purchasing products.

LEVEL OF MEASUREMENT

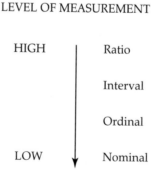

Figure 6.1 Scales of measurement

An *interval scale* is an ordered scale in which the difference between the measurements is a meaningful quantity that does not involve a true zero point (i.e., zero is an arbitrary point). The numbers used allow us to consider the extent of differences that exist between any two measurements.

1. A quantitative scale is used where units in one measurement can be transformed to another using suitable conversion (e.g., income in pounds transformed to income in dollars or francs using a conversion rate of pound to dollar or franc).
2. When we measure temperature by the Fahrenheit scale, we can say that the difference between 60°F and 50°F is the same as that between 10°F and 0°F; however, we cannot say that 50°F is 'five times as hot as 10° (i.e., a 5 : 1 ratio)'. The reason for this is that the zero point on the Fahrenheit scale is arbitrary and does not reflect the 'true' zero of the underlying characteristic (i.e., absence of heat). This requires the use of the Kelvin scale where absolute zero is −273.15°C.

A *ratio scale* is the highest level of measurement and has all the properties of the interval scale plus an absolute zero point (i.e., zero represents the absence of the characteristic being measured) so that ratios of measurements are sensible to consider.

1. A person who is 78 inches tall is twice as tall as someone who is 39 inches tall. In general, measurements of length are ratio scales.
2. The speed of a motorcycle in kilometres or miles per hour. On a ratio scale a reading of zero actually corresponds to absence of speed (i.e., the motorcycle is stationary). Moreover, we can say that driving at 224 miles per hour is four times as fast as 56 miles per hour (a ratio of 4 : 1) or, converting into kilometres, that 360 km per hour is four times as fast as 90 km per hour (also a ratio of 4 : 1). (*Note*: 1 mile = 1.609 km.)

Measures of Central Location

An average value (sometimes referred to as the measure of central location or measure of central tendency) is the most important single statistic used to summarize data. This is the most 'typical' or 'central' value, which is in some way representative of the entire set of observations for the variable concerned. Apart from summarizing a dataset, these measures allow us to make comparisons between different datasets.

Raw data represents the information collected from the respondents in an ungrouped form (for example, the income of an individual, say, £30 per week). However, when the data collected is aggregated into convenient groups with corresponding frequencies, it is called grouped data (for example, the number of respondents with income between £20 to £29 is 35).

Two frequently used measures of location are the mean and the median and the definition of these measures of location is given in Figure 6.2.

Measures of central location

Mean (or arithmetic mean)	Median
This is obtained by finding the sum of observations divided by the number of observations.	This is the middle value of an ordered list of data, in other words, the value that has half of the observations below it and half above.

Figure 6.2 What are mean and median?

Mean

This is obtained generally by finding the sum of observations divided by the number of observations.

Raw Data

Raw data represents the information collected (measurements) from the respondents in an ungrouped form:

$$\bar{X} = \frac{\sum X_i}{n}$$

Example 1 (Raw Data)

The times in minutes taken by 9 respondents to complete a questionnaire are: 22, 34, 21, 19, 27, 32, 30, 25, 32. To calculate the mean we use the formula:

$$\bar{X} = \frac{22 + 34 + 21 + 19 + 27 + 32 + 30 + 25 + 32}{9} = \frac{242}{9} = 26.89 \approx 27 \text{ minutes}$$

If we had information for the tenth respondent as 90 minutes, the mean $\bar{X} = 332/10 = 33.2 \approx 33$ minutes. The extreme value of the tenth respondent affects the mean. It has now moved more towards the higher end of data values. In such a situation, either anomalous values are usually discarded or a median is used.

Frequency Distribution

$$\bar{X} = \frac{\sum fX}{\sum f}$$

Ungrouped $X =$ Actual observation. The number of times (frequency) an observation occurs (f) is recorded against the unit of measurement, e.g, how many days it takes for a packet of washing powder to be sold.

Example 2 (Ungrouped Frequency Distribution)

The number of packets of washing powder sold at a corner shop each day were recorded for a sample of 140 days. No packets were sold for 20 days, 1 packet was sold on 30 days, 2 packets were sold on 55 days, 3 packets on 20 days, 4 packets on 10 days and 5 packets on 5 days. The frequency distribution of the number of packets sold is given in Table 6.1.

Calculation of the mean uses the formula:

$$\overline{X} = \frac{[(20 \times 0) + (30 \times 1) + (55 \times 2) + (20 \times 3) + (10 \times 4) + (5 \times 5)]}{(20 + 30 + 55 + 20 + 10 + 5)} = \frac{265}{140} = 1.89 \approx 2$$

The corner shop, on average, sells 2 packets per day.

Grouped x = Midpoint or class mark. When the data collected is aggregated into convenient groups with corresponding frequencies, it is called grouped data, for example, number of outlets with annual sales of mobile phones between £10 million and £14 million is 35.

Example 3 (Grouped Frequency Distribution)

Table 6.2 shows the annual sales (£ million) of mobile phones of a random sample of 150 outlets.

Table 6.1 Sales of packets of washing powder

Number of packets of washing powder (X)	0	1	2	3	4	5
Number of days (f)	20	30	55	20	10	5

Table 6.2 Annual sales of mobile phones and number of outlets

Annual sales of mobile phones (£m)	Number of outlets (f)
5–9	18
10–14	35
15–19	41
20–24	21
25–29	15
30–34	13
35–39	7
Total	150

The mean of annual sales of the outlets is calculated by using the formula

$$\text{Mean} = \bar{x} = \frac{\sum fx}{\sum f}$$

Table 6.3 shows the calculations necessary to calculate the mean.

$$\text{Mean} = \bar{x} = \frac{\sum fx}{\sum f} = \frac{2785}{150} = £18.57 \approx £19\text{m}$$

Median

This is the middle value of an ordered list of data, in other words, the value that has half of the observations below it and half above it.

Raw Data

First arrange the data in order of magnitude (either ascending or descending order). Find the position of the median which is $(n + 1)/2$, where n is the number of values considered. In the case where the position is halfway between two integers (i.e., when n is an even number), the average of their corresponding values is selected.

Example 4

The times in minutes taken by nine respondents to complete a questionnaire are:

22, 34, 21, 19, 27, 32, 30, 25, 32   ($n = 9$, i.e., 9 observations)
Arrange in an ascending order   19, 21, 22, 25, 27, 30, 32, 32, 34

The position of the median $= (9 + 1)/2 = 10/2 = 5$, so the value lying on the fifth position is the median, i.e., *median* = 27.

Table 6.3 Calculation of mean annual sales

Annual sales (£m)	Class mark (x)	Number of outlets (f)	(fx)
5–9	7	18	126
10–14	12	35	420
15–19	17	41	697
20–24	22	21	462
25–29	27	15	405
30–34	32	13	416
35–39	37	7	259
Total		$\sum f = 150$	$\sum fx = 2785$

If the tenth respondent's value of 90 is added, then arranging in ascending order we have 19, 21, 22, 25, 27, 30, 32, 32, 34, 90. Then the median is $(27 + 30)/2 = 28.5 = 29$. The median is less influenced by the extreme value than the mean. Therefore, if extreme values are present, the median is preferred to the mean.

Example 5

The numbers of packets of product A sold in eight local shops were as follows:

11, 15, 18, 5, 7, 5, 9, 12   ($n = 8$, i.e., 8 (even) number of observations)

which when arranged in order are **5, 5, 7, 9, 11, 12, 15, 18**
The position of the median $= (8 + 1)/2 = 9/2 = 4.5$, so the median lies halfway between the fourth and fifth values. So, median $= (9 + 11)/2 = 20/2 = 10$.

Example 6 (Ungrouped Frequency Distribution—using the data in Example 2 above and Table 6.4.)

For number of observations greater than 30, the position of the median

$$= \frac{n}{2} = \frac{\sum f}{2} = \frac{140}{2} = 70\text{th}$$

which lies on 2, hence the median $= 2$.

Example 7 (Grouped Frequency Distribution—using the data in Example 3 above.)

As with the ungrouped frequency distribution, we need to obtain the cumulative frequency for the number of days for packets sold as shown in Table 6.5.
The median is given by the formula

$$L + \frac{\left(\frac{n}{2} - (\sum f)_l\right)}{f_{\text{median}}} \times C$$

where $L =$ lower class boundary of the median class (15–19), e.g., 14.5*
   $n/2 =$ position of the median $(150/2 = 75)$.
   $(\sum f)_l =$ cumulative frequency up to the median class 10–14 $(= 53)$
   $f_{\text{median}} =$ frequency of the median class 15–19 $(= 41)$.
   $C =$ class width as difference between the upper class boundary (ucb) and lower class boundary (lcb) of the median class $(19.5 - 14.5 = 5)$.

Table 6.4 Cumulative frequency of the number of days for sales of packets

Number of packets of washing powder (X)	0	1	2	3	4	5
Cumulative number of days (f)	20	50	105	125	135	140

*Value is 14.5 at the lower boundary and 19.5 at the upper boundary. The boundary values are rounded down and up respectively.

Table 6.5 Cumulative frequency of annual sales of mobile phones

Annual sales (£m)	Class mark (x)	Number of outlets (f)	Cumulative frequency (F)
5–9	7	18	18
10–14	12	35	53
15–19	17	41	94
20–24	22	21	115
25–29	27	15	130
30–34	32	13	143
35–39	37	7	150
Total		$\sum f = 150$	

Thus,

$$L = 14.5, \; (\textstyle\sum f)_l = 53, f_{median} = 41, C = 5$$

$$\text{Median} = 14.5 + \frac{\left(\dfrac{150}{2} - 53\right)}{41} \times 5 = 14.5 + 2.7 = 17.2$$

The median value of annual sales is £17.2 million.

Measures of Dispersion (or Variation)

While measures of central location identify 'average' values in a set of data, they tell us nothing about the extent to which the individual values are similar or different from one another. A second important property that describes a set of data is variation. Measures of variation summarize the degree of dispersion (or 'scatter' or 'spread') in a variable. They all equal zero when there is no variation and increase in value with greater dispersion in the data.

Figure 6.3 shows the various measures of dispersion.

Range

This is the easiest measure to calculate and is defined as the difference between the highest and lowest values in the data.

Example 8

The following figures represent the times in minutes of 10 workers in completing a short task: 25, 19, 21, 14, 29, 22, 33, 17, 30, 26.

$$\text{Range} = \text{highest value} - \text{lowest value} = 33 - 14 = 19$$

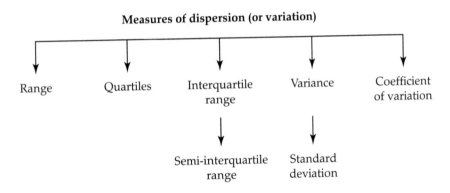

Figure 6.3 Measures of dispersion

Quartiles

Quartiles are the three values which split the distribution into four equal parts and there are three quartiles:

$$Q_1 = \text{first (or lower) quartile}$$
$$Q_2 = \text{second quartile (median)}$$
$$Q_3 = \text{third (or upper) quartile}$$

Raw Data

To calculate the upper quartiles, Q_1 and Q_3, follow the same steps as in the calculation of the median (Q_2). The only difference here is the positions of Q_1 and Q_3 which are $(n + 1)/4$, and $3(n + 1)/4$, respectively.

Ungrouped Frequency Distribution

Follow the same approach as in the calculation of the median but note that the positions of Q_1 and Q_3 are now $(n/4)$ and $(3n/4)$ respectively as the number of observations are large.

Interquartile Range

This is defined as being the difference between the upper and lower quartiles. That is,

$$\text{Interquartile range} = Q_3 - Q_1$$

This value gives the range containing the central 50% of the data. The average difference of the interquartile range is called the *semi-interquartile range* or sometimes the *quartile deviation*:

$$\text{Semi-interquartile range} = \frac{Q_3 - Q_1}{2}$$

Consider the information of sales of mobile phones from Table 6.6 (Example 7).

$$\text{Third quartile} = Q_3$$

$$\text{Position of } Q_3 = \frac{3n}{4} = \frac{3 \times 150}{4} = 112.5$$

Therefore, the class containing the third quartile is (20–24).
Then using $L_1 = 19.5$, the class interval is determined using the following equation:

$$L_1 = 19.5, \quad C = ucb - lcb = 24.5 - 19.5 = 5$$

$$f_{Q_3} = 21 \ (\textstyle\sum f)_l = 18 + 35 + 41 = 94$$

Using the formula

$$Q_3 = L_1 + \frac{\left[\dfrac{3n}{4} - (\textstyle\sum f)_l\right]}{f_{Q_3}} \times C = 19.5 + \frac{(112.5 - 94)}{21} \times 5$$

$$= 19.5 + 4.405 = 23.905 = 23.9$$

Therefore, $Q_3 = £24$ million. 75% of the outlets have annual sales of mobile phones of £23.9 million or less or 25% of the outlets have annual sales of more than £23.9 million.

$$\text{First quartile} = Q_1$$

$$\text{Position of } Q_1 = \frac{n}{4} = \frac{150}{4} = 37.5$$

Table 6.6 Cumulative frequency of annual sales of mobile phones

Annual sales (£m)	Class mark (x)	Number of outlets (f)	Cumulative frequency (F)
5–9	7	18	18
10–14	12	35	53
15–19	17	41	94
20–24	22	21	115
25–29	27	15	130
30–34	32	13	143
35–39	37	7	150
Total		$\sum f = 150$	

Therefore, the class containing the first quartile is (10–14). Then

$$L_1 = 9.5, \quad C = ucb - lcb = 14.5 - 9.5 = 5$$

$$f_{Q_1} = 35, \ (\textstyle\sum f)_l = 18$$

Using the formula

$$Q_1 = L_1 + \frac{\left[\dfrac{n}{4} - (\sum f)_l\right]}{f_{Q_1}} \times C = 9.5 + \frac{37.5 - 18}{35} \times 5$$

$$= 9.5 + 2.8 = 12.3$$

$$\text{Semi-interquartile range} = \frac{Q_3 - Q_1}{2} = \frac{23.9 - 12.3}{2} = 5.8$$

Variance and Standard Deviation

The two commonly used measures of variation that do take into account how all the values in the data are distributed around the mean are the *variance* and its square root, the *standard deviation*.

$$\text{Standard deviation} = \sqrt{Variance}$$

Notation: $S^2 =$ sample variance $\qquad S =$ sample standard deviation

$\qquad\qquad \sigma^2 =$ population variance $\qquad \sigma =$ population standard deviation

Variance is defined as the average of the squared differences between each of the observations in a set of data and the mean.

Formulae for the standard deviation:

Raw data

$$S = \sqrt{\frac{\sum (X - \bar{X})^2}{n}} \quad \text{or} \quad S = \sqrt{\frac{\sum X^2}{n} - \left(\frac{\sum X}{n}\right)^2}$$

Frequency distribution (grouped data)

$$S = \sqrt{\frac{\sum f(X - \bar{X})^2}{\sum f}} \quad \text{or} \quad S = \sqrt{\frac{\sum fX^2}{\sum f} - \left(\frac{\sum fX}{\sum f}\right)^2}$$

Example 8

Table 6.7 shows the calculations for standard deviation for the following raw data of time taken (X) by 10 respondents to complete a questionnaire.
The mean will be

$$\bar{X} = \frac{236}{10} = 23.6$$

Then

$$S = \sqrt{\frac{332.4}{10}} = \sqrt{33.24} = 5.765 \approx 5.8$$

or

$$S = \sqrt{\frac{5902}{10} - \left(\frac{236}{10}\right)^2} = \sqrt{590.2 - (23.6)^2} = \sqrt{590.2 - 556.96} = \sqrt{33.24}$$

$$= 5.765 \approx 5.8 \text{ mins.}$$

Example 9

Using the data from Example 7 in Table 6.6, Table 6.8 provides details of the necessary calculations.

Table 6.7 Calculation of standard deviation for time taken to complete a questionnaire

Time (X)	($X - \bar{X}$)	($X - \bar{X}$)^2	X^2
25	1.4	1.96	225
19	−4.6	21.16	361
21	−2.6	6.76	441
14	−9.6	92.16	196
29	6.4	29.16	841
22	−1.6	2.56	484
33	9.4	88.36	1089
17	−6.6	43.56	289
30	6.4	40.96	900
26	2.4	6.76	676
$\sum X = 236$		$\sum(X - \bar{X})^2 = 332.4$	$\sum X^2 = 5902$

Table 6.8 Calculation of standard deviation

Annual sales (£m)	Class mark (x)	Number of outlets (f)	(fx)	(fx²)
5–9	7	18	126	882
10–14	12	35	420	5040
15–19	17	41	697	11849
20–24	22	21	462	10164
25–29	27	15	405	10935
30–34	32	13	416	13312
35–39	37	7	259	9583
Total		$\sum f = 150$	$\sum fx = 2785$	$\sum (fx^2) = 61765$

Then

$$\text{Variance } S^2 = \frac{\sum fx^2}{\sum f} - \left(\frac{\sum fx}{\sum f}\right)^2 = \left(\frac{61765}{150}\right) - \left(\frac{2785}{150}\right)^2$$

$$= 411.77 - 344.72 = 67.05$$

$$\text{Standard deviation } S = \sqrt{S^2} \Rightarrow \sqrt{67.05} = 8.19 \text{ mins.}$$

Coefficient of Variation (CV)

This is defined (Berenson and Levine, 1999) as the standard deviation divided by the mean and is expressed as a percentage. For instance,

$$CV = \frac{S}{\bar{X}} \times 100$$

The coefficient of variation is independent of the units of measurement and can be used as a more realistic measure of comparison when we have two or more data sets with significantly different means. A dataset with a smaller coefficient of variation is preferred over one with larger coefficient of variation.

Example 10 (Using data from Example 8)

$$\bar{X} = 23.6 \quad S = 5.8$$

$$CV = \frac{5.8}{23.6} \times 100 = 0.24576 \times 100 = 24.576 \cong 24.6\%$$

Normal Distribution

The normal distribution plays an important role in marketing surveys. Measurements such as income, profits, turnover, distance travelled and other interval scaled measurements follow a normal distribution. It is also known that the estimates from a sample selected randomly follow approximately a normal distribution with population mean as its mean and a corresponding standard error (see Chapter 8). This is true even if the original measurements do not themselves follow a normal distribution. For example, if we surveyed a group of workers about their attitude (agree or disagree) to a proposed change, the initial measurements will have a binomial distribution (with only two alternatives) though the estimate, the proportion (p) of workers in favour of the change will have a normal distribution.

The normal distribution is specified by the parameters—mean μ and the variance σ^2. The distribution is symmetrical around its mean, the shape of the distribution is bell-shaped and relates to a continuous variable. Different types of measurements of variables will generate different distributions and to obtain the probability values for any such variable, different tables will be necessary. This is resolved by the use of the probability tables for what is known as a standard normal variable, denoted by Z. This variable Z has 0 as its mean and 1 as its variance. The standard normal variable is obtained by using the formula: $Z = (x - \mu)/\sqrt{\sigma^2}$. The total area (probability) under the normal curve is 1 and half of the area is to right of the mean and the other half to the left of it. Since the distribution is symmetrical, only values to one side of the distribution are given and we can work out the values of the region on the other side of the mean by simply changing the sign of the Z value.

Standardization

This is a procedure one uses for changing any normal distribution into the standard normal distribution (see Figure 6.4). Any normal distribution, $x \sim N(\mu, \sigma^2)$ is converted to a standardized normal distribution $Z \sim N(0, 1)$, by the equation

$$\text{Standard normal variable} = \frac{\text{Normal variable} - \text{mean}}{\text{Standard deviation}}$$

$$Z = \frac{x - \mu}{\sigma}$$

The relationship between normal (x) and standard normal (Z) distributions is shown in Figure 6.4.

Example 11

The average (μ) distance travelled by all employees of a company with 5000 employees is known to be 15 km with a standard deviation (σ) of 2 km. Once we

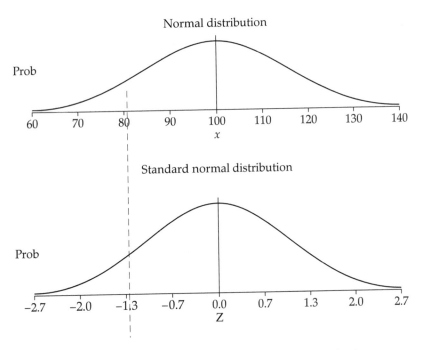

Normal distribution

Prob

60   70   80   90   100   110   120   130   140

x

Standard normal distribution

Prob

−2.7   −2.0   −1.3   −0.7   0.0   0.7   1.3   2.0   2.7

Z

Figure 6.4   Relationship between normal and standard normal distributions

know the distribution of the distance travelled to be normal, we can work out how many employees will travel:

1. More than 20 km
2. Less than 14 km
3. Between 14 km and 20 km

We can also work out the minimum distance travelled by 10% of the employees. This can then be used in deciding the travelling allowance (rate per km) the company might pay to its employees.

In all cases, it is useful to draw the normal distribution and indicate the area under the curve we require by shading it as shown in Figures 6.5 to 6.8.

1. We know $\mu = 15$ km and $\sigma = 2$ km. and $x_1 = 20$ km. Figure 6.5 illustrates the area under the normal distribution curve for x_1. This used to find the probability of the desired value of the number of employees travelling more than 20 km. Then

$$Z = \frac{x_1 - \mu}{\sigma} = \frac{20 - 15}{2} = 2.5$$

141

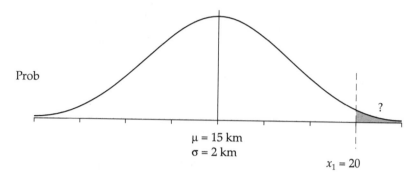

Figure 6.5 Area under the normal distribution curve for x_1

From the tables (Appendix II), the area under the curve (probability) is 0.00621. Therefore, the number of employees travelling more than 20 km will be $5000(0.00621) = 31$.

2. We know $\mu = 15$ km and $\sigma = 2$ km. and $x_2 = 14$ km. Figure 6.6 illustrates the area under the normal distribution curve for x_2. This used to find the probability of the desired value of the number of employees travelling less than 14 km. Then

$$Z = \frac{(x_2 - \mu)}{\sigma} = \frac{(14 - 15)}{2} = -0.50$$

From the table (Appendix II), the area under the curve (probability), using the positive value of $Z = 0.5$ as the distribution is symmetrical, is 0.3085. Therefore, the number of employees travelling less than 14 km will be $5000(0.3085) = 1543$.

3. We know $\mu = 15$ km and $\sigma = 2$ km. We now have two values of x. $x_1 = 20$ km and $x_2 = 14$ km.

$$x_1 \rightarrow Z_1 = 2.50$$

$$x_2 \rightarrow Z_2 = -0.50$$

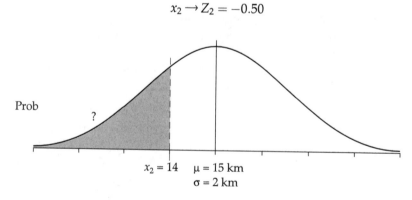

Figure 6.6 Area under the normal distribution curve for x_2

Then using the two Z values calculated above, the areas are 0.00621 and 0.3085 respectively (using Appendix II). Therefore, the area that we require is one which does not include the areas already calculated. This desired area is obtained by subtracting the two areas calculated from 1. Figure 6.7 illustrates the area under the normal distribution curve. This is used to find the probability of the desired value of the number of employees travelling between 14 km and 20 km. Thus the area required will be $1 - (0.0062 + 0.3085) = 1 - 0.31471 = 0.6853$. Therefore, the number of employees travelling between 14 km and 20 km will be $5000(0.68529) = 3426$.

In order to calculate the minimum distance travelled by 10% of the employees, what we know is that the area is 10%, i.e., the area is 0.10. We need to reverse the process to find the value of Z which gives the area to be 0.10 in the table (Appendix II). This value from the tables is -1.28.

Figure 6.8 illustrates the area under the normal distribution curve for x_4. We now know all the values in the Z formula except the required value of x giving the minimum distance travelled:

$$-1.28 = \frac{(x - \mu)}{\sigma} = \frac{(x - 15)}{2} \quad \text{giving } x = 12.44 \approx 12 \text{ km}$$

The minimum distance travelled by 10% of the employees will be 12 km.

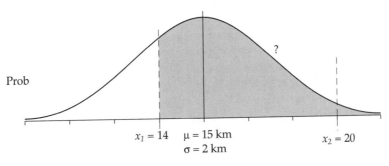

Figure 6.7 Area under the normal distribution curve for x_3

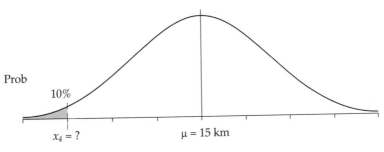

Figure 6.8 Area under the normal distribution curve for x_4

143

Drawing a Scatter Plot

In studying the relationship between two variables the first step is to draw a scatter plot or diagram; a graph of the observed pairs of observations. Values of the independent variable X are assigned to the horizontal axis. The vertical axis is used to represent the dependent variable Y. A dot is placed on the graph at the intersection of each pair of values of X and Y. Consider the following data in

Table 6.9 Market share by relative price/advertising share

Year	Market share (%) (ms)	Relative price (rp)	Advertising share % (as)
1	20	100	20
2	25	100	25
3	40	95	35
4	35	95	35
5	45	80	35
6	35	90	30
7	40	85	35
8	55	80	35
9	50	85	40
10	45	85	55
11	30	105	45
12	20	110	25
13	25	95	20
14	25	100	25
15	30	95	30

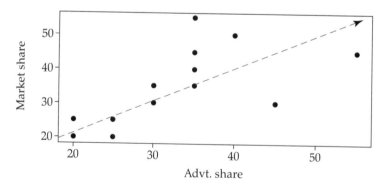

Figure 6.9 Scatter plot for market share with advertising share

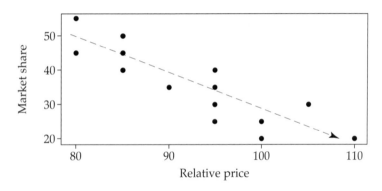

Figure 6.10 Scatter plot for market share with relative price

Table 6.9, showing: (1) the market share (ms) as a percentage of the total market, (2) relative price (rp) as an index with retail price index for the industry as base and (3) advertising share (as) a percentage of the total advertising expenditure, for a particular company, over a period of last 15 years.

Figures 6.9 and 6.10 show scatter diagrams for these data. The pattern provides a means for visual inspection of the data that a list of values for the two variables cannot. Both the direction and the shape of a relationship are conveyed in a plot. Figure 6.9 shows that, in general, when advertising share is high there is a tendency to have high market share and indicates a positive correlation. Figure 6.10 shows that the company will have lower market share when the relative price increases and indicates a negative correlation. When stronger relationships are apparent, the points cluster close to the (imaginary) straight line (shown as the dotted arrow on each graph) while, for weaker relationships, the points are more diffused and further from the line.

Sample Estimates and Standard Errors

Marketing researchers are generally interested in finding either average ($\bar{x}$) income or proportion (p) of buyers or the total ($n\bar{x}$) turnover of the outlets. A point estimate is a single value (such as average income of consumers, proportion of buyers for a product or total turnover of outlets) from the data. For large samples (sample size n greater than 30), the sampling distribution of the estimates is, in most cases, a normal distribution. The standard deviation of the sample estimate is called the standard error. Note that the standard error *always* relates to the sample estimate and the standard deviation (square root of the variance) relates to the population values. Table 6.10 gives some of the parameters, the estimates, and the corresponding standard errors. The standard errors are used in hypothesis testing which is dealt with in Chapters 8 and 9.

Table 6.10 Estimates and standard errors

Sample size		Parameter		Estimate	Standard Error
Large	Single sample	Mean	μ	$\bar{x}$	$\sqrt{\dfrac{\hat{\sigma}^2}{n}}$
		Proportion	π	p	$\sqrt{\dfrac{\pi(1-\pi)}{n}}$
	Two samples	Means	$\bar{\mu}_1 - \bar{\mu}_2$	$\bar{x}_1 - \bar{x}_2$	$\sqrt{\dfrac{\sigma_1^2}{n_1} + \dfrac{\sigma_2^2}{n_2}}$
		Proportions	$\pi_1 - \pi_2$	$p_1 - p_2$	$\sqrt{p(1-p)\left(\dfrac{1}{n_1} + \dfrac{1}{n_2}\right)}$

where

$$p = \frac{n_1 p_1 + n_2 p_2}{n_1 + n_2}$$

Sample size		Parameter		Estimate	Standard Error
Small	Single sample	Mean	μ	$\bar{x}$	$\sqrt{\dfrac{\hat{\sigma}^2}{n-1}}$
	Two samples independent	Means	$\bar{\mu}_1 - \bar{\mu}_2$	$\bar{x}_1 - \bar{x}_2$	$\sqrt{\hat{\sigma}_p^2\left(\dfrac{1}{n_1} + \dfrac{1}{n_2}\right)}$

where

$$\hat{\sigma}_p^2 = \frac{(n_1 - 1)\hat{\sigma}_1^2 + (n_2 - 1)\hat{\sigma}_2^2}{n_1 + n_2 - 2}$$

Sample size		Parameter		Estimate	Standard Error
	Paired	Mean	μ	$\bar{d}$	$\sqrt{\dfrac{\hat{\sigma}_d^2}{n-1}}$

Conclusion

Data can be described by four scales according to the level of measurement. Information can be represented as raw data or grouped data. The two measures of location—mean and median—are commonly used to summarize data in marketing research. The degree of dispersion is summarized by the variation in the data. Two commonly used measures of dispersion are the standard deviation and the semi-interquartile range. The coefficient of variation is a measure used to compare two sets of data. Normal distribution plays an important role in marketing surveys as the estimates from a randomly drawn population follow a normal distribution. The standard error of the estimates is used in testing hypotheses (see Chapters 8 and 9).

References

Berenson, M. and Levine, D. (1999). *Basic Business Statistics*, London: Prentice-Hall.
Siegel, S. (1956). *Non-parametric Statistics for Behavioural Sciences*, London: McGraw-Hill.
Taylor, M.B. (1983). 'Ordinal and interval scaling', *The Journal of the Market Research Society*, 25, No. 4.

Work Assignments

1. The table below shows the annual sales (£ million) of desktop computers of a random sample of 140 computer showrooms of a distributor.

Annual sales of desktop computers (£m)	Number of showrooms (f)
9–13	12
14–18	28
19–23	42
24–28	35
29–33	14
34–38	9
Total	140

(i) Calculate the mean and standard deviation of the annual sales of desktop computers.
(ii) Calculate and interpret the first quartile for the annual sales of desktop computers.
(iii) Given that the third quartile of the distribution is equal to 26.8, calculate the interquartile range.

2. The table below shows the time spent on training during a year by male and female market research executives in the South East of England.

Time spent (minutes)	Number of executives	
	Male	Female
60	120	20
55	100	60
50	200	100
45	355	450
40	350	450
35	500	300
30	350	250
25	20	100

(i) Calculate the average time spent by male and female executives and comment on the results bringing out the advantages of using average as a measure of location in this situation.

(ii) Calculate the standard deviation for both groups.

(iii) Which group is more variable in time spent?

An Introduction to Sampling

7

Learning Outcomes

After reading this chapter you will be able to

- Understand why samples are used and the sampling process.
- Appreciate the role of a sampling frame and choice of a sampling method.
- Choose an appropriate sampling method.
- Determine how large a sample should be.
- Select a sample for a research project.

Introduction

Sampling is an important procedure in marketing research because it is not often possible to collect data from every relevant person within a population. *A population under investigation* can be defined as a set number of units of people that collectively exhibit similar traits or features. The sample is the subject of study. In marketing research, it is possible to distinguish between two different types of approach to sampling. The first is where a marketing researcher studies the whole population, and this is referred to as a *census*. The second is where a sub-set of this population is studied—a *sample*. There are a number of reasons why marketing researchers use sampling rather than census studies and these are outlined below:

- *Cost* Interviewing all units of a population would in many cases be impossible due to the very high costs associated. For instance, it would involve considerable amounts of money for Tesco to interview every couple in Britain (and in the other markets where they have a presence) in relation to their shopping habits.
- *Time* The interviewing process takes time. In many business situations, time is a critical factor since information is usually needed for action to occur within a

specified deadline, e.g., test-marketing a new chocolate bar among consumers then modifying the product subject to the marketing research study's conclusions, then releasing the product on general sale before any other manufacturer can launch a similar product.

- *Accuracy* A census is far more accurate than a sample and the results from censuses are, therefore, more generalizable across the population. Censuses are used more often when highly accurate data are required and populations are small. Where populations are large, marketing researchers have to use large samples which are specifically designed to be as representative of the general population as possible. Samples also allow access to respondents who otherwise are not easily accessible, e.g., those living in residential homes or prisons. Accuracy is also increased as samples enable the use of trained interviewers for investigations requiring specialized technical knowledge of the subject under investigation, e.g., use and impact of pharmaceutical products.
- *Destructive nature of the measurement* If a car manufacturer was testing cars for safety features, it would be unwise to crash every car into a wall in order to test its safety features since to do so would cause the manufacturer to have no stock left to sell.

Census studies tend to be conducted mainly when population units are extremely varied and, thus, sampling becomes difficult due to the problems in defining a suitably stratified sample. As a result, such studies are used predominantly where populations are smaller and, in particular, in business-to-business marketing research (see Chapter 12).

The process of sampling is important because it determines who is selected to provide information for the marketing research problem and how they are selected. As a result, the sampling procedure that is used by a researcher tells an observer how valid the resulting information is in relation to the population of interest. There is a wide range of sampling methods, some of which are more scientific than others. These methods tend to use probability sampling procedures, although commercial marketing research organizations also use complex subjective methods.

The Sampling Process

Jobber (1995) states that the sampling process encompasses five stages as shown in Figure 7.1.

Stage 1—Population Definition

According to Tull and Hawkins (1994), the population should be defined in terms of (a) element, (b) sampling unit, (c) extent and (d) time. The population element relates to the type of person in the sample that is to be interviewed. For instance, in a grocery survey, the population element may be the chief shopper of a household between the ages of 18 and 64. The sampling unit contains one or more population elements and usually relates to the household, street, postcode or shopping centre.

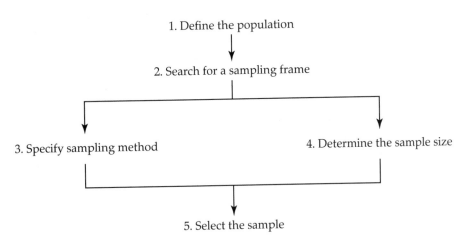

Figure 7.1   Stages in the sampling process
Source: Jobber (1995). Reproduced by permission of McGraw-Hill.

Tull and Hawkins (1994) define this as the 'initial contact point that contains the elements to be sampled'. The extent describes the criterion for selection and, this, in a grocery survey could be persons who have bought a product (e.g., cat food) within the last six months. The time factor relates either to when the survey was performed or to the product consumption time limit where this is specified (as in the above example).

Stage 2—Search for Sampling Frame

It would be useful to begin with a definition of what a sampling frame is. It can be defined as a list or means of representing the sampling units containing the elements of a population. Frequently, this is a telephone directory or membership listing. It could be argued that there are five criteria that are essential in determining how useful a particular sampling frame is and these are outlined below:

- *Accuracy*—Lists need to contain current population elements rather than historic population elements. Thus, an old telephone directory would not provide an accurate sampling frame because many of the numbers would have changed. People may have been disconnected and many new telephone numbers would not be represented.
- *Adequacy*—The list should represent the characteristics of the elements of the sample population that are to be measured. For instance, in a survey on supporters' attitudes at a football match, it would be misleading to compile a sampling frame from season ticket holders only, except where season ticket holders represent the whole population (as they do currently at Newcastle United which changed its policy from selling match-day tickets to season tickets only).

151

- *Completeness*—All members of a sample population need to be represented in order to reduce sampling bias as much as possible. Failure to do so could seriously affect the validity of the results.
- *Convenience*—If a list is ideal but not available (or too expensive to compile or buy in), a marketing researcher will have to find alternative solutions.
- *Duplication*—Population elements should not be duplicated since this will lead to an over-representation of individual elements and sampling bias will result. This may occur in telephone directories and mailing lists and de-duplication should be performed prior to the use of the sampling frame in any probability sampling procedure.

It is difficult to find a sampling frame that fulfils all the above criteria and sampling frames which contain omissions and uncorrected dual listings contribute to sampling frame error due to the fact that the listing does not accurately reflect the general population. National sampling frames currently used in the UK are the electoral registers (lists containing everyone registered to vote for parliamentary, European or local elections) and the postcode system. This system allows the identification of any address in the UK because every street is represented in the code. It was developed to allow automatic mail sorting and postcode details and services relating to them can be obtained from the Royal Mail's marketing department.

Stage 3—Selection of Sampling Method

The researcher first needs to determine whether to use a probability or non-probability sampling method. Each method is particularly appropriate for specific situations. Non-probability sampling methods use judgemental techniques whereby the sample is selected using procedures that are not related by chance. These procedures generally involve the selection of respondents using the judgement of the researcher (where the researcher places restrictions on the type of person that can be interviewed) or the interviewers themselves. In probability sampling procedures, the respondents are selected according to a process which involves a random or chance element. Thus, non-probability sampling procedures are subjective and probability sampling procedures are more objective. As a result, non-probability sampling methods produce results in which there is no guarantee that the sample will be representative of the actual population.

Probability samples require that every individual element of the population be known beforehand so that a percentage chance of selection can be placed upon each individual unit, which is often impossible. Therefore, the practicalities of the situation and the desired objectivity of the survey determine the process of selecting a sampling method.

Since probability samples require that every individual element of the population be known beforehand, in order that a percentage chance of selection can be placed upon each individual unit a suitable sampling frame is required, which is often impossible.

Both sampling procedures can be further sub-divided into specific sampling methods that are appropriate for different circumstances (see Figure 7.2) and each of these methods is explained below. Apart from the method of selecting the units, simple random sampling is the same as systematic sampling and stratified random sampling is the same as quota sampling.

Probabilistic Methods

Simple random sampling is a probability sampling procedure where each population element is assigned a number and the desired sample is determined by generating random numbers appropriate for the relevant sample size. Although this method allows the generation of data which is easily comprehensible and the results are far more likely to be representative (providing an appropriate sample size and frame are used), it is often difficult to use this method as a comprehensive sample frame is simply not available.

The population is assumed to be homogeneous (similar in characteristics) for the purpose of investigation. All samples of a particular size have an equal chance of selection. The units in the population are all identified and can be numbered, thus we should have a sampling frame. The sample selection is done by using different methods such as: (a) for finite populations, use of an urn (football teams), a drum (National Lottery), a bowl or a hat where individual units are identified by numbers, placed in the urn, drum, bowl or hat and selection is done randomly and (b) for larger (infinite) populations use is made of random number tables.

Random number tables (see Appendix II) give a set of numbers which allow the selection of units from a population such that every unit has the chance of selection

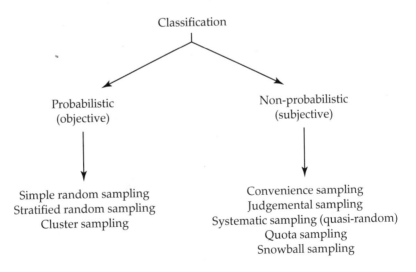

Figure 7.2   Classification of sampling methods

and there is no pattern in the numbers selected. When generating random numbers, the random number is determined by multiplying a random number from 0 to 1 by the population size. Suppose the population (register of customers) has $N = 2500$ names and our required sample size is 250 customers. We would then generate 250 random numbers.

For infinite (very large) populations, use is made of computers as in the case of Post Office Premium Bonds. Millions of customers hold bonds in large numbers. To allow every Bond number an equal chance of winning the first prize, a machine (ERNIE—Electronic Random Number Indicating Equipment) is used. In this situation a customer can win more than one prize, depending on their ownership of the bonds.

Stratified random sampling is a probability sampling procedure that selects sample elements randomly from sub-sections of the main sample defined by some pertinent characteristic. This technique is usually used where there is considerable diversity within the population. The researcher then has to determine whether to use disproportionate sub-sections (strata) or proportionate strata. The researcher may choose to study disproportionate strata where the sub-sample being studied is of particular interest.

In most research situations the target population under investigation is not homogeneous. The population is known to have characteristics that are different but can be split into sub-populations, called *strata* or *groups*, which are homogeneous, themselves. For example, a company may have three marketing regions.

The conditions for using stratified sampling are:

1. Groups homogeneous within (outlets are similar within each region).
2. Groups heterogeneous between (outlets are different between regions).
3. Groups together constitute the population ($N = N_1 + N_2 + N_3$). The outlets in three regions make up all the outlets of the company. No outlets are omitted as not belonging to any region.
4. Groups are non-overlapping. (No single outlet is in two or more regions.)

Samples can be selected using two different procedures. One takes into account *only* the size of the strata populations, called a 'proportional allocation' and the selection of sample units is made using the same proportion in each stratum. The other uses not only the size of the strata populations but also the variation and the cost per unit of conducting the research in each stratum. This is called an 'optimum allocation'.

If the same sampling fraction ($n/N = k = 0.1$) is used in all groups, e.g., taking a 10% sample, then we have what is known as *proportional allocation*. Figure 7.3 illustrates the allocation of sample size using proportional allocation by population size. In proportional allocation we assume the variation (σ_i) in each and cost of conducting investigation per unit (c_i) for each to be the same for all groups.

Proportional allocation does not take into account the variation and the cost of conducting the investigation per unit. When we consider all three factors, the

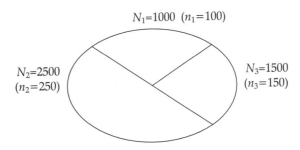

$N_1=1000 \ (n_1=100)$

$N_2=2500$
$(n_2=250)$

$N_3=1500$
$(n_3=150)$

Figure 7.3   Population size and sample size by group

group size (N_i), the variation in each group (σ_i) and the cost per unit of conducting the investigation (c_i), we have *optimum allocation*. We have seen that for larger populations we need proportionally larger samples, i.e., the sample size is proportional to the stratum size ($n_i \propto N_i$). Similarly, populations with larger variation require larger samples than those with smaller variation. We should take a smaller sample for a population where the unit cost of the investigation is high and, conversely, a larger sample in a population where the unit cost is lower.

Thus, in optimum allocation,

$$n_i \propto N_i$$

Sample size in stratum i is proportional to the population size in stratum i.

- For larger population strata, a larger sample is selected, e.g. when the population size is 2000 we select a sample of size 200 while when the population size is 1200, we select a sample of size 120.

$$n_i \propto \sigma_i$$

Sample size in stratum i is proportional to the population standard deviation in stratum i.

- When the variation is large, a large sample is required, e.g., when the standard deviation in a stratum is 20, a larger sample is needed to cover the variation in the stratum compared to a stratum with a standard deviation of 18, which will require a smaller sample:

$$n_i \propto \frac{1}{\sqrt{C_i}}$$

Sample size in stratum i is inversely proportional to the square root of the cost per unit for the stratum of the population.

- When cost per unit is high, a smaller sample is taken, e.g., when in a stratum the cost per unit is 36p, we take a smaller sample in that stratum because of higher cost compared to when in another stratum the cost per unit is 25p.
  When all three factors are taken together, we have

$$n_i \propto \frac{N_i \sigma_i}{\sqrt{C_i}}$$

Sample size in stratum i is proportional to the product of the population stratum size, the standard deviation in that stratum is divided by the square root of the cost per unit for that stratum.

- Sample size is determined by taking all the factors jointly into account. Thus, for optimum allocation, the sample size in the stratum is obtained by taking into account the stratum size, its variability and the cost per unit of conducting research in a stratum.

Figure 7.4 provides the formulas for determining sample size using both proportional and optimal allocation methods.

Example 1

We wish to study a population which has 5000 members by selecting a sample of approximately 500 from it. The aim is to estimate the average income of members, with the greatest accuracy within limited resources. In this example, the population is stratified into two regions, A and B, and within those regions, into two age groups, 1 and 2. The populations in the four categories are given below:

	Region A	Region B
Age group 1	$N_1 = 2000$	$N_2 = 1200$
Age group 2	$N_3 = 1000$	$N_4 = 800$

For stratified samples

If proportional allocation

$$n_i \propto N_i$$

If optimum allocation

$$n_i \propto \frac{N_i \sigma_i}{\sqrt{C_i}}$$

Figure 7.4 Formulas for sample size using stratified sampling

A pilot survey has indicated the approximate amount of variation (σ_i) in income for each of the groups and cost per sampling unit (c_i) in the four categories and these are as follows:

	Region A	Region B
Age group 1	$\sigma_1 = 20$	$\sigma_2 = 18$
	$c_1 = 25p$	$c_2 = 36p$
Age group 2	$\sigma_3 = 14$	$\sigma_4 = 12$
	$c_3 = 49p$	$c_4 = 64p$

Estimation of sample size for each stratum using optimum allocation is performed using the formula:

$$n_i = n \cdot \frac{\dfrac{N_i \sigma_i}{\sqrt{c_i}}}{\sum \dfrac{N_i \sigma_i}{\sqrt{c_i}}}$$

Table 7.1 shows details of the calculations of sample size using the optimal allocation method.

It can be seen here that the optimum allocation selects more units with large sub-populations and very large variation in the sub-populations than the proportional allocation. Considerable gains in precision are obtained by using stratified sampling.

Then

$$n_1 = 500 \left(\frac{8000}{14800} \right) = 270$$

Similarly n_2, n_3 and n_4 can be estimated.

Table 7.1 Calculation of sample size using optimum allocation

	Stratum	N_i	σ_i	$\sqrt{c_i}$	$\dfrac{N_i \sigma_i}{\sqrt{c_i}}$	n_i
Region A	Group 1	2000	20	5	8000	270 (200)
	Group 2	1000	14	7	2000	68 (100)
Region B	Group 1	1200	18	6	3600	122 (120)
	Group 2	800	12	8	1200	41 (80)
				Total	14800	501

Note: Figures in parentheses show stratum sample sizes if proportional allocation with a sampling fraction of 0.1 or a proportion of 10% was used.

Cluster Sampling

This is a probability sampling technique that uses random sampling methods to select clusters of elements which act as the sampling unit, rather than solely the population element. Thus, if each postcode within a constituency was assigned a number and k number of them were selected at random this would constitute use of a simple cluster sampling procedure. The levels of complexity can increase, with areas being selected randomly and then areas within those areas, and so on. At the same time, areas may be selected by using a probability procedure that takes into account the size of the area. Thus, areas with larger populations, for instance, might be more likely to be selected.

The cluster sampling method is similar to stratified random sampling except that the groups consist of units which are different (heterogeneous) within and the groups are similar (homogeneous) between. A cluster is selected randomly and all units of the cluster constitute a sample. In this method all units (housewives in a block of flats or all pharmacists in a road) are interviewed or investigated. The rationale is essentially economic since it saves on cost of travel for the interviewer. The major disadvantage is high sampling error but this can be reduced by using a large number of small clusters rather than a small number of large ones. Cluster sampling is not used very much in UK marketing surveys although it is quite popular in the USA, as cluster formation is possible due to the geographical size of the country.

Non-probabilistic Methods

These methods have selection of units carried out subjectively but the outcome (estimates) are not as reliable as the probabilistic methods. There is one-to-one correspondence between simple random sampling with systematic sampling and stratified random sampling with quota sampling.

- *Convenience sampling* This is a non-probability sampling procedure where the selection of the respondent is left entirely to the interviewer and/or researcher. This method generates considerable sampling error because the sample is unlikely to be representative of the population in general. It is most used where the population is generally difficult to access, for example conducting interviews at a trade fair in industrial marketing research. It is the least expensive and the least time-consuming method.
- *Judgemental sampling* This is a non-probability sampling procedure where the sample is selected according to the judgement of the researcher or the interviewer. In this method, the researcher uses his or her knowledge of the sample to determine who should be selected as a respondent. This method still incorporates a great deal of sampling error since the researcher or interviewer's judgement could be completely wrong. However, it tends to be used for small well-defined populations where larger probability samples would produce too few (and, therefore, meaningless) results.

- *Systematic sampling* (also called quasi-random sampling) This is a semi-probability sampling method where each element is assigned a number and a random number is generated as a starting point in the sequence of numbers. Every kth element is then selected until the sample size criterion is fulfilled. If the researcher reaches the end of the sequence, he or she simply carries on to the start, essentially 'folding' the sequence. This selection procedure may generate periodicity, which occurs when selected units are similar to each other. For instance, if one only samples members of the electorate at specific times of the day, that might correspond with the national news before a general election and, therefore, bias the results.

  Systematic sampling, like simple random sampling, generally requires a sampling frame but the selection of units is subjective. The population is split into groups of equal size of the sampling fraction ($n/N = k$) and every kth member is chosen for inclusion in the sample. The selection of the start unit in the first group is conducted randomly. In the case of 5000 employees with sampling fraction $k = 0.1$ (10%), we will have 500 groups of size 10. The first employee (say, number 4) is selected randomly in the first group. From then on, the rest of employees are selected in a systematic way. Since the sampling fraction is 10, every tenth employee from the fourth is selected, i.e., 14, 24, 34, 44, 54, ... we obtain 500 employees required in the sample. This method is more convenient than simple random sampling, and approximates to simple random sampling if the sampling frame is randomly ordered. When the sampling frame is deliberately ordered (e.g., number of employees in a firm), a more representative sample may well be drawn, resulting in smaller standard errors. However, where there is a systematic pattern (periodicity), the sample may be very unrepresentative (e.g., selection of households in a locality where the households are two blocks of four houses of which two are terraced and the other two are end-of-terrace). The selection may result in systematically selecting only terraced households.

- *Quota sampling* This is a non-probability sampling procedure that restricts the selection of the sample by controlling the number of respondents by one or more criterion. This restriction is usually by demographic or socio-economic status. Thus, an interviewer may have to select 20 respondents. The make-up of his sample, therefore, has to mirror the composition of the population if it is to be truly a quota sample. Otherwise, it is simply a judgemental sample. Thus, if 20% of the population is between the ages of 16 and 24, 20% of the sample should also be between these ages. This procedure could be used to research the habits of grocery shoppers by imposing a quota on the sample which takes into account whether they are male or female, and whether they have loyalty cards.

  Quota sampling is a commonly used sampling method in marketing research, since fieldwork costs are less compared to stratified random sampling. The interviewer is told to interview a certain number of people with specific characteristics as against people who have been selected randomly in each stratum. The population is split into sub-populations (strata) according to known characteristics in the population. For example, we may have 5000 pubs (outlets of a brewery), where the pubs are classified into three marketing regions, further divided in each region according to their turnover (say, up to £400 000, labelled T_1 and above £400 000, labelled T_2). These then being further split into managed (M) by the brewery or those being franchised (NM). The stratification of outlets is, in this case, by three characteristics: region, turnover and type of management. Figure 7.5 shows the quota allocation of the sample according to three characteristics: the type of region the pub belongs, its turnover and the type of management.

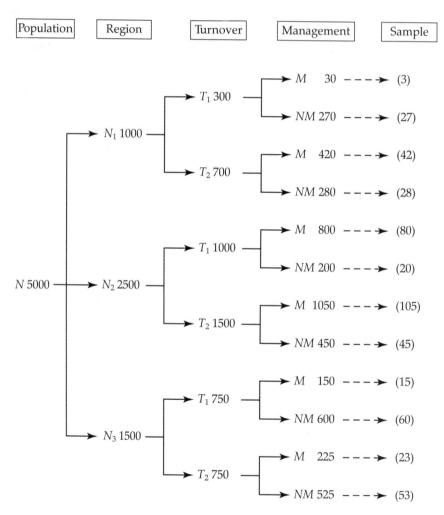

Figure 7.5 Quota allocation of outlets by region, turnover and management
Source: Baines, Chansarkar and Ryan (1999)

Figures in parentheses are sample sizes for each of the stratum obtained by taking a 10% proportion of the corresponding stratum population size.

If we were to take a 10% sample, the quota (sample size) for each selection is shown in the last column of the figure. For example, the interviewer is asked to select three outlets, which are managed, with turnover below £400 000 and belong to region 1. This constitutes the set of outlets in region 1 and the selection is not random, therefore every outlet does not have the same chance of selection. Extra controls (supervision of the fieldwork, etc.) are used to remove such 'bias'.

● *Snowball sampling* This is a non-probability sampling procedure used for sampling rare populations. It usually uses an initial random procedure to select a small sample from a given population. The sample elements generated are then asked if they know of a number of other respondents who possess a specific characteristic of interest to the researcher. These referred respondents are contacted for further referrals and so on. This procedure would be particularly useful for studying the lapsed supporters of a football club. Here, the current season-ticket holders could provide the initial sample, and they could then be asked whether they knew anyone who no longer came to watch the matches. Another possibility could be to place an advertisement in the local newspaper asking for former supporters to come forward and then generate referrals from them. This method obviously involves a considerable amount of selection bias and it is very time-consuming, but it does allow the measurement of characteristics of rare populations. A disadvantage of such sampling is that there is much repetition of respondents due to overlap, as the list tends to have the same names coming from different respondents.

Other sampling methods exist which are only slight variants of the methods mentioned above. It is possible to sample an element more than once in order to provide more information about specific elements of particular importance, for example *double sampling*. It is also possible to increase the percentage chance of an element being sampled in probability sampling in order to find out more information about specific elements of particular importance. Marketing researchers can also select a sample and then 'top it up' if the sample is not sufficiently large to offer statistically significant data. This is termed *sequential sampling*.

Tracking polls are a derivative of this type of sampling technique since they continuously collect data from a sample. In political polling, marketing researchers may collect 5 days' worth of data from around 400 people per day and only keep three days' worth of data, dropping a day's data from each end every day. This allows the pollsters to monitor changes in opinion and voting behaviour.

Essentially, selection of the sampling method involves a determination of how much time is available in order to collect the data, how much budget a researcher has to perform the research and how representative the data should be of the general population. Where budgets are low and time is a critical factor, simple non-probability sampling techniques tend to be used (e.g., convenience or judgemental sampling). When the data collected needs to represent the actual population, probability methods tend to be used. Where the researcher is interested in specific areas, cluster sampling is the best method, while stratified sampling is used to collect representative data from a diverse heterogeneous population with differing characteristics.

Stage 4—Determine Sample Size

Once the sampling method has been determined, the marketing researcher needs to assess how many population elements need to be sampled. This has important implications because it tells observers how likely the sample is to be representative of the actual population.

The size of a sample depends on a range of factors. Generally, a sample is large where the commissioning organization requires a high degree of confidence in the information obtained from the data, i.e., the accuracy of the values obtained from the sample in relation to the population. This might be particularly necessary if the population is heterogeneous and, therefore, there may be many sub-sets of the population that would need to be analysed. Samples tend to be smaller where time and resources are limited, since collection of the data tends to be one of the largest costs involved in a marketing research project. However, telephone and mail surveys do not increase marginal costs as much as personal interviews, so it is possible to have larger sample sizes without increasing total costs as much.

The size of samples also depends on the type of study that is being undertaken. For instance, TV or radio advertising might use a sample of around 300 whereas problem identification research might involve a sample size of around 1000. This is due to the extent to which the information needs to be valid and significant in order to solve marketing research problems of differing complexity.

The sample size needed can be determined for a given accuracy, once we know the standard error (refer to Chapter 6) which involves both σ and n as SE(mean) $= \hat{\sigma}/\sqrt{n}$, where σ is the standard deviation of the sample values and n is the sample size. For example, suppose the standard deviation is 5 and we wish to measure the mean with a standard error of 0.5. Using the relationship we will need a sample of size 100. With increasing sample size there is a reduction in the sampling error. Table 7.2 shows this relationship over a range of values.

Table 7.2   Relationship of sample size and sampling error

Sampling error in relation to the standard deviation	Required increase in sample size
Half	× 4
Third	× 9
Quarter	× 16
Fifth	× 25
Tenth	× 100

Estimating sample size is easy once we know the standard error of the estimate we are going to use. We need to know (1) the likely standard error associated with the question being asked (estimate), (2) the acceptable error, i.e., sample value—population value (or the width of the confidence interval) and (3) what level of error or confidence we are prepared to accept in our significance test.

For large populations when sample size is greater than 30 units, the results (estimates) can be used for drawing conclusions about the population values using a normal distribution (Z values, Chapter 6). The general formulae for estimating the sample size (n) when dealing with the mean and proportion are as follows:

$$n = \frac{z^2 . \hat{\sigma}^2}{e^2}$$ Sample size to be used for estimating μ population mean using sample mean $\bar{x}$.

$$n = \frac{z^2 . p(1-p)}{e^2}$$ Sample size to be used for estimating π population mean using sample proportion p.

where: n = sample size
z = standard score (from Z table, Appendix I) for the required confidence interval,
e.g., for 95% $z = 1.96$; for 99%, $z = 2.58$
p = estimated sample proportion
e = half of the desired width (because of the symmetry of the distribution of the estimate) of the acceptable error
$\hat{\sigma}$ = estimated sample standard deviation.

Example

The government has recently introduced an increase in prescription charges (an additional increase of 10p per prescription from April 2001) and it is anticipated that this increase will reduce the number of patients using prescribed-only medicines (POM). To gauge the effect of this increase we wish to undertake a study of a sample of pharmacists. From a previous study (Chansarkar and Colwell, 1993), it is known that a drop in the average number of patients using POM for similar prescriptions increases in the past is about 10%. We are willing to accept a 5% error in the outcome. How large a sample should we take so that we are 99% confident of the outcome?

In this situation, estimated proportion of number of patients not using POM is 10%, $p = 0.1$. Therefore those using POM will be 0.9. Acceptable error is 0.05. The z value corresponding to 99% confidence will be 2.58 (from Appendix II). The required sample size is given by

$$n = \frac{z^2 . p(1-p)}{e^2} \rightarrow n = \frac{(2.58)^2 \times (0.9)(0.1)}{(0.05)^2} = 239.6 \cong 240$$

Thus, we will select 240 pharmacists.

Stage 5—Select the Sample

The sampling plan involves the specification of how each of the decisions made in each of the earlier stages are to be implemented. Thus, a number of questions will need to be answered. A few examples might include:

- Does the sampling frame need to be compiled or does it exist already?
- What does the interviewer do if someone refuses to be interviewed?
- If an interviewer is selecting respondents based on an socio-economic quota, how will the interviewer determine whether a respondent fits a particular category?
- How many interviewers should be used to collect the data?

Each of these questions has significant implications for the conduct of the research. For instance, it may be that what the researchers originally defined as the sampling frame is simply not possible to reproduce. Therefore, they would need to find a more realistic sampling frame. The second question regarding the respondent's refusal to answer questions has significant implications where a sample population is small and where probability-sampling methods are used.

The definition of the individual variables that are used in a specific study for quota sampling purposes is necessary since without clear definition the interviewer could select respondents in a biased manner. This has obvious implications for the results and their significance. How many interviewers to use in marketing research is a question that needs to be addressed to determine the extent to which interviewer bias can creep into a survey. However, it is obviously not possible to interview a large number of respondents with too few interviewers.

Many other questions will need to be asked and answered before the fieldwork can be conducted and the data is presented to the commissioning organization. In practice, marketing research tends to be much more iterative than suggested here since questions tend to be raised and answered at different stages of the whole sampling process.

Conclusion

This chapter explains the need for using a suitable sampling method in relation to the objective of the research. After explaining briefly both the probabilistic and non-probabilistic methods of sampling, the importance of the sample size and its relation to reliability are highlighted. The calculation of the sample size is illustrated and this should enable us to decide what size the sample we should take in a given investigation. We need to take a proportionately large sample to increase the accuracy of the results derived from the sample.

References

Aaker, D.A. and Day, G.S. (1996). *Marketing Research*, Chichester: John Wiley.

Baines, P., Chansarkar, B. and Ryan, G. (1999). *Introduction to Marketing Research*, London: Middlesex University Press.

Chansarkar, B. and Colwell, J. (1993). 'Higher prescription charges: implications to pharmacists', *The British Pharmaceutical Journal*, August.

Jobber, D. (1995). *Principles and Practices of Marketing*, London: McGraw-Hill.

Tull, D.S. and Hawkins, D.I. (1994). *The Essentials of Marketing Research*, London: Macmillan.

Zikmund, W.G. (1997). *Exploring Marketing Research*, London: The Dryden Press.

Work Assignments

1. Suggest a suitable sampling method for each of the following situations:

   (a) You are a manager of company dealing in FMCG products with outlets spread across the United Kingdom. In recent months your company sales have shown a decline. To stop this decline you intend to introduce a new line in takeaway food. You wish to assess the demand for this new line and decide on its acceptability with a view to intensive nationwide advertising of the new line.

   (b) You are a marketing consultant employed by a company dealing in FMCG products. You have been asked to investigate the new layout of your stores, and whether the company should adopt from a choice of three new layouts against the existing one.

2. How large a sample should you take in a product test where the intention to purchase is 30%? You would allow a margin of error of ±5% on the expected intention to purchase and have 95% confidence in your result.

3. You wish to study a population with 6000 members by selecting a sample of approximately 600 from it. The aim is to achieve the greatest accuracy within limited resources. You have stratified the population into two regions, A and B, and within those regions, into two age groups, 1 and 2. The populations in the four categories are given below:

	Region A	Region B
Age group 1	$N_1 = 2000$	$N_2 = 1800$
Age group 2	$N_3 = 1000$	$N_4 = 1200$

   A pilot survey has indicated the approximate amount of variation (σ_i) and cost per sampling (c_i) unit in the four categories and these are as follows:

	Region A	Region B
Age group 1	$\sigma_1 = 20$	$\sigma_2 = 18$
	$c_1 = 25p$	$c_2 = 36p$
Age group 2	$\sigma_3 = 14$	$\sigma_4 = 12$
	$c_3 = 49p$	$c_4 = 64p$

   Estimate the sample size required.

4. A company markets its merchandise through sales agents who operate within their respective marketing zones. It is known that the destination of 'miles travelled to customer location' in the company is normally distributed with mean = 18.2 km and standard deviation = 4.8 km.

The company plans to introduce variable travelling expenses for the agents on the basis of distance travelled and has collected information from a random sample of 400 agents of the company. The agents are divided into four country zones. It is found that the 12% are A, 18% are B, 35% are C and 25% are D. 10% are unknown.

(a) Obtain the sample size of each of the groups within the different zones.
(b) Use the sample sizes to obtain the standard error of the sample mean for each of the zones.
(c) Find the probability that the agents, on average, would travel more than 19 km within each zone.

Hypothesis Testing and Tests of Association

8

Learning Outcomes

After reading this chapter you will be able to:

- Understand the procedure of hypothesis testing.
- Understand concepts of level of significance and degrees of freedom.
- Decide appropriate measures of association/relationship.
- Choose critical values from statistical tables.
- Calculate measures of association—Chi-square statistic, rank correlation and product–moment correlation.
- Conduct a test of significance for these measures and decide on the strength of the relationship.

Introduction

This chapter begins with explaining hypothesis testing and gives the essential steps used in conducting such a test. It looks at the relationship between variables and shows how to choose an appropriate measure of association or relationship between two variables. It then shows how to conduct a Chi-square test of association between two nominal measurements and gives an interpretation of the calculated value of the test statistic. Two further measures of correlation—Spearman's rank correlation and Pearson's product-moment correlation—are then explained and a test of significance of the relationships is shown with detailed calculations. The chapter finally explains how to choose an appropriate test for the type of measurements made.

Hypothesis Testing

We are often interested in investigating whether the data (sample estimates) that represent actual population values (generally called 'parameters') have changed over time. For example, we may wish to know whether an advertising campaign has increased awareness of a particular brand, or whether there are real differences between different populations, for example whether there is a real difference in percentage of customers in two regions, say, A and B, who prefer a certain type of product. Analysis of the data collected is used to see how consistent they are with the hypotheses. The researcher is generally interested in finding either an average ($\bar{x}$) income; or the proportion (p) of buyers or the total ($n\bar{x}$) turnover of the outlets.

When we estimate a single value (such as average income of consumers, proportion of buyers for a product or total turnover of outlets) from the data, it is called a 'point estimate'. When interval values are proposed they are known as 'interval estimates'. Since we are invariably dealing with sample values (estimates) a hypothesis cannot be proved *per se*, as there may not be evidence in support of the hypothesis. A hypothesis can be rejected as being inconsistent with the observations on the basis of sample estimates. If it is consistent then we accept the hypothesis in the sense that we 'fail to reject it' with some confidence given to the available data.

A statistical hypothesis is generally of the *null* type which is regarded as a negative statement. Consider the following example statements: (a) Is the coin biased? Null hypothesis: 'It is not biased.' (b) Is a new drug more efficient than the one currently used? Null hypothesis: 'No difference in cure potential between the new drug and the current one.' The hypothesis can equally be expressed in the positive and this is known as the alternate hypothesis. An example using the drug example above could be: 'there is a difference between the new drug and the current one'.

In making any decision using a sample, two types of errors can occur. The type I error (the risk) is when we reject a true hypothesis, while the type II error (the risk) is when we accept a false one. Of the two errors, the type II error is more serious as we accept a false hypothesis. For example, as an extreme situation, consider a drug

		HYPOTHESIS	
		Accept	Reject
HYPOTHESIS	True	✓	Type I (α)
	False	Type II (β)	✓

Figure 8.1 Type I and type II errors

which, in small doses, is useful but in large ones is lethal. We accept that it will not result in the death of the patient. This type II error is much more serious than rejecting that drug as not effective (type I error) and as a result will not be used. Most of the marketing research situations we will encounter in hypothesis testing use type I errors. Figure 8.1 illustrates the four situations that can occur in hypothesis testing.

A test of a statistical hypothesis is a procedure for deciding whether to accept the hypothesis on the basis of the significance of the observed result from the sample. The detailed procedure for such a decision is given in the next section.

Steps in Hypothesis Testing

The five basic steps in any hypothesis testing are given in Box 8.1.

Box 8.1   Basic steps in hypothesis testing

1. Statement of null hypothesis (H_0).
2. Statement of alternate hypothesis (H_1)
3. Choice of level of significance (α)
4. Choice of test statistic
5. Decision rule based on the 'critical value' obtained from the tables

---

1. *Statement of null hypothesis* (H_0)   The null hypothesis is generally formulated to test whether the observation implying that there is no difference between population values should be rejected. It should be stated in a negative way. For example, we may be interested to know if there is a difference in average income of male and female workers of a certain company. Two independent samples are taken, one of male employees and the other of female employees, and the average monthly income over a specified period is recorded for both samples. The null hypothesis in this case would be that 'there is no difference in the population means of male and female employees'. If these means were μ_1 (average income of male) and μ_2 (average income of female) respectively, then

$$H_0: \mu_1 - \mu_2 = 0$$

Since we are dealing with sample estimates, $\bar{x}_1$ and $\bar{x}_2$, we would expect *some* difference. Significance testing establishes whether this difference is real (i.e., statistically significant) or whether it is due to random sampling error.

2. *Statement of alternate hypothesis* (H_1)   If the null hypothesis is rejected we will conclude that some other hypothesis is acceptable. This is the alternate

hypothesis (H_1) which is a statement indicating our belief in the nature and level of possible difference. In our case the alternate hypothesis could be:

either H_1: $\mu_1 - \mu_2 \neq 0$, i.e., there is a difference in average income of male and female employees. The direction of change is not indicated, which means we do not know whether the average income of one group (say, male) is higher than the second group (female) (two-tailed test). This test is exploratory and therefore two-tailed as it uses the probability of the observed estimate falling on either side of the tail ends of the sampling distribution of the sample estimate.

or H_1: $\mu_1 - \mu_2 < 0$, i.e., the average income for male employees is higher than that of female employees (one-tailed test). This test is confirmatory and therefore a one-tailed test should be used. It uses the probability of the observed estimate falling on one side of the tail end of the sampling distribution of the sample estimate. If $\bar{x}_2 > \mu_1$, no test is required as it lies on the other side of the expected difference. Obviously there can be a decrease in average values.

As a rule, when the test is *exploratory* (we wish to find the direction of the change), a *two-tailed* test is used (using $\alpha/2$) while a *confirmatory* test uses a *one-tailed* test (as the expected direction of the change is known using α).

3. *Choice of level of significance (α)*   There are, as shown before, two types of errors which can be made. Rejecting the null hypothesis (H_0) when it is true is the type I error and the probability of this is generally denoted by α. Accepting a false hypothesis is a type II error and is denoted by probability β. Usually in marketing research we are interested in controlling the probability of making a type I error (α) more closely than a type II error (β). This probability is called the level of significance of the test. The level of α should be determined in advance of carrying out the test, taking into consideration the relative importance of the investigation and the implications of the test to the outcome. When not specified, it is customary (as a default) to use 5% level of significance, i.e., a 1/20 chance of committing a type I error. In our case let us choose $\alpha = 0.05$.

4. *Choice of test statistic*   In conducting a test of hypothesis, we use a test statistic, a general formula for which is given in Box 8.2. The concepts of estimate, parameter and standard error of the estimate are explained in Chapter 6.

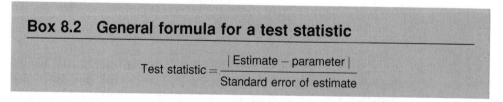

Box 8.2   General formula for a test statistic

$$\text{Test statistic} = \frac{|\,\text{Estimate} - \text{parameter}\,|}{\text{Standard error of estimate}}$$

For large samples (usually $n \geqslant 30$) and samples being taken randomly and independently, we can make certain assumptions such as 'the distribution of

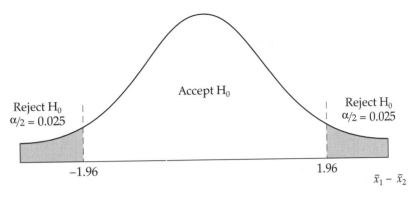

Figure 8.2 Decision rule for Z test: two means

sample means is normal'. These assumptions allow us to undertake what are known as 'parametric tests'. Non-parametric tests require no such assumptions and are generally used for small samples. The choice of the test statistic further depends on how many samples are used—one sample only, two independent samples or a paired sample (which uses the same respondent for observing the effect) or more than two independent samples. We need to determine the sampling distribution of the test statistic to calculate the standard error. For large samples the sampling distribution of the test statistics is, in most cases, normal. Note that the standard error *always* relates to the sample estimate and the standard deviation (square root of the variance) relates to the population values. In our case, the test statistic will be a Z value (normal) for two independent samples.

5. *Decision rule based on the 'critical value' from the tables* The tables for the distribution of the test statistic will give a value for the chosen level of significance. This value, called the 'critical value', is used in formulating the decision rule. Thus in the case of a two-tailed test the critical value will be the Z value at 0.05 level of significance, i.e., 1.96. To obtain this, we take $\alpha/2 = 0.025$ and get the appropriate value using Appendix II.

   If the calculated value of the Z statistic from the sample data is greater than 1.96 and therefore lies in the shaded area as shown in Figure 8.2, we reject H_0; otherwise we accept H_0.

Choosing Appropriate Measures of Association between Two Variables

Relationship between variables

In many marketing situations it is of interest to know how the value of one variable is associated with the value of another variable in some systematic way. Consider the attitude of customers to different wrappings of a product, how profits vary with turnover, frequency of repairs and the age of the equipment, sales in relation to advertising, or demand variation with price. The link between the variables could be of great use to the researcher and decision maker because it enables them to study the relationship between one variable and another. The correlation analysis allows the researcher to establish how strong these linkages are and is then used to measure what type of linkages between the variables exist. Two statistics commonly used to explore relationships between variables are the Chi-squared statistic and the correlation coefficient. When the measurements are classificatory (nominal) in nature we use cross-tabulation procedures. Cross-tabulation is a statistical examination of two or more variables that are described simultaneously. This results in a contingency table (reflecting the joint distribution of the variables). The categories of one variable are cross-classified with the categories of one or more variables. Thus, the frequency distribution of one variable is subdivided according to the values or categories of the other variable. Each square in the table is called a cell and the number indicated in the cell is called the cell-frequency. For example, in testing attitude to new wrappings of a product, three attitudes (like, dislike and indifferent) to three different wrappings (A, B, C) are cross-classified. This will result in a three by three contingency table as shown in Table 8.1. For example, the cell-frequency for wrapping A and customers liking it is 280.

The reasons for the wide use of the contingency table are:

1. The clarity of its interpretations
2. Easy comprehension of its results
3. It provides greater insights than a single multivariate analysis
4. It is simpler to conduct.

Situation 1

When the measurements of two variables are of a classificatory nature (that is, measurements are classes or nominal scales), the association between the variables is tested by using a Chi-squared test (χ^2 test). This is based on the idea of the null hypothesis that the two variables are not associated and the hypothesis is either

Table 8.1 Attitudes to different wrappings of a product

Box design	Opinion			
	Like	Dislike	Indifferent	Total
A	280	96	24	400
B	266	67	67	400
C	300	60	40	400
Total	846	223	131	1200

accepted or rejected on the basis of the evidence obtained from the data (sample values). A summary of the chi-squared test process is shown in Box 8.3 and the detailed procedure follows.

Box 8.3 Summary of Chi-squared test process

Testing association between two categorical measurements

Null hypothesis: There is no association between the two variables

$$\text{Calculate expected values using } \frac{\text{Marginal row total} \times \text{Marginal column total}}{\text{Grand total}}$$

$$\text{Calculate the Chi-squared test statistic using } \chi^2 = \sum \frac{(O-E)^2}{E}$$

Decide the significance of calculated χ^2 against the critical value from the tables using $(r-1)(c-1)$ degrees of freedom.

The procedure for the Chi-squared test of association between two categorical variables is:

1. Set a null hypothesis (H_0) that there is no association between the two variables.
2. Set an alternate hypothesis (H_1) that there is an association between the two variables.
3. Choose a level of significance (α) for accepting or rejecting the null hypothesis.
4. Calculate the degrees of freedom for the Chi-squared value $= (r-1)(c-1)$.
5. Formulate a decision rule using the degrees of freedom and the Chi-squared tables.
6. Calculate the Chi-squared test statistic, using the following equation:

$$\chi^2 = \sum \frac{(O-E)^2}{E}$$

where O = observed values
  E = expected values

7. Decide on the significance of the calculated χ^2 and draw a conclusion about the association between the two variables.

It should be noted that in using the Chi-squared test of association it is necessary to have expected frequencies for a cell to be at least 1 because the Chi-squared distribution is the distribution of a continuous variable. Further, 20% of the cells should have expected frequencies greater than 5. If necessary, adjacent cells can be combined to ensure E (expected cell value) is greater than 1.0. Additionally, when the degrees of freedom is 1, it is desirable to use Yates' correction for continuity, since Chi-square is a continuous distribution. In using Yates' correction the procedure is the same as before, except while calculating the Chi-square statistic the following modified equation is applied:

$$\chi^2 = \sum \frac{(|O - E| - 0.5)^2}{E}$$

where $|O - E|$ is called the modulus of the difference and is always the positive value of the difference. Thus if $(O - E)$ is negative (say, -5), then the modulus will be $+5$.

Example 1

We have developed two box designs (B and C) for washing powder (X). These two new box designs are compared with the existing one (A) by testing the opinions of a total of 1200 randomly selected customers. Each of the boxes was tested by 400 customers. The result of the tests are as shown in Table 8.2.

Is there a difference in opinions of the box designs and, if so, what should we recommend to the company?

Solution

First, we need to decide (answers in parentheses):

1. How large is the sample size? (*n* large and equal to 1200)
2. How is the selection of the sample made? (Probability based using random sampling)
3. What is being tested? (Association of box designs and opinions towards it. Therefore data is categorized and a Chi-squared test is prescribed.)

Once the test criterion is established we can conduct the appropriate test.

H_0 (null hypothesis):   There is no association between the type of box design and opinion.

Table 8.2 Opinions on different box designs of a product

Box design	Opinion			Total
	Like	Dislike	Indifferent	
A	280	96	24	400
B	266	67	67	400
C	300	60	40	400
Total	846	223	131	1200

H_1 (alternative hypothesis):	There is an association between the type of box design and opinion.
Choose level of significance α:	0.05 (95% confidence in the outcome of the test)
Degrees of freedom:	$= (r-1)(c-1)$ where $r =$ number of rows $= 3$
	$= (3-1)(3-1)$ $c =$ number of columns $= 3$
	$= 4$
Decision rule:	From the χ^2 distribution tables at the 0.05 level with 4 degrees of freedom the critical value $= 9.488$. If the calculated value of χ^2 is greater than 9.488, then reject H_0; that there is no association between the type of box design and the opinions and the hypothesis is rejected at the 5% level of significance.

Table 8.3 illustrates the observed and expected frequencies (in parentheses). The expected frequency (E) for box design A and like it, under the null hypothesis that there is no association between box design and attitude is

$$\frac{\text{Marginal total A} \times \text{Marginal total like}}{\text{Grand total}} = (400 \times 846)/1200 = 282$$

Table 8.4 shows the detailed calculations for the Chi-squared test and Figure 8.3 shows the graph for the decision rule about the test statistic.

Since the calculated value of $\chi^2 = 32.506$ is greater than the value in the tables of 9.488, we reject the null hypothesis. Therefore there is an association between the type of box design and the opinions of the customers. At this stage, it will be useful to see which box design is liked most and which is disliked least. For this we need to calculate the proportion of customers in each of the categories and this is given in Table 8.5.

Table 8.3 Observed and expected frequencies for opinions on box designs of a product

Box design	Opinion			Total
	Like	Dislike	Indifferent	
A	280	96	24	400
	(282)	(74.4)	(43.6)	
B	266	67	67	400
	(282)	(74.3)	(43.7)	
C	300	60	40	400
	(282)	(74.3)	(43.7)	
Total	846	223	131	1200

Table 8.4 Calculation of a Chi-squared test

Box design	Observed frequency (O)	Expected frequency (E)	(O − E)	(O − E)²	$\dfrac{(O-E)^2}{E}$
A Like	280	282.0	−2.0	4.00	0.014
Dislike	96	74.4	21.6	466.56	6.271
Indifferent	24	43.6	−19.6	384.16	8.811
B Like	286	282.0	4.0	16.00	0.057
Dislike	67	74.3	7.3	53.29	0.717
Indifferent	67	43.7	23.3	542.89	12.423
C Like	300	282.0	−18.0	324.00	1.148
Dislike	60	74.3	−14.3	204.49	2.752
Indifferent	40	43.7	3.7	13.69	0.313
Total	1200				32.506

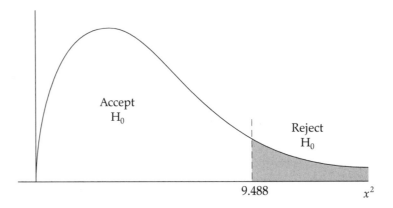

Figure 8.3 Decision rule for the Chi-squared test

Table 8.5 Proportion of those who like and dislike the box design

Box design	Like	Dislike	Indifferent
A	280/400 = 0.70	0.06	0.24
B	266/400 = 0.67	0.17	0.16
C	300/400 = 0.75	0.10	0.15

As the proportion of those who like C is the largest and those who dislike it is not high, we should choose box design C in preference to the existing box design A.

This is further confirmed by the analysis of the opinions by using only those who showed a specific preference and were not indifferent. The analysis follows the same procedure, but this time using only those who clearly indicated a definite opinion, either like or dislike. A new table for this is given in Table 8.6.

$$\chi^2 = \sum \frac{(O - E)^2}{E} = 1.037 + 3.933 + 0.023 + 0.088 + 0.800 + 3.035 = 8.916$$

From the tables the χ^2 value at 2 degrees of freedom at the 0.05 level = 5.991. Since the calculated value of χ^2 is greater than 5.991, we reject H_0. That there is no association between the type of box design and the opinions is rejected at the 5% level of significance. Again, analysis of the proportions confirms our previous finding that C is the best box design when the customers who are indifferent are excluded from the analysis.

Situation 2

When the measurements of two variables are of a ranking nature (ordinal scale), the relationship between the two variables is tested by using Spearman's rank correlation coefficient (r'). A summary of the Spearman's rank correlation test process is shown in Box 8.4 and the detailed procedure follows.

Table 8.6 Observed and expected frequencies for opinions (excluding indifferent) on box designs of a product

| Box design | Opinion | | Total |
	Like	Dislike	
A	280 (297.5)	96 (78.4)	376
B	266 (263.5)	67 (69.5)	333
C	300 (285.0)	60 (75.1)	360
Total	846	223	1069

Box 8.4 Summary of Spearman's rank correlation coefficient test process

Testing the relationship between two ordinal (rank) measurements

Null hypothesis: There is no relationship between the two variables

Calculate rank correlation using $r' = 1 - \dfrac{6\sum D^2}{n(n^2 - 1)}$

Calculate t – test statistic, using $t = r'\sqrt{\dfrac{n - 2}{1 - r'^2}}$

Decide the significance of calculated t against the critical value from the tables using $n - 2$ degrees of freedom.

The procedure for Spearman's rank correlation coefficient test between two variables measured on ordinal scale or at least one of the variables measured on an ordinal scale (ranks) is as follows:

1. Set a null hypothesis (H_0) that there is no relationship between the two variables.
2. Set an alternate hypothesis (H_1) that there is a relationship between the two variables.
3. Choose a level of significance (α) for accepting or rejecting the null hypothesis.
4. Test statistic will be

$$t = r'\sqrt{\frac{n - 2}{1 - r'^2}}$$

5. Formulate a decision rule, using the critical value based on a t distribution with the degrees of freedom $n - 2$.
6. Calculate the rank correlation, using the following equation:

$$r' = 1 - \frac{6\sum D^2}{n(n^2 - 1)}$$

where D = difference in ranks of the two variables
n = number of pairs of observations.

7. Decide on the significance of the calculated rank correlation and draw a conclusion about the relationship between the two variables.

The following example illustrates the calculations and decision-making process more explicitly.

Example 2

Ten industries are ranked in order of their annual turnover and the annual profits of these industries was recorded for the same year. The information obtained is given in Table 8.7.

H_0 (null hypothesis): There is no relationship between annual turnover and annual profits of the industries.

H_1 (alternative hypothesis): There is a relationship between annual turnover and annual profits of the industries (two-tailed test).

Choose the level of significance (α): 0.01 (99% confidence in the outcome of the test)

Degrees of freedom: $n - 2 = 10 - 2 = 8$ where $n =$ number of pairs of observations.

Decision rule: If the calculated value of t is greater than 3.355 (Appendix II), then reject H_0, that there is no relationship between annual turnover and annual profits of the industries, at the 1% level of significance.

Figure 8.4 illustrates the decision rule associated with the testing the hypothesis for the Spearman rank correlation using the example data.

When one of the variables is not recorded as ranks, the ranking of that variable should be in the same order as the ranking of the variable which is already ranked. In our example in Table 8.7, the annual turnover of industry I is ranked first, having the highest annual turnover. When some of the observations have equal measurements, as industries A, B and C have the same annual turnover, the ranking is initially done as if they were all different (column 4) and then, taking the average of equal ranking observations, the adjusted rank ordering is worked out (column 5) (see Table 8.8). For example, industries A, B and C are ranked as 10, 9, and 8 with equal annual profits of £14m. The adjusted ranking is $(10 + 9 + 8)/3 = 9$.

Table 8.7 Rank ordering of industries by turnover and profits

Industry	Rank ordering according to annual turnover	Annual profits (£m)
A	10	14.0
B	8	14.0
C	9	14.0
D	7	18.0
E	6	20.0
F	5	22.5
G	3	28.0
H	2	25.6
I	1	30.8
J	4	22.5

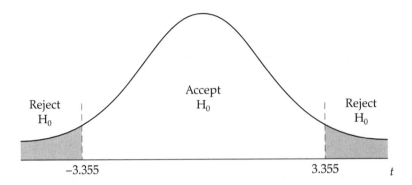

Figure 8.4 Decision rule for test of Spearman's rank correlation coefficient

To calculate the rank correlation coefficient, r', we need to rank the variable which is not measured as rank ordering, e.g., annual profits in this case. The procedure for calculating r' is shown in Table 8.8.

Then using the formula

$$r' = 1 - \frac{\sum D^2}{n(n^2 - 1)} = 1 - \frac{6(4.5)}{10(10^2 - 1)} = 1 - \frac{27}{990} = 1 - 0.03 = 0.97$$

The r' value calculated will always be between -1 and $+1$. 0 indicates no correlation and a value near to $+1$ indicates a high positive correlation (near to -1 indicates high negative correlation).

Table 8.8 Calculation of rank correlation between turnover and profits

Industry (1)	Ranking annual turnover Rx (2)	Annual profits £m (3)	Ranking profits (4)	Adjusted ranking profits Ry (5)	$D = Ry - Rx$ (6)	D^2 (7)
A	10	14.0	10	9	−1	1.00
B	8	14.0	9	9	1	1.00
C	9	14.0	8	9	0	0.00
D	7	18.0	7	7	0	0.00
E	6	20.0	6	6	0	0.00
F	5	22.5	4	4.5	−0.5	0.25
G	3	28.0	2	2	−1	1.00
H	2	25.6	3	3	1	1.00
I	1	30.8	1	1	0	0.00
J	4	22.5	5	4.5	0.5	0.25
						$\sum D^2 = 4.50$

Then

$$t = 0.97 \sqrt{\frac{10-2}{1-(0.97)^2}} = 0.97 \sqrt{\frac{8}{0.0591}} = 0.97(11.64) = 11.29$$

The calculated value of t is greater than the critical value (3.355) and the null hypothesis is rejected. Therefore there is a significant highly positive relationship or correlation between annual turnover and annual profits of the industries. As annual turnover increases, so do annual profits and this relationship can then be measured further by using regression analysis.

Situation 3

When the measurements of two variables are interval or ratio scaled, the relationship between the variables is tested by using Pearson's product–moment correlation (r). A summary of Pearson's product–moment correlation coefficient test process is shown in Box 8.5 and the detailed procedure follows.

Box 8.5   Summary of Pearson's correlation coefficient test process

Testing relationship between two interval scale measurements

Null hypothesis: There is no relationship between the two variables
Calculate Pearson's correlation using

$$r = \frac{\sum(x - \bar{x})(y - \bar{y})}{\sqrt{\sum(x - \bar{x})^2 \, \sum(y - \bar{y})^2}} = \frac{n\sum xy - (\sum x)(\sum y)}{\sqrt{[n\sum x^2 - (\sum x)^2][n\sum y^2 - (\sum y)^2]}}$$

Calculate the t-test statistic, using $t = r \sqrt{\dfrac{n-2}{1-r^2}}$

Decide the significance of calculated t against the critical value from the tables using $n-2$ degrees of freedom.

The procedure of Pearson's product–moment correlation coefficient test between two variables measured in interval scale is:

1. Set a null hypothesis (H_0) that there is no relationship between the two variables.
2. Set an alternate hypothesis (H_1) that there is a relationship between the two variables.
3. Choose a level of significance (α) for accepting or rejecting the null hypothesis.

4. The test statistic will be (Harnett and Soni, 1991):

$$t = r \sqrt{\frac{n - 2}{1 - r^2}}$$

5. Formulate a decision rule with a critical value based on a t distribution with degrees of freedom $n - 2$.
6. Draw a scatter diagram (plot of two variables, the dependent on the Y axis and the independent on the X axis) and judge the nature of the relationship (linear, positive, etc.).
7. Calculate the product–moment correlation r, using the equation

$$r = \frac{\sum(x - \bar{x})(y - \bar{y})}{\sqrt{\sum(x - \bar{x})^2 \sum(y - \bar{y})^2}} = \frac{n \sum xy - (\sum x)(\sum y)}{\sqrt{[n \sum x^2 - (\sum x)^2][n \sum y^2 - (\sum y)^2]}}$$

where n = number of pairs of observations.
8. Decide on the significance of the calculated product–moment correlation using the t value and draw a conclusion about the relationship between the two variables.

The following example illustrates the calculations and decision-making process more explicitly.

Example 3

Information about annual turnover and annual profits of 10 industries was collected to test the relationship between the two variables. Table 8.9 provides further details.

Table 8.9 Annual turnover and profits of industries

Industry	Annual turnover (£bn)	Annual profits (£m)
A	1.4	14.0
B	1.8	14.0
C	1.6	14.0
D	2.0	18.0
E	2.2	20.0
F	2.3	22.5
G	2.6	28.0
H	2.8	25.6
I	3.6	30.8
J	2.5	22.5

Figure 8.5 shows the scatter diagram for annual turnover and profits and indicates that as annual turnover increases, the annual profits also increase. Therefore there appears to be a positive relationship between the annual profits and annual turnover.

H_0 (null hypothesis):   There is no relationship between annual profits and annual turnover of the industries.

H_1 (alternative hypothesis):   There is a relationship between annual profits and annual turnover of the industries.

Choose level of significance (α): 0.05 (95% confidence in the outcome of the test)

The test statistic will be $t = r\sqrt{\dfrac{n-2}{1-r^2}}$

Degrees of freedom: $n - 2 = 10 - 2 = 8$ where $n =$ number of pairs of observations.

Decision rule: If the calculated value of t is greater than 2.306, then reject H_0, that there is no relationship between annual profits and annual turnover of the industries at the 5% level of significance.

To calculate the product–moment correlation coefficient, r, we need to create additional columns 4, 5 and 6 as shown in Table 8.10.

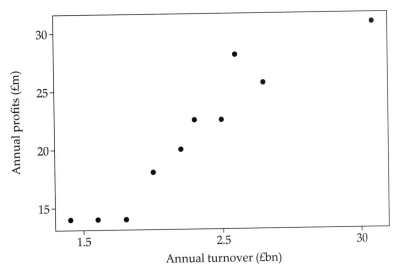

Figure 8.5   Scatter diagram for annual profits and annual turnover

Table 8.10 Calculation of product–moment correlation between turnover and profits

Industry (1)	Annual turnover (£bn) (X) (2)	Annual profits (£m) (Y) (3)	(X^2) (4)	(Y^2) (5)	(XY) (6)
A	1.4	14.0	1.96	196.00	19.60
B	1.8	14.0	3.24	196.00	25.20
C	1.6	14.0	2.56	196.00	22.40
D	2.0	18.0	4.00	324.00	36.00
E	2.2	20.0	4.84	400.00	44.00
F	2.3	22.5	5.29	506.25	51.75
G	2.6	28.0	6.76	784.00	72.80
H	2.8	25.6	7.84	655.36	71.68
I	3.6	30.8	12.96	948.64	110.88
J	2.5	22.5	6.25	506.25	56.25
Total	$\Sigma X = 22.8$	$\Sigma Y = 209.4$	$\Sigma X^2 = 55.70$	$\Sigma Y^2 = 4712.50$	$\Sigma XY = 510.56$

Then

$$r = \frac{n \sum XY - (\sum X)(\sum Y)}{\sqrt{[n\sum X^2 - (\sum X)^2] \cdot [n\sum Y^2 - (\sum Y)^2]}}$$

$$r = \frac{10(510.56) - (22.8)(209.4)}{\sqrt{10(55.7) - (22.8)^2][10(4712.50) - (209.4)^2]}}$$

$$= \frac{5105.60 - 4774.32}{\sqrt{(37.16)(3276.64)}}$$

$$= \frac{331.28}{348.94} = 0.95$$

The value 0.95 indicates a very high positive correlation.
Then

$$t = 0.95 \sqrt{\frac{10 - 2}{1 - (0.95)^2}} = 0.95 \sqrt{\frac{8}{0.0975}} = 0.95(9.058) = 8.61$$

The calculated value of t is greater (as can be seen from Figure 8.6) than the critical value (2.306), and the null hypothesis is rejected. Therefore, there is a significant high positive relationship or correlation between annual turnover and annual profits of the

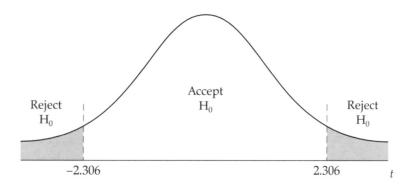

Figure 8.6   Decision rule for test of Pearson's correlation coefficient

industries. This implies that as annual turnover increases, so do annual profits and this relationship can then be measured further by using regression analysis.

Conclusion

There are four basic steps in hypothesis testing: setting the null and alternative hypotheses, choosing the appropriate level of significance and forming a decision rule based on the sampling distribution of the test statistic. When studying an association or a relationship between two variables the type of test we can perform depends on the type of measurements. If the measurements are nominal (categories) we should use a Chi-square test, if measurements are ordinal (ranks) we should use Spearman's rank correlation while if the measurements are interval scales, we should use Pearson's correlation.

References

Anderson, D.R., Sweeney, D.J. and Williams, T.A. (1995). *Qualitative Methods for Business*, St Paul: West Publishing.

Churchill, G.A. (1995). *Marketing Research: Methodological Foundation*, 6th edn, Orlando, FL: The Dryan Press.

Harnett, D.H. and Soni, A.K. (1991). *Statistical Methods for Business and Economics*, Harlow: Addison-Wesley.

Malhotra, N.K. and Birks, D.F. (2000). *Marketing Research: An Applied Approach*, Englewood Cliff, NJ: Prentice-Hall.

Waters, D. (1997). *Quantitative Methods for Business*, Harlow: Addison-Wesley.

Weiss, N.A. (1995). *Introductory Statistics*, Reading, MA: Addison-Wesley.

Work Assignments

1. You are a market research manager of a firm with outlets across most of the United Kingdom. Your major competitor has recently introduced a new own-brand

product onto the market with a nationwide launch. You notice that there is a drop in your market share. In response, you propose to introduce a similar new product with its own-brand name to maintain your share of the market. To investigate the effect of the introduction of the own-brand product, you conduct a test in randomly selected outlets in four marketing regions for a period of four weeks. This provides the following results:

Marketing regions: sales (000) units of new own-brand product

Size of the outlet	Region			
	A	B	C	D
Large	145	120	65	170
Medium	135	130	45	90
Small	120	110	30	40

Conduct a test of significance at the 5% level of the association between the size of the outlet and the marketing region.

2. A marketing manager of a retail outlet is reviewing the results of a survey of adult women. This involved a random sample of 250 respondents and was conducted in a typical (Midlands) test area. The table below gives the cross-tabulation of the data on the working status of the respondents and the amount of money spent on washing-up liquids in a month.

Expenditure on washing-up liquid	Working full-time	Working part-time	Not working	Total
Less than £5	15	10	30	55
£5–£10	25	30	35	90
Over £10	25	40	40	105
Total	65	80	105	250

Can the marketing manager infer that there is an association between working status and expenditure on washing-up liquids?

3. The table below shows (1) the market share (ms) as a percentage of the total market, (2) relative price (rp) as an index with the retail price index for the industry as a base and (3) advertising share (as) as a percentage of the total advertising expenditure, for a particular company over the past 15 years.

Year	Market share % (ms)	Relative price (rp)	Advertising share % (as)
1	20	100	20
2	25	100	25
3	40	95	35
4	35	95	35
5	45	80	35
6	35	90	30
7	40	85	35
8	55	80	35
9	50	85	40
10	45	85	55
11	30	105	45
12	20	110	25
13	25	95	20
14	25	100	25
15	30	95	30

(i) Calculate the rank correlation coefficient between the market share with relative price and test its significance.

(ii) Calculate the product–moment correlation coefficient between the market share and the advertising share and test its significance.

(iii) Comment on which correlation coefficient calculated in (i) and (ii) you would prefer.

Hypothesis Testing and Tests of Differences

9

Learning Outcomes

After reading this chapter you will be able to:

- Choose an appropriate test of significance—monadic (single sample) or comparative (two sample), Z-test (large sample) or t-test (small sample).
- Calculate the value of the test statistic.
- Decide on the significance of the test performed.
- Draw a conclusion and make information-based marketing recommendations.

Introduction

This chapter begins with the considerations we have to take into account in conducting a test of significance when determining the differences in means or proportions between two parameters. It then deals with a monadic test of significance for a single large sample and a comparative test for two large samples. The concept of degrees of freedom is briefly explained. This is followed by a t-test of significance for a single small sample. The t-test for the significance of sample values for two independent samples is demonstrated next. The importance of using a comparative t-test for estimates using the same respondents (paired t-test) is demonstrated. You will find Figure 9.1 useful showing how you can choose an appropriate test.

In attempting to choose a particular significance test, at least four questions should be considered:

1. Has the selection of the sample been done using probabilistic methods? It is necessary that respondents are chosen with a probabilistic method for conducting a test of significance as the test uses the standard errors of the estimates.

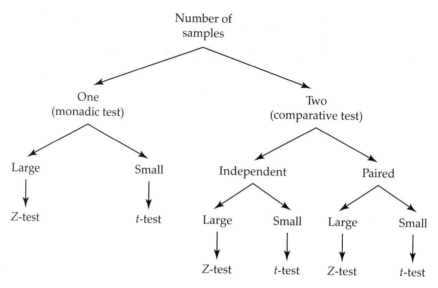

Figure 9.1 Choosing an appropriate test

2. Are the measurement scales nominal, ordinal or interval? Depending on the nature of the scale, different tests should be used. You have seen examples of this in Chapter 8, when the Chi-square test was used for nominal scales.
3. You need to decide whether the test involves one or two samples or more than two samples. Depending on how many samples are used, you will adopt different tests, e.g., you use the monadic test for a single sample, and a paired test for two samples.
4. When using two or more samples, are the individual cases independent or related?

In marketing research investigations we frequently use samples of large size ($n \geqslant 30$) and in experimental situations smaller samples are used. If the samples are drawn randomly, the distribution of the sample estimate (mean or proportion or total) in both situations is approximately normal. This allows us to conduct the tests of significance.

We will consider here some of the techniques related to large samples ($n \geqslant 30$) and others related to small samples. Figure 9.1 shows which test should be selected if the researcher knows the number of samples and their size.

Large Single Sample ($n \geqslant 30$)—Monadic Test for Average

When we select a random sample of size 30 and over, a Z-test of significance should be used. When a single sample is used, the test is called a monadic test.

When two independent samples are used the test is called a comparative test. The summary of the monadic Z-test process is shown in Box 9.1 and the detailed procedure follows.

Box 9.1   Monadic Z-test for a single large sample

The procedure depends on which parameter (*mean* μ or *proportion* π) is being tested.

Null hypothesis: Either   There is no difference in the sample average from the population value.

or   There is no difference in the sample proportion from the population value.

Calculate the appropriate test statistics:

$$\text{For mean } Z = \frac{\bar{x} - \mu}{\sqrt{\dfrac{\sigma^2}{n}}} \qquad \text{for proportion } Z = \frac{p - \pi}{\sqrt{\dfrac{\pi(1 - \pi)}{n}}}$$

Decide the significance of the calculated Z-test statistic against the critical value from the table of the standard normal distribution.

Example 1

A random sample of 96 sales executives, in a multinational corporation (MNC), each with responsibility for their own territory, was selected in a research study evaluating sales revenue. Analysis showed that the average revenue was £9.6 million with a standard deviation of £2.6 million. The average revenue (μ) for similar territories for executives in other companies, according to a recent industry report, is £8.2 million. Does the sample indicate that the executives from the MNC obtain higher revenue from their territories than their industry counterparts?

Solution

H_0:   There is no difference in the average revenue of the MNC executives from their industry counterparts.

H_1:   MNC executives have higher average revenue than their industry counterparts. (One-tailed test as we are confirming that MNC executives have higher revenue. See Chapter 8 for a more detailed explanation of when one- and two-tailed tests should be used.)

α: 0.05 (The choice of the level of significance is made by the researcher. It is common to use 5% when the level is not specified.)

Test statistics: Z; critical value of Z_α (from Appendix II) $= 1.64$
Decision rule: If the calculated value of Z is greater than the critical value of $Z_\alpha(1.64)$ then reject H_0, otherwise accept H_0.

Z is calculated by using the equation

$$Z = \frac{\bar{x} - \mu}{\sqrt{\dfrac{\hat{\sigma}^2}{n}}} = \frac{\bar{x} - \mu}{SE(\bar{x})}$$

$$= \frac{9.6 - 8.2}{\sqrt{\dfrac{(2.6)^2}{96}}} = \frac{1.4}{0.27} = 5.19$$

As the calculated value of $Z = 5.19$ is greater than the critical value from the Z table, we reject H_0. The decision rule is shown in Figure 9.2. MNC executives have a higher revenue than their counterparts.

The estimated average revenue for the MNC executives (point estimate) is £9.6 million. In practice we are interested in finding a confidence interval for the average revenue and this is done by using the equation

$$\bar{x} \pm Z_{\alpha/2}SE(\bar{x})$$

$$9.6 \pm 1.96 \, (0.27)$$

$$9.6 \pm 0.53$$

Lower   9.1   10.1   Upper

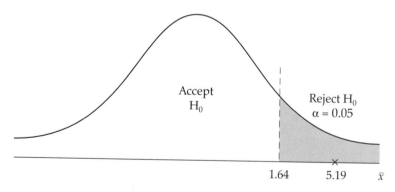

Figure 9.2 Decision rule for a Z-test for a single large sample

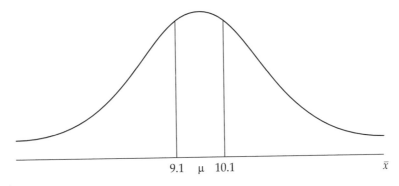

9.1   μ   10.1 $\bar{x}$

Figure 9.3   Confidence interval for the average (revenue)

We will be $(1 - \alpha)\% = 95\%$ confident that the average revenue for all executives of the company will lie between £9.1 million and £10.1 million. The confidence interval is shown in Figure 9.3.

Two Large Samples: Comparative Test of Proportions

We are often interested in making decisions about two populations rather than considering a single population. Typically, the question of interest is whether there is a difference between two populations and, more specifically, whether a difference exists between either two population means or population proportions. For example, we may be interested in investigating whether two marketing regions of a company have the same average turnover or whether there is any difference in the opinion of customers about two varieties of a product. When two independent samples are used, the test is called a comparative test and when the samples are large, it is a Z-test.

The summary of the comparative Z-test process is shown in Box 9.2 and the detailed procedure follows.

Box 9.2   Summary of comparative Z-test process

Testing the significance of two large independent samples

The procedure depends on which parameters (*means* μ_i or *proportions* π_i) are being tested.

Null hypothesis: Either   There is no difference in the two population averages.
                    or   There is no difference in the two population proportions.

Calculate the appropriate test statistics:

$$\text{For means } Z = \frac{\bar{x}_1 - \bar{x}_2}{\sqrt{\dfrac{\sigma_1^2}{n_1} + \dfrac{\sigma_2^2}{n_2}}} \qquad \text{for proportions } Z = \frac{p_1 - p_2}{\sqrt{p(1-p)\left(\dfrac{1}{n_1} + \dfrac{1}{n_2}\right)}}$$

$$\text{where } p = \frac{n_1 p_1 + n_2 p_2}{n_1 + n_2}$$

Decide on the significance of the calculated Z-test statistic against the critical value from the table of the standard normal distribution.

Example 2

The managing director of the company recommends a travel allowance of a flat rate of £1.00 per mile. Two samples of sizes 40 and 130 are chosen respectively from the executives and the other employees of the company. Thus, 81% of the executives are in favour of the recommendation while 72% of the other employees are in favour. The managing director is interested in determining with 99% of confidence whether there is any difference in the proportion of executives and the other employees in favour of the recommendation.

Solution

H_0:   There is no difference in the proportion of all executives in favour from the proportion of all employees in favour of the recommendation. ($\pi_1 - \pi_2 = 0$)

H_1:   There is a difference in the proportion of all executives in favour from the proportion of all employees in favour of the recommendation. ($\pi_1 - \pi_2 \neq 0$).
(Two-tailed test)

α: 0.01 (99% of confidence)

Test statistic: Z; critical value $Z_\alpha = 2.58$ (from Appendix II)

Decision rule: If the calculated value of $Z > Z_\alpha(2.58)$, then reject H_0, otherwise accept H_0. This is shown in Figure 9.4.

$$\text{Standard error of } (p_1 - p_2) = \sqrt{p(1-p)\left(\frac{1}{n_1} + \frac{1}{n_2}\right)}$$

$$\text{where } p = \frac{n_1 p_1 + n_2 p_2}{n_1 + n_2}$$

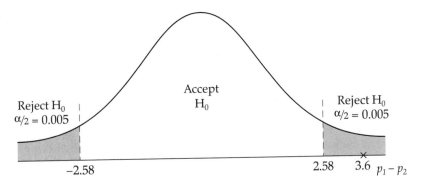

Figure 9.4 Decision rule for a Z-test for comparison of two proportions

p is the estimate of proportion of respondents in the population in favour of the recommendation. You need to do this because the two samples come from the same population.

The following equation should be used to calculate the Z-test statistic when using proportions:

$$\frac{p_1 - p_2}{\sqrt{p(1-p)\left(\dfrac{1}{n_1} + \dfrac{1}{n_2}\right)}}$$

The sample values were

$$p_1 = 0.81 \qquad p_2 = 0.72$$

Then

$$p = \frac{40(0.81) + 130(0.72)}{40 + 130} = \frac{32.4 + 93.6}{170} = \frac{126}{170} = 0.74$$

$$n_1 = 40 \qquad n_2 = 130$$

$$Z = \frac{0.81 - 0.72}{\sqrt{0.74(1 - 0.74)\left(\dfrac{1}{40} + \dfrac{1}{130}\right)}} = \frac{0.09}{\sqrt{0.1924(0.0327)}} = \frac{0.09}{0.025} = 3.6$$

The calculated value of Z (3.6) is greater than the critical value (2.58), therefore reject H_0 that there is no difference in the proportions of executives and all other employees in favour of the recommendation at the 0.01 level of significance.

Therefore, the percentage (81%) of all executives in favour of the recommendation is higher than the percentage (72%) in favour for all other employees, and we will be 99% confident in making this decision.

Small Samples (*t*-test)

When the sample size is small but the population follows a normal distribution or the population is sufficiently large, then the sample estimates follow a *t* distribution (Student's *t* distribution). This distribution is symmetrical around the mean, like the normal distribution, and for large values of *n* (sample size) tends to be a normal distribution. The shape of the distribution depends on the number of observations (strictly, the degrees of freedom). The degrees of freedom are the number of independent observations for the variable. For example, if the weekly incomes in pounds for five workers are 220, 200, 180, 160, 240 then these values have 5 degrees of freedom. However, if we take the total, which is 1000, then only four of the above incomes are independent, since knowing the total and any four values the fifth income can be worked out.

Like the normal distribution, tables are given for the standardized *t* variable but for different degrees of freedom. Thus for tables of the *t* distribution, we decide the level of confidence (α), degrees of freedom and then find the values for the area under consideration. An example of this is as follows:

For sample size, $n = 20$, with degrees of freedom 19 using a two-tailed test,

α	0.05	0.01
t distribution	2.086	2.845

If a simple random sample of size n ($n < 30$) is taken from a population with mean μ and standard deviation σ, the sampling distribution of the sample mean $\bar{x}$ is distributed as a *t* distribution, with mean μ and standard error $\sigma/\sqrt{n}$. This is known as the Central Limit Theorem. Once the distribution is known, we can perform the test of hypothesis as the standard error of the estimates can be calculated.

However, for small samples the standard deviation (usually unknown) is calculated by using

$$\hat{\sigma}^2 = \frac{1}{n-1}\sum(x - \bar{x})^2 \text{ instead of } \hat{\sigma}^2 = \frac{1}{n}\sum(x - \bar{x})^2$$

as this gives a more reliable or unbiased estimate of the population standard deviation.

Small Single-sample Monadic *t*-test for Average

When samples are selected randomly from a large population, hypothesis testing for estimates is done by using the *t*-test. When we use a single sample, it is a monadic test like a Z-test. The degrees of freedom for the test statistic in the case of a small sample are $n - 1$. The rest of the procedure is the same as in the case of a Z-test. A summary of the monadic *t*-test process is shown in Box 9.3 and the detailed procedure follows.

Box 9.3   Summary of monadic *t*-test process

Testing the significance of a single small sample

The procedure depends on which parameter (*mean μ* or *proportion π*) is being tested.

Null hypothesis: Either   There is no difference in the sample average from the population value.

   or   There is no difference in the sample proportion from the population value.

Calculate the appropriate test statistics

$$\text{For mean } t = \frac{\bar{x} - \mu}{\sqrt{\dfrac{\sigma^2}{n}}} \qquad \text{for proportion } t = \frac{p - \pi}{\sqrt{\dfrac{\pi(1 - \pi)}{n}}}$$

Decide the significance of the calculated *t*-test statistic against the critical value from the table of the *t* distribution with n-1 degrees of freedom.

Example 3

A product manager for a line of apparel intends to introduce a line in a new market. A recent survey of 25 households in that market showed the mean income ($\bar{x}$) to be £13000 with a standard deviation (σ) of £8000. On the basis of past experience and comprehensive studies of the current market, he strongly feels that the product line will only be adequately profitable in markets where the average household income μ (based on all households) is greater than £12000. Should he introduce the product line?

H_0: $\mu = £12000$ There is no significant difference between average household income of the sample from the average population household income of £12000.

H_1: $\mu > £12000$ Average household income is greater than the average population household income of £12000 (one-tailed test).

α: 0.05   95% confidence.

df: $(n - 1) = 24$

197

Test statistic: t; critical value $t_{n-1,\alpha} = 1.71$ (from Appendix II)

Decision rule: If the calculated value of t is greater than the critical value of $t_{n-1,\alpha}$ (1.71) then reject H_0, otherwise accept H_0. This is shown in Figure 9.5.

The calculation for the t-test statistic is as follows:

$$t = \frac{\bar{x} - \mu}{\sqrt{\dfrac{\hat{\sigma}^2}{n-1}}} = \frac{13000 - 12000}{\sqrt{\dfrac{8000^2}{25-1}}} = \frac{1000}{1633.3} = 0.61$$

The calculated value of t is 0.61 and is less than the critical value of t which is 1.71. It lies in the acceptance region (non-shaded area of the figure), therefore we accept H_0, that there is no difference in average household income, and the product manager should not enter the market.

Example 4

A pharmaceutical manufacturer claims that its slimming aids will achieve an average weight reduction of 5 lb in the first week of use, provided that the instructions are followed strictly. A chemist selling the product enlisted the help of ten women randomly selected who bought the product on a particular day to test this claim. They reported back as follows:

Women	A	B	C	D	E	F	G	H	I	J
Weight loss (lb) in first week of diet	3	8	2	5	0	−1	2	3	0	4

On the assumptions that the instructions have been followed strictly, a test to determine whether the results are consistent with the manufacturer's claim yielded a statistic of 2.84. Does this result show significant change at the 5% ($\alpha = 0.05$) level?

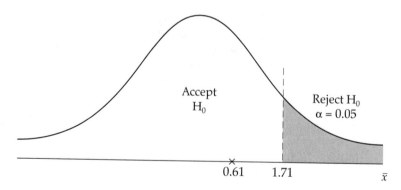

Figure 9.5   Decision rule for a monadic t-test

Solution

Ten women ($n = 10$) were selected to test the manufacturer's claim. The selection is random from a large population; the testing will be done using a *t*-test.

H_o: $\mu = 5$ lb   the average weight reduction does not differ from 5 lb.
H_1: $\mu < 5$ lb   the average weight reduction is less than 5 lb (one-tailed test)
$\alpha = 0.05$
$df = (n - 1) = 9$

$$\text{Test statistic} = \frac{\bar{x} - \mu}{\sqrt{\dfrac{\sigma^2}{n-1}}}$$

Critical value $t_{n-1,\alpha} = t_{9,0.05} = 1.833$ (from Appendix II)
Decision rule: If the calculated value of t is greater than the critical value 1.833, then reject the H_o, otherwise accept H_o. This is shown in Figure 9.6.

Average loss in weight

$$\bar{x} = \frac{\sum x}{n} = \frac{26}{10} = 2.6$$

$$\hat{\sigma}^2 = \frac{\sum(x - \bar{x})^2}{n - 1}$$

$$\hat{\sigma} = 2.67$$

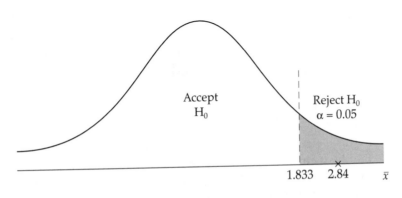

Figure 9.6   Decision rule for a test average weight loss

Then

$$t = \frac{\bar{x} - \mu}{\dfrac{\hat{\sigma}}{\sqrt{n}}} = \frac{2.6 - 5.0}{\dfrac{2.67}{\sqrt{10}}} = 2.84$$

The calculated value of t (2.84) is greater than the critical value of 1.833, therefore reject H_o, the hypothesis that the average weight reduction is not different from 5 lb is rejected. Therefore the average weight reduction is different and an estimate of new average reduction is 2.6 lb.

Two Independent Small Samples: Comparative t-test for Averages

A summary of the process of conducting a test of differences between two independent small samples is given in Box 9.4.

Box 9.4   Summary of comparative t-test process for two independent small samples

Testing the significance of two independent small samples

Null hypothesis: $\mu_1 - \mu_2 = 0$ There is no difference in the two population averages.

Calculate the appropriate test statistics using:

$$t = \frac{(\bar{X}_1 - \bar{X}_2) - (\mu_1 - \mu_2)}{\sqrt{\hat{\sigma}_p^2 \left(\dfrac{1}{n_1} + \dfrac{1}{n_2} \right)}}$$

Decide the significance of the calculated t statistic, against the critical value from the table (Appendix II) of the t distribution with $n_1 + n_2 - 2$ degrees of freedom because we are using two samples.

Example 5

A health agency designed a public service campaign to promote physical fitness and the importance of regular exercise. The experiment was conducted in two cities, Birmingham and Bristol, the latter acting as a control. A random survey of two samples using 20 respondents in Birmingham and 10 respondents in Bristol measured the average time spent in a particular day on an exercise by a typical adult. The adults in Bristol were not exposed to the campaign. The agency was interested in assessing whether the campaign made any difference in average time spent by adults when keeping fit, as a way of evaluating their campaign's effectiveness.

We are given:

Birmingham $n_1 = 20$ $\bar{x}_1 = 35$ minutes $\hat{\sigma}_1 = 25$ minutes
Bristol $n_2 = 10$ $\bar{x}_2 = 30$ minutes $\hat{\sigma}_2 = 22$ minutes

H_0: $\mu_1 - \mu_2 = 0$ There is no difference in the average time spent on exercise between the two cities.
H_1: $\mu_1 - \mu_2 \neq 0$ There is a difference in average time spent on exercise between the two cities (two-tailed test).
α: 0.05 (95% confidence)
df: $n + n_2 - 2 = 28$
Test statistics: $t_{n_1 + n_2 - 2, \alpha}$; critical value $t_{n_1 + n_2 - 2, \alpha} = 2.05$ (from Appendix II)
Decision rule: If the calculated value of t is greater than the critical value of $t_{n_1 + n_2 - 2, \alpha}$ (2.05) then reject H_0, otherwise accept H_0.

The value of the test statistic is calculated by using

$$t = \frac{(\bar{x}_1 - \bar{x}_2) - (\mu_1 - \mu_2)}{\sqrt{\hat{\sigma}_p^2 \left(\dfrac{1}{n_1} + \dfrac{1}{n_2} \right)}}$$

where $\hat{\sigma}_p$ is called the pooled variance as it is the variance of the two samples combined together. This is done because it is assumed that the two samples have the same variance:

$$\hat{\sigma}_p^2 = \frac{(n_1 - 1)\hat{\sigma}_1^2 + (n_2 - 1)\hat{\sigma}_2^2}{n_1 + n_2 - 2} = \frac{11875 + 4356}{20 + 10 - 2} = 580$$

$$t = \frac{|35 - 30|}{\sqrt{580 \left(\dfrac{1}{20} + \dfrac{1}{10} \right)}} = 0.54$$

The calculated value of t is 0.54 and it is less than the critical value of 2.05, therefore we accept H_0, that there is no difference in the average time spent on exercise. Thus the campaign did not make any significant difference in the average time spent by adults in keeping fit. The health agency might wish to rethink its campaign.

Paired Small Sample: Comparative *t*-test for Averages Using Same Respondents

When two independent samples are used, the variation due to the respondents in each sample contributes to the variability, which is not taken into account. It is therefore desirable to use the same respondents to remove this variability. In such situations the same sample is used to test the effect of the factor investigated, thus eliminating the differences in respondents, which would be present if two independent samples were used. A test that uses the same respondents to study the effect of the factor investigated is called a 'paired' *t*-test.

Example 6

Sales (£000) of a particular product A for a period of one month were recorded for 10 outlets before and after an advertising campaign. The manager is interested in finding out how effective his campaign has been. The information in Table 9.1 was obtained:

H_0:	$\mu = 0$. There is no difference in average sales as a result of the advertising campaign.
H_1:	$\mu > 0$. There is an increase in average sales as a result of the advertising campaign (one-tailed test).
α:	0.05 (95% confidence)
df:	$(n - 1) = 9$
Test statistic:	t_{n-1}; critical value $t_{n-1;\,\alpha} = 1.833$ (from Appendix II)

Table 9.1 Calculation of paired *t*-test for small samples

Outlet	Sales (£000) Before	Sales (£000) After	d^*	d^2
1	5.4	6.0	0.6	0.36
2	5.2	5.0	−0.2	0.04
3	6.5	7.0	0.5	0.25
4	5.9	6.2	0.3	0.09
5	6.0	6.0	0.0	0.00
6	6.8	6.2	−0.6	0.36
7	7.1	7.0	−0.1	0.01
8	5.9	6.1	0.2	0.04
9	6.8	7.1	0.3	0.09
10	5.6	5.7	0.1	0.01
			$\sum d = 1.1$	$\sum d^2 = 1.25$

$d^* =$ difference between sales after and before.

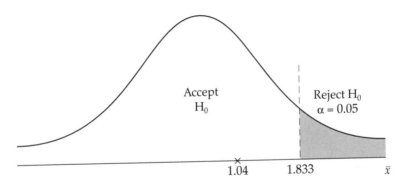

Figure 9.7 Decision rule for small sample paired *t*-test.

Decision rule: If the calculated value of *t* is greater than the critical value of $t_{n-1;\,\alpha}$ (1.833) then reject H_0, otherwise accept H_0.

$$\bar{d} = \frac{\sum d}{n} = \frac{1.1}{10} = 0.11$$

$$t_9 = \frac{\bar{d}}{\sqrt{\dfrac{\sigma_d^2}{n}}} = \frac{\sum d/n}{\sqrt{\dfrac{1}{n}\left[\dfrac{\sum d^2}{n} - \left(\dfrac{\sum d}{n}\right)^2\right]}}$$

$$= \frac{1.1/10}{\sqrt{\dfrac{1}{10}\left[\dfrac{1.25}{10} - \left(\dfrac{1.1}{10}\right)^2\right]}} = \frac{0.11}{\sqrt{\dfrac{1}{10}(0.1129)}} = \frac{0.110}{0.106}$$

$$= 1.04$$

The calculated value of *t* (1.04) is less than the critical value of *t* (1.833), therefore accept H_0. This is shown in Figure 9.7. Therefore, advertising has not increased average sales.

Conclusion

This chapter explains the type of tests we would use when we have samples of different sizes. When the sample size is large ($n \geqslant 30$) we should use a Z-test. The test is monadic when using a single sample while it is comparative when using two independent samples. When the sample size is small ($n < 30$) we should use a *t*-test. When using two samples as far as possible we should use a paired *t*-test as the same respondents are used, thus removing the respondent differences present in the test with two independent samples.

In practice, most of the market research reports use only the *t*-test because the probabilities of the *t* distribution for large sample sizes are the same as for the *Z* distribution. The decisions based on *t* distribution thus can cover both small and large samples.

References

Anderson, D.R., Sweeney, D.J. and Williams, T.A. (1995). *Qualitative Methods for Business*, St Paul, MN: West Publishing.

Churchill, G.A. (1995). *Marketing Research: Methodological Foundation*, 6th edn, Orlando, FL: The Dryden Press.

Malhotra, N.K. (1996). *Marketing Research: An Applied Orientation*, Englewood Cliffs, NJ: Prentice-Hall.

Waters, D. (1997). *Quantitative Methods for Business*, Harlow: Addison-Wesley.

Weiss, N.A. (1995). *Introductory Statistics*, Reading, MA: Addison-Wesley.

Work Assignments

1. It is claimed that the average expenditure per adult on an overseas holiday is £450. A travel survey of 1400 such adults gives an average expenditure of £425 with a standard deviation of £80. Test at the 1% level of significance if the difference is significant.

2. An advertiser claims that 'eight of ten housewives cannot tell Swan margarine from butter'. Consumers group sets out to test this claim and finds that among 100 of their member selected randomly, 30 can distinguish between Swan and the butter. Would this cause you to doubt the advertiser's claim?

3. Fast-food service companies try to devise wage plans that provide incentive and produce salaries for their managers that are competitive with corresponding positions in competing companies. A random sample of 12 unit managers for one company shows that they earn an average salary of £36750 with a standard deviation of £3100.

   (a) Calculate a 95% confidence interval for the mean salary of the company's managers.

   (b) Do the data suggest that the mean salary earned by the company's unit managers differ from £38500, which is the mean salary paid by a competitor firm? Use a significance level of 5%.

4. A company selects nine salesmen at random and their sales figures for the previous month are recorded. Then they undergo a training course designed by a business consultant and their sales figures for the following month are recorded:

Previous month	75	90	94	85	100	90	69	70	64
Following month	77	101	93	92	105	88	73	76	68

Has the training course caused an improvement in the salesmen's ability? (You may assume that the standard deviation for the difference $= 4$.)

5. A manufacturer of orange juice develops a new container and tests the sales of the drink in relation to its existing container in ten randomly selected shops over a period of one month. The results are shown below:

	Units sold in different outlets									
Container	A	B	C	D	E	F	G	H	I	J
Existing	36	61	60	63	57	58	61	48	54	75
New	58	58	76	63	50	54	63	64	65	87

(a) Do these results provide evidence that the existing and new containers have different mean sales?

(b) Suppose that, instead of two different groups of shops, one group of shops sold the drink in the existing container and after a month sold it in the new container. Can you now conclude that the sales are different? What is the methodological importance of the one-month gap?

PART III

Contexts in marketing research

International Marketing Research 10

Introduction

This chapter provides an overview of the international environment and will focus more specifically on the challenges of conducting research across several countries and cultures. Trade liberalization and advances in technology have changed the world considerably compared with the world of 20 years ago. The Internet has provided large corporations as well as micro-companies and individuals with wide access to the world markets in which to promote their products and services.

We often have preconceived ideas about other cultures and people. Many in the West may be disgusted by the Chinese banqueting on turtle soup, snake and particularly dog, or the Guineans snacking on insects. Customs and habits are deeply ingrained in people's minds and perpetuated through family values, education, peer groups and ideology. For instance, in Scandinavian countries, consumers are used to recycling cans and bottles at the supermarket although this is not yet the part of the consumer culture in the UK. In California, smoking in bars is not permitted and the practice of smoking is actually positively discouraged socially even where it is allowed. Drinking alcohol is not permitted in many Islamic countries. However, at the same time, tastes and habits could also be said to be converging. Young people around the world are seen parading the Nike swoosh on various garments, listening to their favourite singer on a Sony Walkman and stopping for a Coke at the local McDonald's. Some aspiring executives could not be seen without their Nokia mobile, Cartier sunglasses, Pierre Cardin suit and Rolex watch.

It has been demonstrated that lack of information was a major hindrance to firms' internationalization, especially for small businesses (Kedia and Chhokar, 1986), or a major cause of failure in the international marketplace (Czinkota and Ronkainen, 1993). Thus, marketing research is necessary because businesses often lack basic knowledge about their potential overseas markets. Craig and Douglas (2000: 10) stress the importance of international research to:

1. Avoid the costly mistakes of inappropriate strategies.
2. Avoid lost opportunities in international markets.
3. Determine how far international operations can be coordinated across countries to take advantage of potential synergies arising from marketing in a global environment.

The first challenge for marketing researchers, therefore, is to develop an intrinsic understanding of the extent to which people can adapt their own traditions to those of other cultures. The second challenge is to learn how and when to adapt research designs to various cultural environments so that the data collected can be compared across countries. For instance, small businesses conduct research in their own way, in a more 'artistic' way, according to Carson and Coviello (1996). Thus, in an international setting, with scarce resources, such firms may rely more on the experience of their friends and colleagues in similar sectors, and on advice provided by specialist government organizations, e.g., the Chambers of Commerce and the Department of Trade and Industry in the UK. Finally, this chapter also intends to provide an appreciation of how to deal with research suppliers to gather data from various countries. Generally, the various challenges arise from differences in the international marketing environment and their impact upon the research process, which is discussed in the next section.

The International Marketing Environment

Differences in the international marketing environment across countries will dictate the way in which data is collected, the type of questions to ask, who will answer, and how to interpret the answers. Malhotra (1999: 683–687) identifies the following seven different environments which impact upon the international marketing research process: the marketing, government, legal, economic, structural, techno-logical and socio-cultural environments.

Marketing

This generally refers to the extent to which the marketing mix (four Ps—product, place, price and promotion—or seven Ps for services—includes people, physical evidence and process) differs in each country. For instance, marketing research regarding pricing for a product launch in the Middle East would need to take account of the bartering that occurs in these cultures. Marketing research into children's tastes in Greece would also need to be aware that advertising to this sector is restricted. Similarly, product law varies according to the country, requiring relatively strict adherence to packaging and labelling regulations in some countries (i.e., the EU).

The extent to which companies have adopted the marketing philosophy and achieved a marketing orientation also determines the type of research undertaken. For instance, companies in developing countries tend to be more production-oriented and, therefore, marketing research would tend to centre more on product characteristics than on market characteristics.

Government

The nature of the government's involvement in geographic markets may impact differently in different countries. For instance, research into telecommunications in Brazil in 1997 would need to take into account the fact that the industry was only starting the privatization process and that for some time it would still be regulated by the government and it would take time to introduce competition. As a result, a foreign telecommunications operator using a research design for business-to-business research in a deregulated market would achieve findings that would not be comparable to those from other markets.

Governments have tended to impose regulations on domestic companies in order to promote competition, and restrictions on foreign competitors in order to protect their markets. For instance, Japan has until recently strongly restricted imports of foreign products into its markets. The government environment has a greater impact upon restricted product and service categories, e.g., petrol, tobacco, alcohol, pharmaceuticals, pensions and insurance. Whether a country's health service is private (as in the USA, Spain) or public (as in the UK) impacts upon the price and distribution of pharmaceutical products. Therefore, research into their use by the consumer would need to reflect the considerable difference in purchasing habits occurring as a result of government intervention in distribution and pricing. As governments change their political allegiance, the extent to which they are prepared to intervene in markets is also often affected. Thus, the traditional, deeply religious conservative administration in Iran is said to be becoming less anti-West and moving a little towards liberal democratic principles. Public opinion polling in Iran, which was previously resisted, is now starting to be conducted to a limited degree.

Legal

Since countries have their own legal systems, the laws relating to marketing, products and services and business in general all differ depending on the country and location in which an organization is based. In the USA different states have different laws regarding gambling and the consumption of alcohol. Therefore, knowledge of these factors would be necessary for a casino chain that wished to gain a cross-state presence.

Advertising law in Greece restricts the promotion of certain products to children, e.g., toys. This is not the case in the UK. However, in the USA, political candidates can advertise on broadcast networks, including terrestrial, satellite and cable, whereas in Britain paid political advertising is illegal. In Indonesia, all research activities are banned prior to an election. Distribution arrangements are also covered by law and differ from country to country. This usually relates to the allocation of territories and restriction of trade. There are differences in the extent to which countries operate under public disclosure of government information. For instance, in the UK, there is no law requiring government departments to release such information, whereas in the USA, there is. This has major implications for those firms that have dealings with government. Essentially, the Freedom of Information Act 1964 operating in the USA allows firms to collect sensitive information, i.e., competitive intelligence. Such information, e.g., anti-trust cases and government enquiries, could provide the diligent market researcher with useful secondary data on market share, proprietary product information and distribution arrangements (see Chapter 3).

In the UK, the Data Protection Act 1998 stipulates that information on members of the public must not be held without their consent and that they have a right to see this information. More recent changes to the legislation limit the use of the electoral roll, ruling that it cannot be used for commercial purposes. Thus, market researchers will have to devise, and maintain, their own sampling frames based on other sources of information. In the EU, the Data Protection Directive (95/46/EC) provides the legislation that encompasses the whole of the European Union. International law may also cover some items, hence negating the need for customized research. An example would include the manufacture of chemical, nuclear and biological materials.

Economic

The wealth of a country generally determines its lifestyle. For instance, the population of a country with a high GDP (Gross Domestic Product) usually has a higher discretionary income per capita. As a result, the populace will tend to have different consumption patterns. A more specific example of the effect of the economy is the difference in interest rates between countries. This will affect the house-buying market that will in turn have an effect upon the construction industry and other ancillary industries. Currency fluctuations will also have an impact upon the consumption of products since they will have a bearing on the ultimate price of a product. For instance, the high value of the pound sterling has affected the exports of British products. In order to compete, British firms have had to focus on added value rather than price. Thus, research aiming to identify lucrative export markets would have to account for the different standards of living enjoyed by the consumer and the consumers' perception of a product's value. This may differ greatly between markets. An example of this was when Unilever launched a branded shampoo product in Kazakhstan with very limited success.

Structural

Infrastructure, communication networks and the nature of the industry all impact upon the marketing activity of a firm. Marketing research into international markets may need to take into account the differences in telephone usage since this affects the use of telephone and computer-assisted telephone interviewing techniques. An understanding of the degree of television penetration (the extent to which television sets are owned by the population), and the nature of the audience breakdown by different channels, is also important since it has an impact upon the conduct of advertising research. The efficiency of the postal service tends to be different in different countries, thereby affecting the decision of whether or not to use a mail survey methodology.

Technological

This area relates to a country's capacity to innovate and its ability to use technological knowledge. In countries where there is a lack of technological innovation, there is usually a tendency to resist products and services that rely on sophisticated technological methods. The degree to which personal computers and information technology have penetrated the culture of a country affect the research process and its design considerably.

For instance, consider Microsoft's recent expansion in the area of Internet access. This has been a growth area for them. If they were interested in the Latin American market, the extent of the usage of information technology would be imperative. Secondary research could provide an indication of the degree of computer, and multimedia computer (i.e., access to the Internet) penetration levels.

In some countries, the fact that there is not the energy available for some products also negates their use. In Latin America, cars are run on a mixture of sugarbeet juice and petroleum. Subsequently, a Western car manufacturer, entering such a market, would have to bear this in mind when performing their research and manufacturing their products since it would affect the running costs of the car, which may be a relatively more important criterion for Latin American car buyers than for their European counterparts.

Socio-cultural

This is perhaps the most important aspect of the international environment as it relates to differences in language, culture, literacy and numeracy. It is clear that a company distributing pork would have to take into account the religion of the people in specific countries since this would determine whether they would buy it. Since the Japanese dislike disagreeing with people in public, this would negate the use of focus groups. At the same time, it would not be possible to interview Saudi Arabian women in the street, because the practice of women talking to men in the street is frowned upon. In addition to affecting the process of research, socio-cultural differences often affect habits, attitudes, opinions and values, all of which can impact upon how products and services are purchased by consumers.

It is possible to cluster some countries in terms of their socio-cultural similarity, in order to perform marketing research using international sampling frames provided the similarities have been shown to exist in previous research. For instance, Ronen and Shenkar (1985) showed that the non-Communist world in the 1980s could broadly be divided into nine different clusters, each cluster including a number of countries. They were defined as Anglo (the UK, the USA and Australia), Germanic (Austria and Switzerland), Nordic (some of the Scandinavian countries), Latin European (Belgium), Latin American, Near East (Greece, Turkey, the former Yugoslavia), Arabic (Oman and Kuwait) and, finally, Independents (Japan and India).

Applying these clusters indiscriminately to a wide range of products and services could understandably lead to the wrong conclusions. A subtle divide exists between the adoption of foreign values and the maintenance of traditional ones. For instance, bicycles are used predominantly for transport purposes in China, but for recreational purposes in the UK. Even when foreign products have been adapted, their usage, positioning, and perception may be different from those in their country of origin. The concept of drive-in and drive-through in the USA has never really transferred to the UK. Although drive-in cinemas and drive-through supermarkets have been successful in the USA, drive-in and drive-through has only really been accepted in the car wash and petrol retailing sectors.

The Challenge of Equivalence in International Marketing Research

The complexity of the international environment makes international marketing research particularly complex because of its effect upon the research process and its design. The fact that many more variables need to be taken into account means that use of local experts is important to avoid any problems inherent in overcentralizing and, therefore, misunderstanding international marketing research. The dichotomy occurs between overcustomization of international marketing research, where separate countries are researched using differing scales, sampling methods and sizes with the corresponding reduction in equivalence, and using a single method for all countries (hence using international sampling frames), where country-specific data would no longer be valid.

The process of researching international markets is no different from researching valid, accurate and relevant information regarding the domestic market (as explained in Chapter 3). However, as seen above, vast cultural differences among countries imply that the implementation of the process, or parts of it, have to be adapted to the national or regional environments in which the research takes place.

Consequently, the main issue faced by international researchers is that of comparability of data when, for instance, access to key respondents is restricted due to differences in cultural values or lack of technology. Western marketing concepts may be inappropriate due to variations in economic development and consumption patterns. How can we find out about women's consumption patterns in countries where access to this segment of the population is limited? How comparable is the data related to the consumption of a fast-moving consumer good (FMCG) manufactured by a German firm and collected through personal interviews in Peru, telephone interviews in Canada and mailed questionnaires in the UK? How is the concept of brand loyalty perceived in Spain and in the Ukraine?

Hibbert (1993) states that 'it is essential that differences are taken into account in the formulation of the initial design of a multi-country survey, and they may well necessitate variations in the research methods used to be applied in individual countries'. Hibbert goes on to say that international marketing research managers must ensure comparability and validity of results across countries and comparable data analysis. In order to do this the manager has to understand how to measure equivalence. This helps the researcher to understand how to ask the right questions in different countries.

Are we talking about the same thing?

Conceptual, functional and translation equivalence

Conceptual Equivalence

Conceptual equivalence is concerned with the extent to which interpretation of behaviour, or objects, is similar across countries. For instance, in Japan it is not polite to openly disagree with someone, whereas this is not necessarily forbidden in Europe. Some concepts like beauty, quality and loyalty are universal. Nevertheless, they may have different meanings in different countries. The concept of service quality, for instance, is different in the UK and the USA. British commuters have a much higher tolerance threshold when faced with overcrowded and unreliable trains than would the Americans, a country where the consumer is king. Therefore, the results of a survey investigating the 'quality of service' in public transportation would have to be interpreted differently in the two countries.

Defining what constitutes the 'household' can be problematic in both question design and when determining the sampling unit. In the Western world, a typical household consists of four people (i.e., two adults and two children). In these same countries, more and more people are living on their own. In London, where rent is expensive, several single people, unrelated by blood, may be sharing the same house. Would they constitute a household? In many countries and sub-cultures within countries, a household may also include the elderly generation where it is generally considered to be the children's duty to look after their parents. This may either be because the social security system does not provide for them, or because it is generally expected that this will be the case (i.e., tradition).

Conceptual equivalence needs to be considered when defining the research problem, in wording the questionnaire and determining the sample unit. There would be no need to investigate 'brand loyalty' in a country in which the competition is restricted and the choice of products is relatively limited.

Functional Equivalence

Functional equivalence relates to whether a concept has the same function in different countries. In the USA, grocery shopping serves a utilitarian purpose and has to be completed as efficiently as possible, once a week. Therefore, it is important for parking spaces to be close to the supermarket and for helpers to be available to pack the goods and place them in car boots. It is this high degree of functionality that has ensured the existence of drive-through supermarkets where the driver never has to leave the car. In Mediterranean countries, women usually conduct the grocery shopping. They generally travel to the local shops or markets on foot on an everyday basis. This serves both a social and a utilitarian purpose. The shoppers meet their friends, chat with the grocers and catch up on the latest news, and this is part of their social environment. A survey on shopping habits, therefore, would have to address different issues in these countries.

Shopping habits are often related to the functions performed by refrigerators and other white goods. In the USA, refrigerators are used to store food for a week, whereas in the Mediterranean countries food is stored in refrigerators for a day or two. This will have an impact on the size of the appliance and the features required. However, refrigerators are not only used to keep food fresh. In some African countries, they are a status symbol and are displayed in the living room in the view of guests. The larger the refrigerator, the greater the family's status. Consequently, a survey on refrigerator preferences designed by a Western researcher without cultural awareness for an African country could lead to the wrong conclusions. There are also extreme situations that make the life of international researchers all the more interesting. One former president of an international market research firm based in Korea reported that one of his colleagues was sent to Papua New Guinea to investigate the reason for an increase in sales of unusually large bras. The investigation revealed that the bras were being used by warriors as bum bags!

These examples show that it is almost impossible to achieve functional equivalence when the products or concepts serve different purposes. More importantly, these functional differences have to be detected before starting the research design. Usunier (2000: 216) suggests that 'one of the best ways to investigate functional equivalence is to examine the social settings in which a product is consumed'. This is in order to ensure validity of data (i.e., making sure that the constructs used in the research measure what they are supposed to measure).

Translation Equivalence

Translation equivalence is a particularly important aspect of the international research process since words in some languages have no real equivalent in others. *Schadenfreude* is a good example of a German word that has no real English translation although it roughly means taking delight in someone else's misfortune. The meaning that one associates with different words is important in questionnaire design since words may convey a different meaning from that intended when directly translated to another language. In order to avoid such translation errors, there are two possible methods that can be used:

(a) *Back translation* this method initially uses a translator fluent in the foreign language into which the research method is being translated and then a translator whose native language was the original language to translate back again. The resulting differences in wording can be identified.

(b) *Parallel translation* where a research instrument (e.g., a questionnaire) is translated using a team of translators fluent in at least two languages until a final version is agreed (Malhotra, 1999: 814).

When questionnaires are developed for countries where there is officially one common language, sometimes they still need to be adapted to the words actually in usage in that specific country. For instance, a lorry in the UK is labelled a truck in the USA and Canada. In France, shopping is translated as *faire des courses* and *magasiner* in Quebec. The spelling should also use the format of the country where the survey is being carried out (i.e., favour in the UK and favor in the USA). A British focus group moderator, conducting discussions on cigarette habits and usage in Washington, DC, would receive a very different response from Americans if they were to use the British colloquialism 'fag' to describe a cigarette in one of their questions compared with their counterparts in Newcastle (for example, 'when do you most fancy a fag?'). This is because 'fag' is a derogatory term in the USA used to describe homosexual males. In other countries, the multi-ethnicity of the population has to be acknowledged in survey design. In Singapore, for example, questionnaires often go out with multiple languages on the same page, commonly Chinese, Malay, Indian and English. The interviewer may even switch between languages if some words are unfamiliar to respondents in one particular language.

Measurement Equivalence

How Long is this Piece of String?

This concept examines the extent to which measurement scales can be compared across countries. When surveys are conducted in countries using metric and imperial systems of measure, the scales have to be translated to reflect the actual content and size of the product in the markets as well as the consumption habits. For instance, a 2-ounce chocolate bar in the USA would be equivalent to 50 grams in France. The same concept of metric equivalence applies to currency and length measurement. Taking into account the measurement system in each country is called calibration equivalence. Because of this problem of equivalence in product quality standards across countries, the international standards organization (ISO) was developed.

Box 10.1   How much do you drink? Investigating wine consumption in the UK, France and Canada

One of the questions on a National Shopper Survey questionnaire sent to British homes was:

How many bottles of wine do you normally buy in a month?

☐ None   ☐ Less than one   ☐ One to two
☐ Three to five   ☐ Six to eleven   ☐ Twelve plus

Such a question could lead to the wrong conclusions if asked in the same way in France because: (1) the French tend to drink wine on an everyday basis; thus the upper range of the scale would tend to be used more often without providing relevant details; (2) wine is bought in bottles or in wider containers from supermarkets, or in bulk from local producers, or made at home. In the wine-producing areas of France, this scale would report unusual low consumption of wine since wine bottles may only be bought occasionally. This scale, therefore, would not accurately measure wine consumption in France.

In Canada, retailers encourage consumers to buy in bulk and often offer discounts on the purchase of cases of 6 to 12 bottles of wine. This is then stored at home for future consumption. In this country, a better way of wording this question would be: How many bottles of wine do you normally consume in a month?

Multi-item scales present a number of challenges for international researchers. First, the anchors on the scale cannot be translated literally from one language to the other. Some languages have fewer words than others to express satisfaction or agreement. It is therefore suggested to use words drawn from national surveys instead of attempting an approximate translation (Usunier, 2000).

Second, some cultures are more open than others at expressing their own opinions and feelings or describing their behaviours. An American would not hesitate at expressing extreme opinions, and therefore would use the full spectrum of values on a Likert scale. The British are more reserved and would rarely use the extreme points on the same scale. This concept is known as metric or scalar equivalence, and concerns how concepts are measured and their equivalence in different cultural systems. Other cultures would tend to answer on the positive side of the scale to please the interviewer. This is a courtesy bias. Consequently, would two samples with different arithmetic average scores on the Likert scale really have different attitudes? In order to reduce this error, different measurement scales are often used in order to attempt to provide comparable results (Sood, 1989). The symbolic value of colours also needs to be considered when designing surveys. Latin countries find bright colours warm and joyful, while these are considered offensive in Nordic countries.

Sampling Equivalence

Who Am I Talking to? Which Population Are You Representing?

Choosing the appropriate target market is an additional challenge in international marketing research and the profile of respondents for the same survey may vary from one country to another. One of the reasons is that the age at which certain activities are allowed is far from standardized across countries, due partly to the cultural background and partly due to the legal environment. In some countries, for instance, women marry at a very young age and are expected to have children almost immediately. This will influence their consumption patterns as well as the way in which they live and view life in general. A survey aimed at looking into the interests of new car drivers would not be able to use the same age groups across the world as the legal age for driving differs among countries. This is also true of alcohol consumption. Therefore, an understanding of these differences is essential before conducting a study.

Decision makers also vary between cultures. In North America, children have a strong influence on the purchase of the food they consume, and the toys and clothes they use. In other countries, parental influence in children's choice is predominant. A survey has demonstrated that major household items are mostly purchased by men in Latin America, while the decision-making process is shared in the USA (Jeannet and Hennessey, 1998).

Decision makers have to be carefully scrutinized for industrial surveys. In countries that favour a centralized decision-making process, only senior executives will have the answers to most questions. In countries where a more informal system exists, lower levels of management might also be helpful.

Representativeness

Another aspect of sampling equivalence is the extent to which the samples chosen can be said to be representative of the population. Where a national sampling frame exists (e.g., a telephone directory or electoral register), samples can usually be taken provided other national statistics are available to allow comparison with other countries' samples (i.e., using census statistics). However, in some countries such sampling frames do not exist, or are inaccurate (telephone directories in Saudi Arabia are incomplete, electoral registers in Bolivia consist of an overrepresentation of men). In these cases, non-probability sampling methods are often used. Quota sampling (see Chapter 7) is a method that has been widely used in developing countries (Malhotra, Agarwal and Peterson, 1996).

Futhermore, one could also argue that trying to achieve national representativeness could lead to the wrong conclusions in countries where 80% of the wealth is concentrated into 20% of the population. Only those potential customers who could afford the product should be surveyed. This implies that extrapolation of the results to wider segments of the population should be undertaken with care as the following example shows.

One soft-drinks company tested a product in a major city in Indonesia. The results were then extrapolated to the Indonesian population at large and a plant was built based on these results. The plant operated much below capacity as the research overlooked the fact that the drink was bought mainly by foreigners and urban Indonesian from the middle classes while Indonesia as a whole consists of over 3000 islands, with mostly a rural population.

Data-collection Methods

It may be that different methods of collecting data are appropriate in different countries. The three main methods are mail, telephone and personal interviews. The differences in using each are explained below.

- *Mail* This method tends to be used more where literacy is high and where the mail system is efficient. Sampling frames usually are compiled from electoral registers, and with the creation of a European Parliament, it is now possible to use the electoral registers compiled in each of the member countries. Recent legislation in the UK, however, has stipulated that the electoral register can no longer be used for commercial purposes. European survey respondents can therefore be targeted efficiently and accurately by mail. However, where there is a lack of mailing lists, this method becomes less useful. It is also difficult to control the sample. An advantage is that letters can be sent from a central location, thereby maximizing efficiency.
- *Telephone* In many countries telephone usage may be limited. Where this is around 95% in the USA, the European figure is around 80% at the current time. Obviously, in Third World and developing countries, these figures will be much lower and, as a result, the potential use of this method for interviewing is reduced. The updating of directories is also important. Using the telephone is advantageous where the sample needs to be controlled and is inaccessible by other means. It also has the advantage that it could be centrally controlled, although this obviously requires the use of native speakers.
- *Personal interviews* This data-collection method is widely used in countries in which personal relationships are important, such as in Latin America. Many European countries tend to use this method, particularly the door-to-door variant as well. However, in some countries, this type of interviewer would be considered suspicious. They are perceived to be linked with burglars in Russia when they ask questions about house content, kidnappers in Mozambique when they inquire about the number of children, and the tax ministry in some Latin American countries when asking questions about income and expenditure. In

such places, the research process has to be managed appropriately and the populations reassured of the true objectives of the research. Shopping mall intercept interviews would not be appropriate in the Arabic countries where women cannot be approached in the street. In these countries, comparability would have to be achieved using door-to-door interviews. In countries where it is rude to openly disagree with someone, such as Japan, it might be wiser to use in-depth interviews, since no-one else will be present. Where there is a low telephone penetration and a lack of comprehensive or reliable mailing lists, this method probably offers the best alternative. In addition, where literacy is low (i.e., in developing and Third World countries), this method may be the only alternative. In these countries, availability of interviewers is often high and the costs are low.

In order to limit interviewer bias in countries with a heterogeneous population consisting of several ethnic groups living together, it is important to select interviewers with the right ethnic origins (Usunier, 2000). Achieving comparability when conducting international surveys can be very difficult. The more countries that are included in an international study, the more likely it is that error will be introduced, and that the results and findings will be inaccurate and, therefore, misinterpreted. It is very difficult to take into account how each of the above concepts differs in their respective countries unless one has an intimate knowledge of the various markets. Therefore, international research requires both a local and an international feel and the extent to which one can internationalize certain operations depends on the objectives of the research.

Coordinating International Marketing Research

Toyne and Walters (1993) suggest that the major decisions governing the organization of international marketing research encapsulate delegation of work to local and regional agencies and corporate staff, control and administration, the type of information to be collected and the budget allocation for the various tasks.

Hibbert (1993) states that a multi-country research using a survey methodology will generally follow an eleven-stage procedure. Each is outlined further below with considerations suggested at each stage.

I. The project is discussed at length with the client

As with a domestic study, it is important to understand the client's motivations for commissioning the research. A clear statement of objectives is very important. Often, some clients require agency input to determine their management problem, whereas other more experienced organizations provide the agency with a clear problem statement. The research design is often determined in draft at this stage with input from the client.

II. The fieldwork agencies for each country are selected

The price of agencies varies greatly in different countries. For instance, in Portugal, the average price of a consumer survey is approximately 58% of the European Union average, while the UK is approximately 112% of the EU average. Central Europe is around 40% of the EU average, North America 149%, Central and South America 84%, Asia 32%, North Africa 55%, Australasia 128% and the Pacific Rim around 85% of the EU average. The difficulty lies in finding agencies that are reliable and reputable. Some local agencies are affiliated to larger marketing research organizations, while other market research providers operate in a large number of countries. For instance, Opinion Research Corporation International is a global market research company, with offices in the USA, Europe, Asia and Latin America. Millward Brown International is a global market research agency employing over 5000 staff in more than 25 countries. Muhlbacher, Dahringer and Leihs (1999) state that when selecting a local agency, the central agency can either select the local agency by geographic location (i.e., the USA or EU), by industry specialization (i.e., telecommunications, pharmaceuticals, etc.) or by using an international agency.

III. The questionnaire is developed centrally

IV. The questionnaire is translated locally and the translation is checked centrally

Toyne and Walters (1993) suggest that the lack of familiarity with each national situation heightens the potential for misunderstandings to occur during problem formulation. Thus, the questionnaire is translated locally to avoid cultural differences in language. However, the translation is checked centrally again to ensure a fit with the original research objectives.

V. The questionnaire is piloted locally

VI. The questionnaire is finalized centrally

To ensure that the questionnaire does not contain unforeseen errors, which may not have been picked up by the local researchers, the questionnaire is piloted locally. Then to maintain the client's research objectives, the questionnaire is finalized centrally rather than locally since this may well dilute the original objectives.

VII. The interviewers are briefed locally by an executive of the central company

It is important that the executive from the central agency meets with local interviewers so that the executive is aware of cultural sensitivities and local difficulties. This information can then be input to future projects. This also allows corporate staff to monitor how the research is being undertaken at the local level and maintain quality, if necessary. At this stage, the fieldwork is carried out in much the same way as it would be in a domestic market research project.

VIII. A coding and editing plan is provided for the local agencies

IX. The edited and coded questionnaires are returned to the head office

> The coding is designed to enable the central research agency to cross-tabulate results across countries if necessary and compare data from one country with another.

X. A coding and editing check is carried out centrally

XI. Computing is carried out centrally

> In order to ensure local compliance with the central coding procedures, the editing and coding checks are carried out centrally. Computing is also generally carried out centrally.
>
> Because of the geographic disparity between central and local agencies there is ample opportunity for misunderstandings, errors, inefficiency and lack of cultural sensitivity. The central agency should identify a number of local market research providers that it trusts on a variety of continents. Often, however, trying to obtain highly comparable data is difficult and so the interpretation of market research reports becomes critical. They should be read with care and caution.

Conclusion

The process of international market research can be seen to be considerably more complex than that devoted to one country only. Not only does the researcher need to ensure that the studies are equivalent in different countries, which may involve considerably different research designs, the researcher also needs to understand the differing environments that bring about the necessary changes in research design. The international researcher also needs to understand how such research designs can be amended while still keeping to the original theme and searching for the original information requirements. The coordination of the international research project provides a number of opportunities to deviate from the original research design and objectives. In order to ensure that the integrity of the original design is maintained, central agencies should work closely with local agencies in designing, piloting and coding the questionnaire. The central agency receives the data and compiles a report centrally, which may be comparative if this is required by the client, or a profile of individual countries.

References

Carson, D. and Coviello, N. (1996). 'Qualitative research issues at the marketing/entrepreneurship interface', *Marketing Intelligence and Planning*, **14**(6), 51–59.

Craig, S.P. and Douglas, C.S. (2000). *International Marketing Research* (2nd edn), New York: Wiley.

Czinkota, M. and Ronkainen, I.A. (1993). *International Marketing* (3rd edn), Orlando, FL: Dryden Press.

Hibbert. E. (1993). 'Research international markets—how can we ensure validity of results?' *Marketing and Research Today*, November, 222–228.

Jeannet, J.-P. and Hennessey, H.D. (1998). *Global Marketing Strategies* (4th edn), New York: Houghton Mifflin.

Kedia, B.L. and Chhokar, J. (1986). 'Factors inhibiting export performance of firms: An empirical investigation', *Management International Review*, 26, 33–43.

Malhotra, N.K. (1999). *Marketing Research: An Applied Approach* (3rd edn), Englewood Cliffs, NJ: Prentice-Hall.

Malhotra, N.K., Agarwal, J. and Peterson, M. (1996). 'Methodological issues in cross-cultural marketing research', *International Marketing Review*, **13**(5), 7–43.

Muhlbacher, H., Dahringer, L. and Leihs, H. (1999). *International Marketing* (2nd edn), London: International Thomson Business Press, 250–251.

Ronen, S. and Shenkar, O. (1985). 'Clustering countries on attitudinal dimensions: a review and synthesis', *Academy of Management Review*, **10**(3), 435–445.

Sood, J. (1989). 'Equivalent measurement in international marketing research: Is it really a problem?' *Journal of International Consumer Marketing*, 2(2), 25–41.

Toyne, B. and Walters, P.G.P. (1993). *Global Marketing Management: A Strategic Perspective* (2nd edn), London: Allyn and Bacon, 381.

Usunier, J.C. (2000). *Marketing Across Cultures* (3rd edn), Englewood Cliffs, NJ: Prentice-Hall.

Zikmund, W.G. (1997). *Exploring Marketing Research* (6th edn), Orlando, FL: Dryden Press.

Work Assignments

1. When is international marketing research necessary?
2. How does the environment affect the conduct of marketing research?
3. Why is it difficult to achieve comparability of data across countries?
4. How are the differing aspects of the research process affected by differences in equivalence between countries?
5. How should international marketing research be coordinated when a global FMCG organization like Coca-Cola wishes to determine how to customize its product for, say, the Indonesian market?

Internet Marketing Research

11

Learning Outcomes

After reading this chapter you will be able to:

- Understand the contribution that the Internet can make to marketing research.
- Know how to collect primary data using the Internet.
- Compare on- and off-line approaches to primary data collection.
- Describe the difficulties associated with data collection in Internet marketing research.

Introduction

In a relatively short period of time, the Internet has become a primary source of information for researchers. In particular, the Web now provides ready access to secondary data on all aspects of business, including estimates of the number of consumers connected to the Internet, analyses of specific market sectors, marketing intelligence reports and competitor profiles. There is a growing amount of useful marketing information available on the Internet, much of it posted by Internet research companies such as AC Nielsen, NOP, Nua, Jupiter MMXI and Forrester (see Kumar, Aaker and Day, 1999, Chapter 6 for a review), but government bodies and academic institutions (e.g., GVU, 1998) have also made significant contributions. In this chapter, however, we will concentrate on the use of the Internet for primary research, and particularly survey research. (See Chapter 3 and Lescher, 1995, for ideas on using the Internet for secondary research.)

So what does on-line marketing research look like? To many observers, the most obvious form is the on-line poll included on many websites. You will probably have seen one or more of these, identifying the best footballer of the twentieth century, rating the top ten films of all time, or asking you to vote on a topical issue or event. These are not 'surveys' in the conventional sense and, as some of the more reputable sites will tell you, they have no scientific basis. They are there for fun—and to attract repeat visits.

The Internet can also be used for more serious kinds of research, such as:

- Estimating potential consumers (on- or off-line) for a product or service—e.g., will my on-line business idea attract enough customers to make it viable?
- Audience qualification study, e.g., how effective is my Web advertising campaign, and will it satisfy my website advertisers?
- Consumer satisfaction survey, e.g., are my customers happy with the Internet service I provide?
- Product or service design and testing, e.g., what feedback can I obtain on-line to improve/extend my product range?

As with other marketing research channels, the Internet can be used at various stages of the marketing process: conceptualization or design; prior to a product launch or relaunch; or after customers have acquired a product or used a service. The Internet can also be used at all stages of the marketing research process: finding potential respondents; questioning respondents; following up initial surveys; and disseminating research summaries to interested parties. In this chapter, we will concentrate on the information-gathering phase, and particularly on consumer-focused research.

The Internet as a Research Medium

Marketing researchers are no strangers to technology. Equipment and software of various kinds are routinely used in the profession for: data gathering (e.g., telephone interviews, computer-based surveys (CATI, CAPI, CASI, CAWI); TV audience measurement (desk-top boxes and hand-held 'peoplemeters'); in-store research (e.g., video-recording); data processing (e.g., statistical and data-visualization software); and data presentation (e.g., CD broadcasting). The Internet is therefore just the latest in a long line of technologies that have been enlisted to improve various elements of the marketing research process.

The Internet has several advantages as a medium for conducting marketing research:

- *Global reach*   In principle, any marketer can undertake research around the world from a single location (see Chapter 10).
- *Speed*   E-mails can be sent and Web pages can be displayed and updated almost instantaneously, and research evidence suggests that more respondents will reply immediately to on-line surveys than to paper-based ones.
- *Low cost*   As spammers know only too well, it costs little to distribute millions of e-mail messages across the Internet, since the printing and mailing costs associated with conventional mailshots do not apply. The principal cost is

setting up a server and/or paying an Internet service provider (ISP), and when respondent information is received, there are few data-entry costs because user responses are already in computer-readable form. Some estimates suggest that e-mail or Web surveys can cost less than a fifth of traditional surveys.

- *Data quality* Because it is possible (using client-side or server-side scripts) to check the user's responses to a Web questionnaire, input errors can be trapped and corrected before the data are accepted for storage and processing. (As we will see later, it is relatively easy for users to fool Web software into accepting bogus information.)
- *Flexibility* By writing scripts or using computer-assisted Web interview (CAWI) software, it is possible to design complex, multi-stage surveys, in which a succession of survey forms is sent to the user based on their responses to previous forms (e.g., Kottler, 1997; Parackal and Brennan, 1999). Using this method, Web-based surveys can include the same kinds of sophisticated techniques (branching logic, item rotation, and randomization) that are commonly used in more traditional questionnaire surveys.
- *Interactivity* It is possible to carry out advertising research on the Web where the subject is contacted and questioned the moment they visit a document or view an advertisement, thereby providing an on-the-spot insight into their reaction that may be difficult to achieve with other advertising media.
- *Generic technology* The same methods that are used to research consumers and their preferences on the Internet can also be employed in the more controlled environments of company intranets and extranets.

However, when it comes to actually undertaking on-line research various problems arise, so it is essential to review some of the negative characteristics of the Internet for the marketing researcher:

- *Overpopulated* With tens of millions of websites, discussion groups, chat facilities, user forums and the like on the Net, it can be a difficult place to get your voice heard. In this kind of environment, it can be difficult for the marketing researcher to attract the attention of respondents to participate in their surveys.
- *Congested* The delivery of a long or multi-part Web questionnaire over the Internet at certain times of day and in some countries can be extremely sluggish, and may lead to loss of interest by respondents. At least one large market research company specializing in Internet surveys attempts to minimize this problem by providing its own Web servers at well-connected junctions on the Internet (Ross, 2001).
- *Stateless* Traffic on the Internet consists of independent 'transactions', which makes it difficult to track the sequence of activities of an individual on-line consumer. Cookies (small text files deposited on a visitor's computer by a Web server) are the standard means of overcoming this problem. Cookies have been used to deliver multi-page questions to respondents, in which the questions on each page were generated on the basis of responses to the previous page (Parackal and Brennan, 1999).

- *Cost* As the commercialization of the Internet proceeds, it may get more, rather than less, expensive to undertake effective on-line marketing research. Among the costs are: purchasing and updating e-mail address lists; renting banner ads on other peoples' websites to advertise or link to a survey form; and providing incentives to encourage higher response rates.
- *Sensory deprivation* Currently, most communication over the Internet involves text messages. Information broadcasting on the Web also includes graphical images, but voice and video input from users is still relatively rare. Interactions involving haptic (touch-related) and olfactory (smell-related) senses are still in their infancy. These sensory limitations of the Internet place considerable limits on the amount of information that market researchers can obtain from on-line respondents, as they have in conventional mail surveys, and it is a particularly strong constraint on research into affective responses to products and services.

Recognizing Multiple On-line Environments

The Internet is not a single, undifferentiated medium for undertaking marketing research. It hosts a variety of on-line environments—the Web, chat rooms, e-mail, discussion groups, etc.—and people often use these environments for very different purposes. As a marketing researcher, you will need to become familiar with each of these environments, the people who frequent them, and the on-line activities that are common to each. Simply knowing about 'surfers', strictly speaking those who inhabit the Web, will provide only a partial view of the on-line world. It is far more important to think in terms of 'Netizens', an inclusive term that refers to inhabitants of any or all of the Internet's on-line haunts.

In these diverse environments it is possible to undertake various types of marketing research: quantitative and qualitative; exploratory and confirmatory; one-off and longitudinal. Clearly, overlapping membership of these environments is relatively common, and this introduces potential problems for the design of surveys aimed at individual or multiple Internet environments. But such problems are worth solving because of the potential benefits.

Comparing On- and Off-line Marketing Research

Most of the marketing research techniques that evolved during the twentieth century have been adapted for the Internet, so that many on-line techniques differ very little from their off-line counterparts. For example, postal questionnaire surveys have their counterparts in e-mail or Web questionnaires, face-to-face interviews are represented by e-mails and on-line chat, focus groups are carried out on-line using discussion groups, chat or conferencing facilities, and customer panels have their counterparts in e-mail or chat customer panels.

Most of the information collected off-line can also be collected on-line, often with little degradation in response rates and accuracy. An example is the personal or socio-demographic information that is usually requested in questionnaire surveys to help establish the characteristics of the sample. One study (Basi, 1999) indicates that, in a well-designed survey, visitors to a sports website had few qualms in divulging personal information, including their name, sex, age, marital status, e-mail address, and nationality. However, there are some methods of gathering consumer information, and notably website registration forms, that tend to generate poorer-quality data. This suggests the importance of establishing some kind of rapport or common-interest relationship with the intended survey respondents.

Broadly speaking, the kinds of quantitative and qualitative information you can expect to acquire through Internet marketing research are the same as those collected through conventional marketing research. However, the technical limitations of the medium used to interrogate the respondents, together with psychological factors influencing their experience of the research episode, will have a bearing on the amount and type of information that can be gathered. Table 11.1 provides examples of qualitative and quantitative data-collection methods.

Fairly conventional questionnaires can be distributed by e-mail or placed on websites (described below), to gather quantitative and other structured information. However, rich consumer information of a 'softer' variety can also be gathered in certain on-line public environments. For example, observing and/or participating in specialist Internet chat rooms or discussion lists can be extremely revealing about people's preferences and activities. Some information can be picked up directly about particular products or sectors (e.g., from highly specific 'alt' newsgroups), while others are sources of broader consumer attitudes and inclinations. (See the DejaNews archives at groups.google.com for a directory of Internet discussion and news groups.) However, there are ethical issues to be considered when using this form of data gleaning.

There are several other methods of gathering qualitative information over the Internet. One is the moderated e-mail group (MEG). The MEG involves a moderator posting questions by e-mail to a small group of respondents, collating and summarizing their answers, and sending these to the group for comment. The process is repeated several times (Adriaenssens and Cadman, 1999). Another approach is represented by the virtual group interview (O'Connor and Madge, 2000), which has been introduced by academic researchers at the University of Leicester using the 'Hotline Client' conferencing software.

Table 11.1 Quantitative and qualitative data-gathering methods on the Internet

Quantitative data	Qualitative data
E-mail questionnaires	In-depth interviews (e-mail, chat)
Web questionnaires	On-line focus groups (chat, newsgroups)
On-line panels	Message boards, discussion group archives
	On-line mystery shopping

Goodwin (1999) suggests that the overwhelmingly quantitative approach currently adopted by Internet surveys (e.g., through e-mails and Web forms) should be complemented by the collection of 'fluffy' data on visitor attitudes, perceptions and motivations (e.g., through in-depth on-line interviews, on-line focus groups, and trawling through discussion group archives). While numerical measures typically build a profile of (past) consumer actions, Goodwin argues that marketing research should also attempt to understand consumers' anticipated actions, through the collection of suitable qualitative data.

How It's Done: On-line Surveys in Practice

As with conventional surveys, undertaking an on-line survey involves a number of clearly defined activities. Three of the main ones will be discussed here, though the sequence is not necessarily strictly chronological.

1. Finding Potential Respondents

There are two main ways of finding people to respond to an on-line survey. The *controlled sample method* involves recruiting people from a reputable sampling frame, so that the sample results are generalizable. Unfortunately, there are few reputable sampling frames for Internet populations. In some cases, where research is aimed at understanding the on-line users of a particular Web service, a list of registered members can be used as a suitable sampling frame, though this will not say anything about other potential users of the service. Another approach is to use a sampling frame gathered off-line for other uses, which contains e-mail addresses.

Omnibus panels amassed by large opinion and market research agencies usually provide a controlled sample of pre-screened individuals. Harris International has over 3.5 million e-panellists on its books, and some on-line market research agencies (e.g., AC Nielsen and Jupiter MMXI) supply members of on-line panels with automatic monitoring software for their home PCs which periodically transmit data for analysis. (Adriaenssens and Cadman, 1999, provide a MORI example.) The use of panels or precontacted samples is one of the most effective solutions to the sampling problems of uncontrolled, open-access surveys. By giving each member a unique ID number, and requesting this when a survey is being completed, it is possible to check for multiple responses by the same person, to adjust survey quotas, and to weight sample responses. Nevertheless, there is concern about people who sign up to multiple panels.

The *'open to all' method* involves broadcasting e-mails to all and sundry, or posting a questionnaire on a public website (with or without attendant publicity), and accepting responses from all who reply, or inviting members of a discussion group or chat forum to contact the researcher. The problem with this approach is well known from conventional street and magazine surveys: the sample is largely self-selected, and the results are therefore unlikely to be representative of the population at large. A version of this approach is represented by the 'snowball' method of sending an e-mail questionnaire to one person and asking them to forward it to others. See Bradley (1999) for a list of the varied sources from which on-line respondents can be obtained.

2. Getting Respondents to Participate

Once you have identified potential respondents, you have to interest them in participating in your survey. There are two issues here: letting respondents know about your on-line survey, and getting them to complete an on-line survey instrument or attend an on-line focus group.

Publicity is especially important for questionnaires posted on a website, where there is so much competition for surfers' attention. The necessary publicity can be obtained in several ways: publish notices in conventional media (e.g., a newspaper or specialist magazine); send e-mails to members of a sampling frame; place links on other websites; or inform members of chat or discussion or news groups (but be sure there is a clear match between the survey topic and the subject of the forum).

Encouraging participants to complete questionnaires can be approached in several ways: send out prior e-mail invitations (these filter out unwilling respondents); design the survey instrument so it encourages completion (e.g., keep it short, use pop-ups); provide incentives (entry in a prize draw, or on-line credit/tokens); and follow-up non-responders (this can be automated in the case of e-mail surveys). Seeking the permission of respondents to send them a questionnaire can reduce the number of incomplete responses and mischievous answers, and also provides e-mail addresses of respondents that can be contacted again for follow-up study (Witmer, Colman and Katzman, 1998).

3. Choosing and Designing a Survey Instrument

There are four main ways of gathering marketing research information from consumers on-line: e-mail questionnaires, Web questionnaires, public chat and discussion groups, and on-line focus groups. In the following sections we will explore these techniques in more detail, outlining the advantages and disadvantages of each.

E-mail Questionnaires

E-mail is a cheap, simple and speedy survey method, which can return useful 'hard' (i.e., quantitative) information. Respondents often find it more convenient to respond to an e-mail questionnaire than to a postal questionnaire, and many will do so almost immediately. However, there are also drawbacks: e-mail address lists are frequently poor in quality; you cannot include fancy formatting; many recipients will discard even *bona fide* e-mail surveys because of previous experience with junk e-mail (i.e., spam); there are ethical and legal hurdles involved in sending out unsolicited e-mails; and the extraction and validation of responses from returned e-mails can often require considerable manual effort.

You can use e-mail in several ways as a survey instrument:

- Embed questions in the body of an e-mail message;
- Include questions in a document attached to the e-mail message (e.g., Word, PDF or HTML form) which the user is invited to extract and complete; or
- Provide a link in an e-mail message to a survey instrument located elsewhere (e.g., on a website).

A variation on the second method is to send a more complex executable program that delivers a multimedia survey to run on the respondent's PC. The benefits of this are that the program may contain multimedia (video, sound, etc.) which can be used to test reactions to new products. The downside is the longer download time involved, and the problem that potential respondents in the workplace might not be able to receive large attachments—or any kind of attachment—because of security restrictions placed on their e-mail server. Also bear in mind that some e-mail reading software does not always handle attachments successfully, and some recipients may not know how to extract attachments.

Most types of question used in conventional questionnaires can be included in e-mail questionnaires. However, you will need to simplify the e-mail version considerably if it is to work on most users' e-mail readers. In particular, you should avoid long lines, tables, tab settings, text fonts and styles, and colour. This is because individual respondents are likely to use different e-mail reading software, and each will interpret the contents of an e-mail questionnaire in different ways. Some will simply ignore formatting characters, and some will not reproduce characters such as the pound sign or the euro. The best rule is to design for the simplest possible technology, and create a questionnaire that consists of short lines of simple text, and text 'boxes' into which users are invited to type a simple response (see Figure 11.1 for an example section of an e-mail questionnaire). Finally, pay particular attention to the wording of the introductory text of the e-mail, which should explain the purpose of the survey, promise anonymity, and possibly introduce the researchers.

As Internet-enabled mobile phones become more frequently used as a way of accessing e-mail, you will also need to start thinking about how to design e-mail questionnaires that will work within the much tighter display constraints of these devices.

Web Questionnaires

Web questionnaires, like their e-mail counterparts, are used largely to gather quantitative or other structured information. The major advantages of Web questionnaires are: they can be made to resemble a printed questionnaire; multimedia elements can be included; the validity of user's responses can be checked; responses can be extracted into data-processing software; and high-volume surveys can be handled rapidly and inexpensively. At least one major consumer goods manufacturer (Unilever) has said that it sees its consumer websites as more important for the consumer data they yield than for the products they sell.

Q6. Where do you live?
(Enter your postcode between the following square brackets)
[ ]

Q7. How often do you shop at Terry's Diner?
Enter an 'X' between the square brackets alongside your
single answer)
Daily [ ]
Weekly [ ]
Monthly [ ]
Occasionally [ ]
Never [ ]

Q8. What are your main reasons for visiting Terry's Diner?
(Enter an 'X' between the square brackets alongside all
reasons that apply)
Good quality food [ ]
Large portions [ ]
Friendly atmosphere [ ]
Low price [ ]
Open 24 hours a day [ ]
Other [ ]

Q8a. If you have selected 'Other', please describe these
within the following square brackets:
[ ]

Figure 11.1 Example section of an e-mail questionnaire

The main drawback of Web questionnaires is the relatively small proportion of people who use the Web and, if an 'open-to-all' approach is used (described earlier), there is the additional problem of the self-selecting sample. There are also several technical problems. First, if the user's browser window is set to a smaller size (or their screen is set to a lower resolution) than that used to design the Web form, its carefully designed layout may be rendered ineffective. Second, if cookies are used as the mechanism for delivering multi-page questionnaires (for an example see Parackal and Brennan, 1999), these may not work if cookies have been switched off by the user.

Third, there may be problems checking the validity of user responses to individual questions—e.g., the user's browser may be too old to support the version of the scripting language used in the Web form to undertake the checking. Finally, if a script is needed on the Web server to process the data returned from the respondent, this will only be possible if the Web host (e.g., a commercial ISP) allows them.

The Web can be used in a number of ways to deliver survey instruments:

- Include questions in a Web document (e.g., at the end of an information-giving page).
- Include questions in a separate document, and invite the user to visit this page (e.g., by a banner or button on an information page or by an e-mail message).
- Present questions in a pop-up questionnaire (see Figure 11.2) that is triggered by some kind of visitor behaviour (e.g., time of day, the navigation behaviour of an individual visitor, the e-mail address of groups of visitors, aggregate visitor traffic levels, etc.). Cookies can be used to ensure that the same questionnaire is not displayed to the same person more than once. Early research evidence

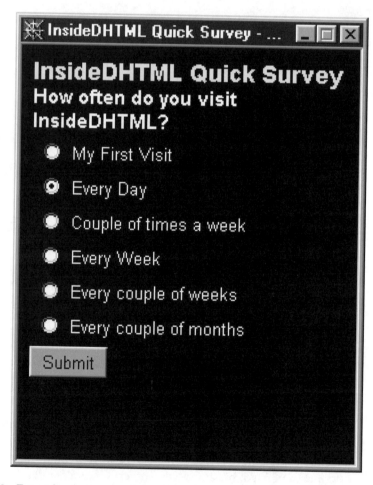

Figure 11.2 Example of a 'pop-up' questionnaire

Source: http://www.SiteExperts.com, Copyright © 1997–2001 InsideDHTML.com, LCC. All rights reserved.

suggests that pop-ups are good at attracting visitor attention, though how long this will last is open to question. (Within Web questionnaires, pop-up prompt cards can be used as convenient substitutes for the printed equivalents (Parackal and Brennan, 1999).)

As with e-mail questionnaires, it is best to keep Web questionnaires simple: avoid scrolling (this leads to reduced response rates); avoid switching between mouse and keyboard entry; and use clear wording and layout. Web questionnaires can be designed in-house and posted on the researcher's own website, or else developed using Web survey design services on third-party commercial sites (an illustrative example is the INWEB service at www.infocorp.co.uk/inweb.htm). Some sites (e.g., SurveyAnywhere.com) provide a free service. Some research or placement students have been able to run a large-scale Web survey on a commercial website as part of their studies.

Finally, there are benefits to be gained from combining e-mail and the Web, along with other conventional survey methods. For example:

- Use an off-line sampling frame (e.g., a market research company's omnibus survey panel) as a controlled source of e-mail addresses, and send e-mail questions to them.
- Use an on-line sampling frame (e.g., registered members of a Web service) to identify respondents to whom printed questionnaires are mailed.
- Announce a survey on relevant discussion lists and/or chat forums, and send an e-mail survey to those indicating their willingness to participate.
- Distribute e-mail invitations requesting participation in a survey, and send consenting respondents the URL of the location of the survey form on the Web (this reduces the likelihood that e-mail recipients will see your e-mail as a form of spamming, particularly those culled from discussion groups), together with a password to access it (this prevents casual surfers from completing the questionnaire, and thus allows you some control over the characteristics of the sample).

Public Chat and Discussion Groups

On-line venues for discussion and chat are an important source of information on the latest ideas and attitudes of Netizens, and are excellent sources for gathering 'soft' data. You can use them in two main ways:

- *Non-participant observation* Most chat forums and discussion groups permit non-registered users to listen in on conversations by members (known as 'lurking'). This can be a fruitful activity at the early stages of an investigation, particularly if you choose groups carefully in relation to your research subject. However, this form of research can be extremely time-consuming, particularly if you decide to trawl through discussion archives (where these are available). The main problem is the low signal-to-noise ratio in the exchanges you are likely to encounter—i.e., the nuggets are often few and far between.

● *Participant observation* If you register with a chat forum or discussion group, then you can join in with on-going discussions. If you are careful to keep within the boundaries of the subject matter of the group you have joined, and pose questions in a non-survey manner, then you may be able to elicit useful responses from other members. However, be wary of 'pumping' members with a succession of questions on your research topic, or you risk getting 'flamed'—i.e., bombarded with negative messages questioning your motives for being in the group, and maybe other things besides!

On-line Focus Groups

One of the best-known methods of gathering unstructured, qualitative information is the focus group (see Chapter 4). There has been considerable success in transferring focus groups into the on-line environment, where they are used for a variety of exploratory investigations—e.g., to evaluate the performance of existing products or services; to brainstorm new ideas; to test new products and services; and to pilot conventional surveys. Box 11.1 summarizes the advantages of on-line focus groups; the disadvantages are summarized in Box 11.2.

Box 11.1 Advantages of on-line focus groups

● Virtually eliminate the time and cost of participation in face-to-face focus group meetings.
● Participants can be drawn from a much wider geographical area (national, international or global) than face-to-face groups—this is valuable in cases where the target respondents belong to a low penetration group, and a viable group size cannot be drawn simply from a local area (e.g., Adriaenssens and Cadman, 1999); and it permits participation by a wider cultural or national range of participants, which is useful in cross-cultural research.
● Useful where the culture of participants might suppress open expression of opinions (Tse, 1999).
● Encourage all participants to have their say, unlike face-to-face focus groups in which a dominant individual can hog the discussion.
● Relatively easy for moderator to apply sanctions on domineering participants (e.g., temporarily silence their input).
● Often encourage more explicit statement of views and opinions by participants.
● Encourage greater participation by group members, particularly when sensitive or personal topics are being discussed.
● Enable participation by 'backroom' experts, supporting either moderator or clients.
● Permit extended discussion over several days or even weeks.
● Provide a digital transcript as soon as the group discussions are completed—there is no need for laborious transcription of handwritten scribbles or listening to a semi-audible tape recording.

Box 11.2   Disadvantages of on-line focus groups

- There may be problems in recruiting suitable on-line participants (representative samples are hard to achieve, and a greater number of registrants fail to 'show up').
- Participant contributions may depend on their typing ability.
- The unusual group dynamics and interaction procedures may be offputting to many participants.
- It can be difficult to gather attitudes based on the feel or smell of new products.
- The moderator can find it difficult to deal with affective issues or to use participants' body language to steer interactions.
- The participants may have to pay for the Internet connection—though this cost can be reimbursed by the market researcher.

It is possible to use standard Internet software (e.g., e-mail, peer-to-peer chat, or threaded discussion group facilities) to run on-line focus groups, though proprietary products such as Cyberqual (from Michel Herbert and Associates in the UK) are also available.

Problems with On-line Surveys

Many of the problems of carrying out marketing research on the Internet are common to conventional marketing research. Those problems that are more likely to be associated with Internet surveys are summarized below.

- *Lack of universal access to the Internet*   Recent figures (e.g., Nua, 2001) suggest that less than 20% of the world's population currently has access to the Internet, and most of these are concentrated in the countries of the developed world. Within particular countries, there is also an in-built bias towards early Internet adopters.
- *Poor on-line sampling frames*   There is no global list of e-mail addresses, so on-line surveys have to make do with alternatives, such as: conventional sampling frames (e.g., printed directories or member lists); Internet-based lists (e.g., website visitors and e-mail address lists); and newsgroups (Witmer, Colman and Katzman, 1998). Automatically harvested lists of e-mail addresses (e.g., from newsgroups) often contain a high proportion of out-of-date or spurious addresses. Even where correct e-mail addresses are available, other problems still reduce their effectiveness as a sampling frame: the growing number of people who have multiple e-mail addresses; people who change their e-mail addresses (e.g., switching from one ISP to another to benefit from low-cost start-up offers); users who fail to check their e-mail regularly; and many consumers belong to a number of different on-line environments.
- *Sampling problems*   Even within countries that have a relatively large on-line population, sampling is made difficult because of biases in the characteristics of people who currently have Internet access—until recently, early Internet adopters in the USA and the UK were white, male, aged 18–59, of above-

average socio-economic and educational status, and either white-collar or professional workers (Schmidt, 1997). This makes it difficult to extrapolate Internet survey findings to the entire population.

It is possible to adjust sampling methods to account for this kind of bias. For example, the demographic profile of early Internet adopters tends to be different from the population at large. Knowing the demographic profile of this group, various steps can be taken to counter this bias: adjust samples to include more laggards; sift responses to weed out those from ineligible groups (Farmer, 1998); weight results to boost the results for under-represented sub-populations; or combine online surveys with conventional surveys that have biases in the opposite direction (McDonald and Wilson, 1999).

The 'open-to-all' Web survey suffers from the same lack of sample knowledge that affects the use of self-completion mail cards inserted in magazines or left on aeroplanes. However, it is not just differential access to the Internet that poses sampling problems and problems of sample representativeness. Bradley (1999) makes the important point that the capabilities of the hardware and software that people use to access the Internet (e.g., PC, TV, Internet-enabled phone) also need to be taken into account, as do the different levels of user capability in relation to the Internet (e.g., do they know how to extract an e-mail attachment?), and user behaviour in the on-line environment (e.g., frequency, time and place of access). These all affect whether a survey instrument will get through to an individual, and thus the structure of the on-line sample. Because these additional factors are still not well understood, this makes it difficult to draw properly constituted samples from on-line populations. Because of this problem, some restrict on-line research to on-line populations, such as visitors to a website, members of an on-line forum, or members of a business extranet.

- *Response rate problems* If a sampling frame is unavailable, then it is difficult to estimate the on-line survey response rate, and to ascertain whether a sample quota has been achieved. Although Internet surveys can obtain equally good response rates as conventional surveys, very low response rates (in the 1–5% range) are not uncommon, even in well-designed and highly targeted surveys (e.g., Basi, 1999). Poor response rates in on-line surveys can be due to several reasons: bad vibes caused by spamming; fears over security and lack of anonymity; and survey fatigue.
- *Data quality issues* The value of data gathered on-line can be compromised by unreliable responses (e.g., users entering spurious details on website registration forms), and lack of geographical specificity (i.e., not knowing where e-mail or Web respondents live).
- *Ethical issues* Internet marketing research shares many of the ethical problems that surround various forms of conventional survey and observational research (see Chapter 1). However, the Internet has thrown up additional problems, the chief of which is the lack of anonymity of e-mail, the selling on of people's e-mail addresses and personal information, and the dangers of data integration (i.e., the collation, integration or fusion of disparate sources of individual data gathered over the Internet).

ESOMAR, the European Association of Research Professionals, has drawn up guidelines on best practice in conducting marketing and opinion research on the Internet (ESOMAR, 1999). These are strongly weighted in favour of the survey respondent, and cover such issues as survey participation, anonymity, data transmission security and intrusion. For the survey user, it also suggests guidelines to prevent misleading people about the reliability and validity of Internet research findings. As a result of recent legislation in the European Community, the majority of on-line research carried out in a few years' time is likely to involve using people who have 'opted in'.

When to Use—and Not to Use—On-line Marketing Research

'Horses for courses' is still the best principle to adopt when choosing between Internet-based or traditional marketing survey methods. Sometimes the on-line version works better than the traditional method (see Mehta and Sivadas, 1995, for a comparison of e-mail with conventional mail, and Weible and Wallace, 2001, for a comparison of mail, fax, e-mail and Web). Typically, however, there is a mix of advantages and disadvantages (Tse, 1999, reviews these for on-line focus groups).

There are several situations where the Internet is a good choice:

- To survey people in distant areas/countries, or dispersed common interest populations (e.g., O'Lear, 1996).
- To investigate sensitive subjects. There is some evidence, for example, that consumers enjoy the perceived anonymity that Web shopping brings, not only to the obvious acquisition of porn but also to car buying and medical diagnosis. In face-to-face encounters, there is always the possibility that some consumers will feel ashamed or embarrassed, and the same feelings may apply when they are polled for their views. The mediating influence of an Internet encounter can reduce or eliminate these potentially negative feelings.
- For studying people who are early technology adopters or regular Internet users (e.g., academics or young people)—i.e., those who are *au fait* with the technology, and who are more likely to respond to on-line questions.
- To study people's on-line activities—e.g., their use of websites.

There are also circumstances where it is probably inadvisable to use the Internet. The Internet is probably not the best choice when it is necessary to draw a representative sample of people whose characteristics, behaviour and attitudes need to be extrapolated to the population at large. Another situation is where it is important to involve naturalistic (i.e., non-mediated) interaction—e.g., where the observation of an individual's body language or of interpersonal reactions is significant. Finally, the Internet may not be effective where respondents need to have physical contact with a product that is being evaluated.

The Past, Present and Future of Internet Marketing Research

Over the past half century, the marketing research industry has gone through a number of technology adoption phases. Indeed, it is possible to define a 'technology cycle' in marketing research. When a new medium becomes available for carrying out research, it is initially used only on a limited scale because of its low penetration. However, as its adoption rate increases, and early adoption makes way to near-universal use, the technology can be used routinely for surveying the majority of the population. Over time, however, overuse and misuse of the medium lead to decreasing response rates, as survey fatigue sets in among respondents, and the industry is ripe for another innovation. This cycle can be seen in the use of mail, telephone, fax, computer, interactive TV, e-mail and the Internet.

It is early days yet for Internet marketing research. However, as more and more people live, work, shop and socialize on-line, it will become increasingly important as a source of information about people's off- and on-line lives. Integration of the Internet with other survey technologies is being actively explored. For example, researchers at Brigham Young University have added a live telephone interviewer (or 'eInterviewer) to the Web survey process (Feld and Wygant, 2000), resulting in dramatically improved completion rates. Voice-over-IP (VOIP) already makes it possible to carry out spoken interviews over the Internet, supplemented by visual interaction where both parties have a webcam. However, the downside is that this reintroduces the need for transcribing the spoken responses, or at best cleaning up the output from voice-recognition software.

Other competing on-line channels—including direct response TV (DRTV), interactive television (iTV) and wireless telephony (cellular or satellite phones)—are rapidly achieving high rates of consumer penetration, and will need to be considered for routine marketing research purposes. In some respects, these information channels share the same characteristics as the Internet, but in others they are significantly different.

One group of innovations that is likely to reduce the differences between off- and on-line research is the combination of multimedia and virtual reality (e.g., Needel, 1995, 1996; Urban et al. 1997). If subjects can manipulate the size, colour, design, price and other characteristics of a product on-line (e.g., a pair of shoes or a car), then the range of options for online marketing research are considerably extended. One of the more intriguing prospects is the ability to deliver smells at the PC, where the user is quizzed about the odour-response to certain products, ranging from foods and perfumes to toiletries and confectionery. This is not so far-fetched as it might seem; at least one Internet start-up (www.digiscents.com) has already developed the necessary desktop technology.

The telephone, computer and the Internet are being integrated in new ways through the introduction of Net-enabled mobile phones. When this bundle is linked to mobile, location-based services (perhaps through satellite link-ups), then this will bring closer the era of instant, intelligent interrogation of consumers about anything and everything they experience, wherever and whenever they may be. Imagine being able to ring someone automatically on their mobile phone as they walk past your shop to ask them what they think about your window display and its special offers. Or imagine monitoring a viewer's responses to products 'placed' in an interactive TV show.

Conclusion

The Internet represents both continuity and innovation in marketing research. Although it brings considerable new opportunities to market researchers, it is not without its problems and challenges. Some of these are technical, others are ethical, and yet others are political. With less than a decade of solid experience behind it, Internet marketing research is still in its infancy. Although it is now relatively clear how to use the medium to investigate Internet users, it is still not quite so clear how it can be used to research off-line activities.

Perhaps the single greatest challenge of the Internet lies in the way that it promises to break down the artificial barriers that currently exist between marketing research and most of the other activities involved in marketing. The Internet provides an opportunity to close the loop, not only between data gathering and data reporting but also between marketing research and selling, and even between marketing research and the product or service design process. As Goodwin (1999: 404) puts it: 'Unlike traditional media, the Internet encompasses the entire "sales" process.' Therefore on-line advertising can be (and is being) integrated with all the other processes of selling, and is becoming an essential element of the broader technology of customer relationship management (CRM).

For on-line marketing, research need no longer be an episodic and expensive activity, involving teams of interviewers descending on people with clipboards or tape recorders in hand. Rather, it can take place frequently, wherever crucial consumer views are required. The Internet can also close the loop between survey research and reporting. Where Web questionnaires are used, for example, it is possible to post interim results back on the Web or deliver them to sponsors in real time, though the co-existence of interim results and a live questionnaire (as in the currently popular website polls) raises all kinds of methodological issues.

Does the Internet represent a new era in marketing research or a false dawn? We have described some of the newer approaches that have been devised to take advantage of the particular characteristics of the world's new on-line environment, but many traditional marketing research activities have also been transferred onto or adapted for the Internet. Since most technological revolutions tend to be absorbed into the social and professional mainstream without causing radical upheavals to existing practice, how likely is it that the Internet will modify rather than revolutionize marketing research? We will leave you to ponder this as an open question.

References

Adriaenssens, C. and Cadman, L. (1999). 'An adaptation of moderated e-mail focus groups to assess the potential for a new online (Internet) financial services offer in the UK', *Journal of the Market Research Society*, **41**(4), 417–424.

Basi, R.K. (1999). 'WWW response rates to socio-demographic items', *Journal of the Market Research Society*, **41**(4), 397–401.

Bradley, N. (1999). 'Sampling for Internet surveys: an examination of respondent selection for Internet research', *Journal of the Market Research Society*, **41**(4), 387–395.

ESOMAR (1999). 'ESOMAR guideline: conducting marketing and opinion research using the Internet', *Journal of the Market Research Society*, **41**(4), 439–441.

Farmer, T. (1998). 'Using the Internet for primary research data collection'. http://www.researchinfo.com/library/infotek/index.shtml (February 2001).

Feld, K.G. and Wygant, S. (2000). 'The impact of eInterviewers on Web-based survey research' (Abstract), http://www.asc.org.uk/Events/Sep00/feld_abstract.htm (19 September 2001).

Goodwin, T. (1999). 'Measuring the effectiveness of online marketing', *Journal of the Market Research Society*, **41**(4), 403–406.

Graphics Visualization Unit (GVU) (1998). 'GVU's WWW User Surveys', http://www.cc.gatech.edu/gvu/user_surveys/ (19 September 2001).

Kottler, R.E. (1997). 'Exploiting the research potential of the World Wide Web', http://ukweb.quantime.co.uk/son/r97a.htm (19 September 2001).

Kumar, V., Aaker, D.A. and Day, G.S. (1999). *Essentials of Marketing Research*, Chichester: John Wiley.

Lescher, J.F. (1995). *Online Market Research: Cost-Effective Searching of the Internet and Online Databases*, Harlow: Addison-Wesley Longman.

McDonald, M. and Wilson, H. (1999). *eMarketing: Improving Marketing Effectiveness in a Digital World*, London: Prentice-Hall.

Mehta, R. and Sivadas, E. (1995). 'Comparing response rates and response content in mail versus electronic mail surveys', *Journal of the Market Research Society*, **37**(4), 429–439.

Needel, S.P. (1995). 'Marrying marketing research and virtual reality: implications for consumer research', http://www.simulationresearch.com/papers/paper1.htm (19 September 2001).

Needel, S.P. (1996). 'Virtual reality and consumer research: the future is here today', http://www.simulationresearch.com/papers/paper2.htm (19 September 2001).

Nua (2001). 'How many online?', http://www.nua.com/surveys/how_many_online/index.html (19 September 2001).

O'Connor, H. and Madge, C. (2000). 'When it's face to face it's harder: online group interviewing' (Abstract), http://www.asc.org.uk/Events/Sep00/oconnor_abstract.htm (19 September 2001).

O'Lear, S.R.M. (1996). 'Using electronic mail (E-mail) surveys for geographic research', *Professional Geographer*, **48**(2), 209–217.

Parackal, M. and Brennan, M. (1999). 'Obtaining purchase probabilities via a Web based survey: some corrections!', *Marketing Bulletin*, **10**, 93–101.

Ross, E. (2001). 'Market research and the Worldwide Web', http://ukweb.quantime.co.uk/son/esrweb.htm (19 September 2001).

Schmidt, W.C. (1997). 'World Wide Web survey research: benefits, potential problems, and solutions', *Behaviour Research Methods, Instruments, and Computers*, **29**, 274–279.

Tse, A.C.B. (1999). 'Conducting electronic focus group discussions among Chinese respondents', *Journal of Marketing Research*, **34**(1), 407–415.

Urban, G.L., Hauser, J.R., Qualls, W.J. and Weinberg, B.D. (1997). 'Information acceleration: validation and lessons from the field', *Journal of Marketing Research*, **34**(1), 143–153.

Weible, R. and Wallace, J. (2001). 'The impact of the Internet on data collection', in P. Richardson (ed.), *Internet Marketing*, New York: McGraw-Hill, 274–283.

Witmer, D.F., Colman, R.W. and Katzman, S.L. (1998). 'From paper-and-pencil to screen-and-keyboard', in S. Jones (ed.), *Doing Internet Research: Critical Issues and Methods for Examining the Net*, Thousand Oaks, CA: Sage, 145–161.

Work Assignments

1. Design and send a simple e-mail questionnaire to identify the on-line shopping habits of your circle of friends and/or acquaintances.

2. Alternative Internet access devices are appearing all the time, including: games consoles, personal digital assistants (PDAs), third-generation mobile phones, kiosks, and interactive TV. Investigate how the display and interaction technology adopted by each of these channels are likely to impact on how you design a marketing research survey aimed at identifying the on-line shopping habits of consumers.

3. Search the Web to find examples of form-based questionnaires. Draw up a list of ways in which these are similar to, and different from, conventional questionnaires, and record your own assessment of their individual strengths and weaknesses.

4. From sources available on the Web, identify the likely response rates you can expect from e-mail and Web questionnaires. How do these compare to response rates for conventional (i.e., off-line) surveys?

5. Research the Web, and find out how attitudes and legislation on the control of unsolicited electronic communication varies between countries. How is this likely to affect the undertaking of on-line marketing research on an international basis?

Business-to-business Markets and Marketing Research

12

Learning Outcomes

After reading this chapter, you will be able to:

- Understand the key differences between business-to-business markets and consumer markets.
- Know how those differences affect the practice of marketing research.
- Use the standard industrial classification system to define a market and specify a research sample.
- Prepare an industry sector profile using secondary data sources.
- Know what techniques are likely to provide the highest response rates for business-to-business market surveys.

Introduction

This chapter focuses on situations in which market research is conducted on markets comprising organizations (e.g., industrial firms, commercial firms, governmental organizations) rather than consumers. It looks at the particular circumstances and problems associated with doing research into business-to-business markets. Consumer marketing, and consumer goods marketing in particular, is the most visible form of marketing in modern economies. That is because there are many millions of consumers, often buying a homogeneous product, and it makes economic sense to communicate with as many of them as possible at the same time—often through the medium of television. Everybody fits into myriad different target markets, and therefore is the recipient of multiple different consumer marketing messages. On the other hand, most people are very unfamiliar with business-to-business marketing. That is because business-to-business markets usually have few buyers, who can be reached economically through precision marketing campaigns, and who respond to highly technical messages. Most of us would neither understand nor care if we were to see a poster extolling the virtues of a new filtration system that reduces the energy required to manufacture cattle feed by 6.3%. That is why nobody wastes their money on such posters, and why we remain largely ignorant of business-to-business marketing. But business-to-business marketing is big business, and the evidence suggests that the top-performing firms make greater use of marketing research than the rest (Hooley and Jobber, 1986).

To begin the chapter there is a discussion of the differences between business-to-business markets and consumer markets, to understand what leads to differences in market research practice. Having understood these fundamental differences, there follows a discussion of the business-to-business marketing research process. The chapter concludes with a discussion of the management of the relationship between the client (the buyer of research) and the market research agency in business-to-business markets.

What Makes Business-to-business Marketing Research Different?

Differences between Business-to-business and Consumer Marketing

Business-to-business marketing is concerned with the marketing of products and services from one organization to another. It is not the nature of the product or service that identifies business-to-business, it is the nature of the customer. The customer is an organization, with organizational goals. When organizations buy goods and services, they do so to pursue organizational objectives, not to derive pleasure or personal satisfaction from using the product. Business-to-business marketing is the process of trying to match our own products and services to the organizational goals of our target customers. This fundamental difference makes business-to-business marketing different from consumer marketing. Gross *et al.* (1993) provide a list of 58 differences between business-to-business and consumer marketing. However, most of these differences are at the level of marketing tactics—for example, the promotional emphasis in business-to-business marketing is on personal selling, to be contrasted with mass advertising in consumer markets. Such tactical differences between business-to-business and consumer marketing can be traced back to the underlying differences between business and consumer markets shown in Table 12.1. It is these differences that affect the conduct of marketing research.

The demand from businesses for products and services is derived from that for their own products and services (hence 'derived demand'). Organizational buying

Table 12.1 What differentiates business-to-business markets?

Characteristic	Business market	Consumer market
Nature of demand	Derived	Direct
Size of buying unit	Group	Individual or family
Market geography	Concentrated	Dispersed
Demand concentration	High	Low
Purchasing motives	Organizational, rational	Personal, self-gratifying
Purchasing decision process	Often complex and lengthy	Often short
Purchasing skills	Professional, trained	Untrained

decisions are usually made by a group of skilled employees, each of whom brings professional expertise to the buying decision. A key area of professional expertise is the specialist skill of the purchasing professional—who will often be a member of a professional body (in the UK, this is the Chartered Institute of Purchasing and Supply). Organizational buyers make their buying decision on the basis of the evidence of which supplier can best help the organization to meet its goals, and this can often involve a complex decision process comparing supplier capabilities against organizational need. Demand in business markets is often more concentrated geographically than consumer demand, because firms in the same industry sector are frequently found in geographical clusters. Finally, demand in business markets is concentrated in the hands of fewer buyers than in consumer markets. There are comparatively few firms in the UK that would want to buy a backhoe loader, for example. Yet a few of these businesses, such as the major construction firms, will buy a large number of industrial diggers.

The differences between consumer and business-to-business marketing research can largely be traced to these differences in market structure and buying behaviour. All these differences between consumer and business markets have implications for the marketing research process, which will be explored in the rest of this chapter.

The Implications for Marketing Research

Secondary market research is used in all areas of marketing, but is particularly important in business-to-business markets. One reason is cost. Secondary research is relatively inexpensive, and marketing budgets are usually less generous in business-to-business marketing than in consumer marketing. Furthermore, since demand in business-to-business markets is derived, it is necessary to study markets beyond the immediate customer market. The marketer must know something about what is happening in the customer's market, and perhaps even in the market of the customer's customer. This is best explained by an example.

In marketing instant coffee to consumers, one must try to understand why it is that they buy coffee and how their tastes may change. In marketing component parts to a manufacturer of industrial diggers, one must look beyond the immediate customer (e.g., a construction firm) to the customer's customers. These might include the government (e.g., road building), commercial firms (e.g., offices and industrial facilities), and private individuals (e.g., house building). This makes the marketing research problem much more complicated, and means that secondary sources must play a greater part. It would be much too expensive to research all these downstream markets using primary research.

Another reason for the emphasis on secondary research in business-to-business marketing is the wide availability of excellent information sources at various levels of detail—from the level of an entire economy, down to that of an industrial sector, a sub-division of an industry, or a single firm. Governments are very interested in gathering data on business activity, and much broad information on industry trends can be found in government sources (e.g., the *Annual Abstract of Statistics*, the *Monthly Digest of Statistics*, *Economic Trends*, and the *Business Monitor* series of publications). For most industries there is an industry association to serve the interests of the firms in that industry (see the *Directory of British Associations* in Appendix I), which collects data on key trends in the industry. At the level of individual firms, commercial information providers such as Reed Information Services and Dun & Bradstreet publish directories containing information on such things as ownership structure, principal lines of business, and key personnel (e.g., *Key British Enterprises, Who Owns Whom, Kelly's, Kompass*—see Appendix I). Firms are keen to be included in such directories, since their primary purpose is as a source of reference for potential buyers. Marketing researchers benefit from the wide availability of accurate and current information. Directories can provide a quick and accurate method of identifying firms that lie within a target market, together with details of their product range and key management personnel.

The nature of business-to-business markets also has implications for the conduct of primary market research projects (Cox and Dominguez, 1979). The organizational buying process often involves group decision making, and can be lengthy and complex. So, in addition to using standard questionnaire techniques to gather descriptive data on the market, business-to-business market researchers often employ in-depth, qualitative interviews with key informants. The key informant is regarded as an expert in a particular field, who is able to provide inside information on the way in which buying decisions are made. He or she can help to identify who is directly involved in the buying process, who else is influential, what decision criteria are applied to select a supplier, and who is the ultimate decision maker.

Conventional market research surveys are also used in business-to-business marketing. The principal factor that differentiates a business-to-business survey from a consumer market survey is the sampling procedure. In a consumer survey the objective is normally to obtain a representative sample from the population of interest. Often quota sampling (a non-random method) or stratified random sampling is used to achieve this. There is no reason to suppose that any single consumer is more important than any other in the sampling process. However, in business markets it is almost always the case that there are a vital few organizations which control a large share of any given market (demand concentration, see Table 12.1). For example, there may be 2000 firms in the target industry, of which the top ten control 75% of the output. Those top ten firms also represent around 75% of the market potential for a firm trying to sell goods or services to the industry. If a *random* sample of 200 firms was chosen from the industry, it is quite possible that none of the top ten firms would be included in it. In practice, therefore, it would be usual to include the 'top few' firms automatically in the sample, and then to take a stratified random sample from the remaining firms in the industry. What is meant by the 'top few' firms depends upon the industry. Car manufacturing is a highly concentrated industry, and the 'top few' might be only four or five firms. Clothing manufacturing is a much less concentrated industry, and the 'top few' might be as many as fifteen or twenty firms.

One further aspect of the concentration of demand in business markets has practical implications for marketing researchers. Many different firms wish to gather data on only a few key target industry sectors—particularly fast-growing sectors like telecommunications, information technology and pharmaceuticals. Each of those sectors is dominated by a few very large firms. Not surprisingly, the 'key informants' in those firms receive many invitations to participate in market research studies. This means that response rates to business-to-business marketing surveys can be very low, an issue that will be discussed in more detail later in the chapter.

The Process of Business-to-business Marketing Research

The Marketing Research Process

Chisnall (1995) has put forward a five-step model of the marketing research process, which applies irrespective of the nature of the market. This process is organization-oriented in that it considers the first two stages of the process outlined in Chapter 2 from the organization's perspective. Thus, problem definition is considered in the research brief stage and deciding the research plan is considered in the research proposal stage. Those five steps are:

1. Research brief
2. Research proposal
3. Data collection
4. Data analysis and evaluation
5. Preparation and presentation of the research report.

Most experts would agree that it is critically important to get things right at the beginning of the process, however, both market researchers and their clients tend to be impatient, wanting to move as quickly as possible to data collection and analysis. Penn (1978) looked at this issue, and focused on the process of problem formulation in industrial marketing research. Problem formulation is at the heart of the first step—research brief—of Chisnall's five-step model. Penn further sub-divided the problem-formulation process into six steps, beginning with in-depth discussion of the problem between all interested parties, and culminating in the submission of the written project proposal (Chisnall's step 2). The work of these authors, and others, confirms that a sound market research project can only be built upon the solid foundations of a carefully honed understanding of the research problem. A key element of understanding the problem, in a business-to-business marketing research project, is to have a clear and unambiguous definition of the industry that is to be investigated. For this and other reasons, the standard industrial classification system is of particular use to business-to-business marketing researchers.

Industry Definition and the Standard Industrial Classification

For most everyday purposes it is perfectly acceptable to talk about 'the car industry' or 'the chemical industry'. In a normal conversation we do not normally need to be any more specific than that. However, it is certainly not good enough for market research purposes. If a client asks a researcher to study the growth rate of the car industry, and to profile the key firms in the industry, then the researcher will immediately set about refining the definition of the industry. 'So, when you say the car industry, do you just mean manufacturers of automobiles, or would you include such things as trucks and buses ... what about construction equipment like backhoe diggers? Is it only the vehicle manufacturers that are of interest, or are you interested in the suppliers of automotive components as well, like exhaust systems, instrument clusters and tyres? Would you say that car repair firms should be included, or not?' And so might the conversation continue. The answers to these questions will depend upon exactly what it is that the client is trying to find out. If the objective is to establish the potential of the UK original equipment market for fuel injection systems for use in passenger cars, then the car industry will be defined quite narrowly as those very few firms that actually assemble passenger cars in the UK. But fuel injection systems can also be sold to firms supplying engines to car manufacturers, and to car repair shops operating in the after-sales market. So the definition of the industry or industry sector is a matter of fundamental importance to the success of a business-to-business marketing research project. If we do not have a clear and agreed industry definition, then we could end up wasting time and energy researching things that are of no interest. Worse, we could end up *not* researching something that is regarded as central to a targeted marketing strategy.

In order to ensure a common understanding of industry definition, a rigorous classification of industries, sectors and sub-sectors is required. Conveniently, governments—in order to measure the output and growth of the economy—have put in place such a system, the *standard industrial classification*. Marketing researchers can make use of this system, first, to ensure that industry sectors are defined rigorously, second, to build lists of similar firms for purposes of primary market research. Although there are several standard industrial classification systems in use throughout the world, there is a fairly high degree of common ground between them. The British standard industrial classification (UK SIC) is, for all practical purposes, identical to the equivalent NACE system devised by the European Union. Both of these systems are identical to the International Standard Industrial Classification of the United Nations (ISIC) at the two-digit level. In North America, the old United States Standard Industrial Classification (US SIC) has now been officially replaced by the North American Industrial Classification System (NAICS), which is used throughout the USA, Canada and Mexico.

The principle behind any standard industrial classification system is to put every form of economic activity into a unique numeric (or alphanumeric) category. A SIC starts with a single letter or digit, which divides an economy into broad industry categories. Each successive digit in the classification then sub-divides that industry into smaller and smaller industry sectors and sub-sectors. Take, for example, the NAICS. Categories 31 to 33 denote manufacturing industries. Category 334 is 'computer and electronic product manufacturing', a sub-division of the manufacturing industry, while category 3346 is 'manufacturing and reproduction of magnetic and optical media', a further sub-division. The NAICS is a six-digit classification system, so that this process of successively dividing up larger units into their component parts continues until the sixth digit is reached (for example, 334611 indicates 'reproduction of software').

For business-to-business marketing researchers, standard industrial classification systems are useful for two key purposes, first, to make an unambiguous definition of an industry or industry sector, and, second, as a means of specifying a sampling frame from which a sample will be drawn for purposes of primary data gathering. Commercial information providers, such as Dun & Bradstreet and Reed Information Services, will provide either hard copy or electronic lists of firms within a specified range of SIC codes. Of course, in addition to marketing research, such lists are very commonly used for purposes of business-to-business direct mail campaigns.

Secondary Research: Compiling an Industry Profile

One of the most characteristic tasks in business-to-business marketing research is the production of an industry sector profile. This is a substantial piece of secondary market research, which will be of direct managerial use in itself, and which may also lead to more detailed investigation of opportunities through follow-up primary research. Usually such sector profiles are produced in-house, rather than by a commercial research agency. The object of the exercise is to provide an objective and current picture of one of the company's key target industry sectors. This can be used as a first step in the strategic marketing process of segmentation, targeting and positioning, and can be used to brief people within the company (particularly the sales force) on current market and company trends. While such industry profiles can vary greatly in terms of scale and scope, there are five components that can be regarded as the core of a sound industry sector profile—industry definition, sector size and concentration, growth rate, key firms analysis, and environmental trends.

Some of the important questions associated with these five elements are presented in Box 12.1.

Box 12.1   Key questions for an industry sector profile

The following are not meant to be exhaustive, rather, indicative of the type of question to be asked when conducting an industry sector analysis based on secondary sources. It is also important to remember one of the key defining characteristics of business-to-business marketing, namely, derived demand. In studying the prospects for an industry sector, one must be alert to downstream influences that might—sooner or later—affect the sector itself.

1. *Define the industry sector*   How do we put boundaries on the sector? How do we know which firms to include and which to exclude? How is your sector defined in terms of standard industrial classification (SIC) headings? What are the important sub-sectors?

2. *Sector size and concentration*   Consider the various ways in which the size of an industry can be defined, examples are the number of firms, aggregate turnover of firms in the sector, employee numbers, output of the sector measured in production units (e.g., litres, kilos). How concentrated is production in the industry? In other words, to what extent is output concentrated in the hands of a small group of producers? What percentage of output is contributed by the top five firms? Which are the 'important few' firms?

3. *Growth rate and sector size projections*   You would normally expect to produce a projection of the future growth rate of the sector over the next five years. Sometimes you may be fortunate enough to find a recent and reliable forecast produced by another analyst. Otherwise you will have to do your own. To do this you could

   (i)   extrapolate from past sales or output trends in the industry
   (ii) compare output trends with overall economic growth, and base your projection on published predictions of future economic growth (usually measured by Gross Domestic Product, GDP)
   (iii) examine the prospects for the industries to which this sector sells its output.

   In practice, it is wise to consider all three of these alternatives, to compare and contrast the predictions from them. Simple extrapolation is all very well, but would past trends continue if there was a general economic recession? And basing your forecast on overall economic growth trends might work, but what if there is major downturn in a key customer sector? For example, in 1998/99 the service sector of the UK economy was growing steadily, but the manufacturing sector was experiencing difficulties—it matters whether your customers are service businesses or manufacturers.

4. *Which are the key firms in the sector?*   For, let us say, the 'top five' firms, you would expect to find in an industry sector profile the following kind of information: ownership structure (immediate and ultimate owners); size, growth, financial viability; market share; strengths and weaknesses; some indication of their strategic priorities.

5. *Key environmental trends*   How is technology developing in the sector? What recent competitive entries or exits have there been? What are the key political and economic forces underlying the development of the sector? For example, the pharmaceutical industry is influenced by government decisions on NHS spending priorities.

Surveys in Business-to-business Marketing Research

Hooley and Jobber (1986) found that the customer survey was the most commonly used method of primary market research in industrial markets, used by 27.4% of top-performing companies, and by 18.9% of other companies. However, the response rate to business-to-business marketing surveys can be very low, because too many companies want to know the views of too few key informants (so-called 'respondent fatigue'). Not surprisingly, therefore, investigations have been conducted to try to find ways of improving business-to-business survey response rates. Faria and Dickinson (1992) found that the type of organizations sponsoring the survey, and the offer of a donation to charity, both affected the response rate. Non-commercial sponsorship (e.g., by a university or charity) of a survey increases response rate, and the offer of a donation to charity for a completed questionnaire also increased the response rate. However, it must be borne in mind when offering charitable donations that this does increase the overall survey cost—Faria and Dickinson found that the average cost per response was increased by the offer of a charitable donation. In other words, the donation to charity had generated an increased response rate, but the cost of running the survey (*including* the donation) had increased by more than the number of responses received.

The trade-off between cost and response rate is a tricky issue for researchers. Diamantopoulos and Schlegelmilch (1996) tried to identify which methods of boosting response rate were cost-effective, and which were not. They concluded that the following are worthwhile methods of boosting response rates in business-to-business postal surveys:

- Obtaining survey approval from an organization valued by the respondent.
- Personalizing the covering letter to include the respondent's name and job title, and having it personally signed (this need not be a chore in the digital age, since signatures can be digitized in various ways, the easiest of which is probably the simple desktop scanner).
- Keeping the questionnaire as short as possible, requesting easily accessible information, and using simple, precoded questions.
- Providing assurances that anonymity and/or confidentiality will be maintained.
- Prenotifying respondents by telephone to expect a questionnaire, conducting the survey during normal business periods (for example, not Christmas), and sending a later reminder and duplicate questionnaire to non-respondents.
- Providing a stamped addressed return envelope.
- Promising the respondent a summary of the study's results without compromising confidentiality.

On the other hand, Diamantopoulos and Schlegelmilch found that there was little to be gained from using coloured paper, from printing only on one side of the paper, or from using expensive forms of postage such as recorded delivery. Any small advantage in terms of a boosted response was not justified by the extra cost incurred.

Management of Business-to-business Marketing Research

Business-to-business Marketing as the Management of Relationships

One of the underlying differences between business-to-business markets and consumer markets that was outlined earlier in this chapter was the concentration of demand among a few key organizational customers. For example, it is obvious that if you are in the business of selling pharmaceutical manufacturing equipment, then there are a few very large firms that will be in your key actual or potential markets, e.g., Astra Zeneca and Novartis. For this reason, it is normal practice in business-to-business markets to manage key customer relationships with great care, and to expend substantial resources on single customers to maintain a healthy business relationship. For many firms, business-to-business marketing has far more to do with the active management of key customer relationships, rather than the manipulation of the marketing mix. At the same time, many of these large customer organizations see benefits to themselves from actively managing the business relationships that they establish with their own key suppliers. They decide that if they have found a supplier who can regularly deliver a quality product or service, at a good price, and with good after-sales support, then it makes sense to nurture the relationship. Such close relationships between buying and selling firms, however, have tended not to be found in the market research industry. In the final section of this chapter, we ask why this is so, and whether it is likely to change in the future.

Business-to-business Marketing Research: the Client/Agency Interface

Peterson and Kerin (1980: 69) argued that 'While guidelines have been offered for obtaining and evaluating commercial marketing research proposals ... critical considerations involved in managing the interface between buyers and sellers of marketing research services go virtually uncharted'. Indeed, not a great deal of research has been done into the management of the client/agency relationship in business-to-business markets. Peterson and Kerin (1980: 72) concluded that effective management of the client/agency relationship required the client to 'Open lines of frank and honest communication with the research seller early in the research process and maintain them throughout project implementation. Provide whatever information you have which bears on the problem at hand.'

Eborall and Nathan (1989) argued that 'Market research is unique among professional and business services in that the competitive project tender is usually the basis for the client/agency relationship. This means that the contact between the two parties may be sporadic rather than continuous, and that the loyalty, commitment and expertise of the agency will be built more slowly than it would otherwise.' In the absence of any commitment on the part of the client, the market research agency will be disinclined to invest substantially in building client-specific

254

expertise. This, in turn, leads to a number of characteristic problems associated with the market research client/agency relationship. These are:

- Researchers often failing to solve clients' problems
- Researchers being unable to participate in the strategic decision-making process
- The low perceived value of market research information, and
- The low status attached to the market research profession.

However, it is important, for both clients and agencies, that these problems are addressed since—with a proliferation of information available ever more easily—increasingly it will be the effective *use* of information which will differentiate successful firms. The use of information, and the management of the research agency/client relationship to maximize the likelihood that information will be relevant and useful, are matters of importance to both parties.

The development of effective research agency/client partnerships, within which the agency can develop an in-depth understanding of the client's business, and the client can develop trust in the work of the agency, cannot readily take place in the context of a series of short-term competitive contracts. As long as there is the prospect of the client simply taking their business elsewhere, it is not rational for the agency to invest heavily in the relationship.

Peterson and Kerin (1980: 73) concluded that 'The marketing research buyer–seller relationship should be treated as a mutually beneficial one, not one of conflict or acrimony'. Broadly, the message from research conducted into research agency/client relationships is that there is a tendency for both parties to adopt a relatively short-term and essentially transactional approach to relationship management. As competitive success depends increasingly upon creating and using relevant marketing information, both agencies and clients could benefit from a longer-term, relational approach to relationship management. This would foster trust, which would:

- Encourage the agency to invest in client-specific skills and knowledge, increasing its effectiveness in providing relevant and usable information
- Predispose the client to make more use of the information provided by the agency.

To bring about such an outcome requires the adoption of a relationship marketing strategy on the part of the agency, and a shift towards supplier partnering by the client. Industrial firms have learned to reap the benefits of supplier partnerships with component suppliers, and might now consider the advantages of a similar approach to research agency management (Brennan, 2000).

Conclusion

Business-to-business marketing is concerned with marketing goods and services to organizations, rather than to consumers. Demand in organizational markets is derived from the sales that those organizations make to other organizations or to consumers; organizations buy goods and services because of the contribution they make to organizational goals, not for the direct satisfaction that they generate. Secondary market research is particularly important in business-to-business markets, since it allows the firm to gain access to information about its customers' customers relatively quickly and at comparatively low cost. When business-to-business market surveys are used, response rates tend to be rather low, and several mechanisms are discussed in the chapter for improving response rates. Market research agencies tend to be used in a very *ad hoc* way by business-to-business marketers; it is suggested that a more long-term view of the client/agency relationship might improve the quality of market research done by agencies for their clients.

References

Brennan, R. (2000). 'Management of the market research client/agency relationship', in A.G. Woodside (ed.), *Advances in Business Marketing and Purchasing*, Volume 9, Connecticut: JAI Press, 119–141.

Chisnall, P.M. (1995). *Strategic Business Marketing*, 3rd edn, Hemel Hempstead: Prentice-Hall.

Cox, W.E. Jr and Dominguez, L.V. (1979). 'The key issues and procedures of industrial marketing research', *Industrial Marketing Research*, **8**, 81–93.

Diamantopoulos, A. and Schlegelmilch, B.B. (1996). 'Determinants of industrial mail survey response: a survey-on-surveys analysis of researchers' and managers' views', *Journal of Marketing Management*, **12**, 505–531.

Eborall, C. and Nathan, L. (1989). 'Caveat emptor, or ours not to reason why? A look at client/agency relationships in business research', *Proceedings of the Market Research Society Conference*, 154–167.

Faria, A.J. and Dickinson, J.R. (1992). 'Mail survey response, speed, and cost', *Industrial Marketing Management*, **21**, 51–60.

Gross, A.C., Banting, P.M., Meredith, L.N. and Ford, I.D. (1993). *Business Marketing*, Boston & Toronto: Houghton Mifflin.

Hooley, G.J. and Jobber, D. (1986). 'Five common factors in top performing industrial firms', *Industrial Marketing Management*, **15**, 89–96.

Penn, W.S. Jr (1978). 'Problem formulation in industrial marketing research', *Industrial Marketing Management*, **7**, 402–409.

Peterson, R.A. and Kerin, R.A. (1980). 'The effective use of marketing research consultants', *Industrial Marketing Management*, **9**, 69–73.

Work Assignments

These tasks will require access to some secondary sources mentioned in the chapter. These sources will certainly be available at any business school library, and are also available at many public libraries.

You work for an American company that plans to enter the UK market for heavy industrial machinery. The market leader is J.C. Bamford Excavators Ltd.

1. What is J.C. Bamford's product range?
2. What are their primary target markets?

The construction industry will be a key target market for your company.

3. What are the key trends currently affecting the UK construction industry?
4. Provide a brief summary of the UK government's current plans for road building.

Answers to Work Assignment Questions

Chapter 1

Question 1

Your company is a leader holding 40% of the market in clothes for young people between the ages of 18 and 30 years and has been trading for the past ten years. The market share of your company has been declining for the last year. The company is facing increased competition in the market and is proposing to introduce a 'new line of clothes'. It needs information on its competition and acceptability of the 'new line of clothes' it is developing. Suggest a suitable research design for:

(i) Collecting information about competition.
(ii) Deciding the need for the 'new line of clothes' and its acceptability.

Answer 1

(i) The research design should be exploratory using desk research.
(ii) The company should have enough background information about clothing for young people between the ages 18–30 years as it has been trading for a long period and is a leader in this market. A descriptive research design will allow the company to find the opinions of the young people both in existing and new markets.

Question 2

Plastique Ltd is a medium-sized company in the plastic mouldings business. They compete for a well-defined market segment, within which they have a 20% market share, making them number two in the market after Alpha Plastics plc, which is believed to have a share of 45%. Plastique Ltd relies heavily on this segment, from which they derive 75% of their revenue and around 90% of their profits. Recent attempts to identify profitable opportunities for product or market development have been unsuccessful, leading the managing director to conclude that the company will have to rely on this market for survival and growth for the foreseeable future. In view of this, the MD was very concerned to hear a rumour that Alpha Plastics plc might have developed a new plastic moulding process, which would enable it to improve quality while reducing prices by as much as 15%. She is determined to find out as much as possible about the Alpha Plastics plc development, as quickly as possible, in order to develop a counter-strategy. In her view, the survival of Plastique Ltd probably depends on her ability to obtain and exploit meaningful information quickly. Her job, and those of the 50 other people working for the company, could be at stake.

She is considering a number of possibilities to obtain the market intelligence that she requires:

(i) Carry out a detailed search of the plastic mouldings trade press to see whether any information has leaked out of Alpha Plastics plc.
(ii) Persuade her production supervisor to apply for the job of production manager at Alpha Plastics (currently vacant) and to use the interview and plant visit as an intelligence-gathering opportunity.
(iii) Speak informally to known customers of Alpha Plastics, and ask them what they know about the new production technique.

Make a judgement on the ethics of the above possibilities and recommend a research design appropriate for this situation.

Answer 2

(i) The approach is ethical as she proposes to use published information. This will be an exploratory design using desk research.
(ii) This approach is not ethical as the production supervisor is not really interested in taking up the job and is using the interview to collect the information. Such intelligence gathering, though used in practice, is not ethical. Causal design using experimental techniques to improve the production process internally should be used.
(iii) This approach of speaking informally to known customers of Alpha Plastics may not result in reliable information about new production technique. As such it is not totally ethical and may not achieve the desired outcome. Exploratory designs should be used to investigate the new development techniques in the plastics industry.

Chapter 2

Question 1

Given more time and money, how would you modify the London Football Club proposal outlined in the Chapter Appendix in order to explore further the management problem?

Answer 1

The researchers have assumed that season ticket holders, matchday attenders and the London club members are all homogeneous groups. However, it is likely that they have shared characteristics across their groupings. One method would have been to design one questionnaire with different sections for these groups with a section that asked common questions. This could then have been extended to a larger sample over a number of different games using a quota-based sample. Such a survey would have allowed a more direct comparison of these different groups. The local community questionnaire would probably best be conducted door-to-door on a weekend over a specified area near to the club. Finally, the whole study is organized around profiling the supporters rather than gaining an understanding of their needs. Only the last study really does this and it could be argued that this was not enough. Therefore, perhaps a larger number of focus groups could have been conducted. More recently, football clubs have started to organize supporter panels whereby a selected group of supporters are contacted to give their views across a range of issues.

Question 2

What are the limitations of the given research designs for each of the projects outlined in the study?

Answer 2

Project 1—Systematic random sampling method is acceptable but does not provide a representative sample made up of different groups where the sample is heterogeneous. The research is supposed to provide 'a measure of shifts in attitudes and perceptions of this important group'. It would not unless compared with a similar previous study.

Project 2—Conducting a census of the members is a good idea since they are a limited group in size. However, the problem comes when these members are sent questionnaires as a result of other surveys. In other words, London Football Club members could also have been sent questionnaires, when questioned on matters related to London Football Club, as part of the other four projects. Since the group is relatively small, one can also question whether they really deserve a separate survey.

Project 3—There is not much detail about how the matchday attenders will receive their questionnaires. Since many of them do not pay by credit card or in advance and do not register their contact details with the club, it is very difficult to access contact details.

Project 4—A convenience sample of the local community might not be particularly useful, particularly since those that do take part in the survey are likely to be self-selecting (i.e., those either particularly favour or dislike the club).

261

Project 5—Eight to twelve supporters in a focus group might be very difficult to handle at one particular time. It might be more useful to have a smaller mini-group of 5 or 6. The groups have been organized by age and sex, which is quite useful but equally they could have been mixed groups organized by type of supporter as in the rest of the study. The point is that all stages should be consistent for comparison purposes.

All the first four projects are descriptive and the final stage is exploratory. This is because the first four projects are collecting quantitative data that provides the researcher with a profile of supporter characteristics and views. The final project, conducted afterwards, uses qualitative methods. None of these methods are causal because this requires the use of an experimental methodology. It is interesting to note that this proposal suggests that the exploratory stage be conducted last since it could have been used in drawing up the questionnaires used in the first four projects. This would have been better and ensured that the responses to the questionnaires were more valid.

Question 3

Suggest appropriate changes to the proposal in order to reduce the bias arising from the limitations determined in question 2.

Answer 3

Project 1—Would benefit more from using a stratified random sample. The research is supposed to provide 'a measure of shifts in attitudes and perceptions of this important group'. It would not unless compared with a similar previous study.

Project 2—London Football Club members could also have been sent questionnaires, or questioned on matters related to London Football Club, as part of the other four projects. Since the group is relatively small, one can also question whether they really deserve a separate survey since they could have been combined with season ticket holders.

Project 3—The proposal needs to outline how matchday attenders will be contacted. This could occur as a convenience survey, questioning fans as they enter and leave the stadium, ideally as a quota sample.

Project 4—It would be better to conduct a survey that uses a random sampling methodology such as cluster sampling (see Chapter 7) among the local community.

Project 5—It might be more useful to have a smaller mini-group of 5 or 6. The groups have been organized by age and sex but equally they could have been mixed groups organized by type of supporter as in the rest of the study. The point is that all stages should be consistent for comparison purposes.

Question 4

What type of research (i.e., causal, descriptive or exploratory) should be commissioned in the following contexts? Explain why.

Answer 4

(a) By a political party that wants to understand why its percentage of the vote has fallen from 45% to 35% within a two-month period.

Descriptive research, in the form of tracking studies, is used to determine why this sort of event is happening. Usually a sample of around 400 respondents is questioned every day, often by telephone, over the relevant period and 1200 responses are analysed as a sample and compared with a similar number from the previous week/month etc.

(b) By a manufacturing firm wanting to determine whether there is a relationship between its recent expenditure on training and the performance of its salesforce.

This would make use of company information related to individual training costs and individual salespersons' sales figures/profit figures/leads generated, etc. This is effectively a data analysis problem and could use *t*- or Z-tests (see Chapter 9) to determine whether there is an association. Such a test would not explain the causal direction of the relationship, however, in other words, whether training enhanced salesperson's performance or whether high-performance salespersons undertook more training. To determine this would require the use of experimental methodologies.

(c) By a toy company that wants to test new ideas for board games.

This would best be conducted using an exploratory design. Qualitative methods, and particularly focus or mini-groups (using the recommended number of people for a game), would be useful in this regard.

(d) By a company wanting information relating to possible competitors, their market share and major suppliers and buyers in a new market.

Some of this data is readily available from secondary sources and requires a diligent desk researcher to uncover it. Market share data and competitor information is usually relatively easy to find compared to uncovering major suppliers and buyers in an established market. This latter type of data is often difficult to access, particularly in new markets. It can be collected through market intelligence methods not covered in this text. Examples include visiting trade fairs and watching different customers as they attend particular stands. Similarly, watching a particular company's HQ to see which suppliers visit is another method. There are ethical concerns with this approach. From a desk research perspective though it is unlikely that this data will be available on a *new* market. Primary data studies could be conducted among likely buyers and suppliers but the difficulty is in compiling the sampling frame.

Question 5

Critically analyse the research design process outlined in Figure 2.1. Point out aspects of the process that you believe might not currently be included. Criticize the sequencing of the process. To help you with this, read the sections related to the London Football Club examples.

Answer 5

The research design process is outlined as a sequence. If you look at the sections related to London Football Club it becomes clear that the process is actually iterative. The brief might be changed after discussion with the MRO and the proposal may be altered after discussion with the client. Part-way through the research, the objectives may change slightly perhaps because of a refocus in the company's mission or strategy, for instance.

Chapter 3

Question 1

Desk research can be used in a number of different marketing decision-making scenarios. Describe three uses of desk research.

Answer 1

The objective of this question is to have students recognize the importance of good information in all areas of marketing decision making. Students should recall that information gathered and assessed through desk research can be used to help at all stages of the marketing research process; to provide insights into how changes in the business environment affect marketing decisions; to make sales and market share forecasts; to gain insights into the characteristics and needs of customers; and as part of the research into potential international markets.

Question 2

Explain how desk research can be used in the marketing research process.

Answer 2

Students may assume that desk research is most useful in gathering background information on the problem/issue to be researched and as the step to be taken before primary research is undertaken in the hope that if adequate and accurate information is found, the company may not need to carry on with the more expensive primary collection process.

However, secondary research can be useful at other stages of the marketing research process as well. In determining the most appropriate research design, marketers may look at the methodology used in previous studies. Already existing lists of customers from internal databases or list brokers can be used to create the sample for marketing research. Finally, once the data has been collected and analysed, researchers can look at previously conducted, similar studies to assess the reliability of the new findings.

Question 3

Consider that you are asked to conduct research into the ice cream market in the UK. You are interested in the size of the market, market shares of key competitors, factors affecting the industry, and target markets for ice cream. Go to the library and identify four appropriate sources of information.

Answer 3

Sources of information of this type of information are: Euromonitor Reports; Mintel; Industry Trade Association Publications; FT Profile; Keynote Reports.

More specific information on key competitors can be found in: *Kelly's Business Directory*; *KOMPASS Register*; *Major UK Companies Index*; *The World's Major Companies Directory, FAME; FT Extol; Moody's International Manual.*

A general search of the current business press, the Internet and article databases will also bring up the most recent information on key competitors.

Question 4

Assume you are conducting research for a large breakfast cereal manufacturer. You are planning to develop a range of organic cereals. Using the Internet and the search engines listed in this chapter, collect as much information as you can about the competition and their marketing programmes.

Answer 4

Students will need to begin by defining whom they view the key competitors to be and then clarifying key search terms. In terms of competitors, they should consider both organic and non-organic cereals ranges, as well as other non-cereal breakfast foods. They should make use of major article databases on the Internet to find the most recent articles on key competitors and on the organics food market, industry and customer base.

Question 5

Describe the criteria to be used when assessing secondary data.

Answer 5

Students should discuss whether the data is accurate, reliable, relevant, current (timely), available and whether it is affordable.

Question 6

Two critical steps in the secondary information search are beginning with a clear definition of your research needs, and keeping records of your sources in a marketing information system. Explain why these steps are so important.

Answer 6

A clear definition and understanding of the research needs are necessary in order to provide a framework and guidelines for the information search and to be sure that the information gathered will be pertinent and useful to the marketer's research problem. Without a well-defined research brief, the researcher's search may be too broad, thus wasting time and resources. Since a well-conducted desk research process may solve the problem at hand and eliminate the need for primary research, a clear definition of what information is needed is critical.

Keeping records of all sources and relevant information in a marketing information system will allow marketers to develop a database of information on customers, markets, and the environment that they can draw and build upon for future decisions and research projects.

Question 7

Explain why desk research alone is not usually sufficient to solve a marketing research problem.

Answer 7

(a) If the problem is of a current or future nature, no secondary research may be available.
(b) If the problem is to identify target markets, assess customers' current attitudes towards the company and its products, or test advertising, then the information may be neither sufficiently up to date nor available.
(c) Secondary information is often outdated or not in the correct frame of reference for the research at hand.
(d) Often it is difficult to assess the accuracy and/or reliability of secondary information.

Chapter 4

Question 1

Use the template below to design a moderator's outline for a focus group study evaluating five different sales promotion campaigns for a new flavour of crisps. Note that the template asks you to ask questions that are introductory, transitional, key and ending questions. This represents the depth of the conceptual flow of the conversation as it goes from general to specific.

Question type	Question	Duration (min)
Opening	1. Going around the table, can you tell us your name and what you enjoy doing most in your spare time?	5
Introductory	2.	10
Transition	3.	5
Key	SHOW PROMOTIONAL CONCEPT STORYBOARDS IN TURN (**ASK RESPONDENTS TO FILL IN BRIEF QUESTIONNAIRE ON EACH**)	30
	Promotion 1 ☐ Promotion 2 ☐ Promotion 3 ☐ Promotion 4 ☐ Promotion 5 ☐	
	What are you first impressions of these promotions? (**PROBE on mechanics and theme for each one, e.g., Would you prefer to link up with Vodafone or Cellnet?**)	
Ending	4.	8
Summary	5. Let me summarize the key points of the discussion. MODERATOR PROVIDES ORAL SUMMARY Is that an adequate summary?	2

Answer 1

Students only need to write the introductory, transitional, key and ending questions but should ensure that they fit the context of the question, which is a sales promotion campaign evaluation for a new flavour of crisps. Possible examples of questions (there are no definite right answers here) are placed within the template in bold italics in the appropriate sections. The key question actually depends on the type of sales promotions being tested. Moderators should probe on mechanics and theme. Thus, questions should be asked about the mechanic (i.e., how the sales promotion works, e.g., money off next purchase, coupon collection scheme, competition). For a promotion that used a coupon collection scheme where consumers collected 30 tokens and could purchase CDs cheaply and were also entered into a competition for free tickets to a major concert (e.g., Britney Spears), example questions might include: Do you think that you would be prepared to collect 30 coupons? Is it too many? Are the cheap CDs worth collecting the coupons for? What's more appealing to you, the cheap CDs or the chance to go and see Britney Spears in concert?

Questions should also be asked about the theme of the promotion. Is music the right sort of product for this promotion? Are there other products you would rather have? Is this particular concert appealing to you?

267

Question type	Question	Duration (min)
Opening	Going around the table, can you tell us your name and what you enjoy doing most in your spare time?	5
Introductory	*This discussion is going to be about crisps. Can you tell me what brand of crisps you usually buy? What are your favourite flavours? Why?*	10
Transition	*Remember back to the time you last tried a new flavour of crisps, one that you had never had before, what made you decide to try them? <ASK QUESTION ABOUT NEW FLAVOUR—e.g., What would you think of XXXX as a flavour?>*	5
Key	SHOW PROMOTIONAL CONCEPT STORYBOARDS IN TURN (**ASK RESPONDENTS TO FILL IN BRIEF QUESTIONNAIRE ON EACH**)	30

Promotion 1 ☐
Promotion 2 ☐
Promotion 3 ☐
Promotion 4 ☐
Promotion 5 ☐

	What are you first impressions of these promotions? (**PROBE on mechanics and theme for each one.**)	
Ending	*Do you think that the promotion complements the new flavour? Why do you say that?*	8
Summary	Let me summarize the key points of the discussion. MODERATOR PROVIDES ORAL SUMMARY Is that an adequate summary?	2

MODERATOR THANKS PARTICIPANTS

Question 2

A UK political party wishes to determine the marketing methods that are used by American political consultants when running US presidential campaigns. However, traditionally political parties usually obtain links with supposedly ideological 'sister' parties. Thus, in this case, the UK party can obtain opinions only from one US party's representatives. Assuming that the party can easily arrange the data-collection process, which qualitative market research method should it use?

Answer 2

The UK political party should use in-depth interviews to determine the marketing methods that are used by American political consultants when running US presidential campaigns. This is because it is unlikely that political consultants would be prepared to allow themselves to be interviewed in one central location. They are very busy, professional people and so would need to be interviewed in their own offices at their own convenience. Another important issue concerns who should be interviewed. In this case, the sample should include only those political consultants that have worked on presidential campaigns. This would cut down the consultant population drastically. This population would probably then constitute a rare population. Such a population could be accessed initially using membership lists (for example, the consultant listings in specialist publications such as *Campaign and Elections*) and then referrals from willing participants. The in-depth interview could adopt either a telephone or personal interview format. This really depends on cost and whether the researcher has the necessary telephone conversation recording equipment.

Question 3

Fictional Bus Company wants to understand the quality of their customer service, the friendliness of the driver, and whether the driver ensures that passengers pay the full fare. What type of research method could be used?

Answer 3

Since Fictional Bus Company wants to understand the quality of their customer service, they require a customer's perspective as they go through the journey. The efficiency of the bus service would be measured by whether the bus turned up on time. If it was late, how late was it? Was it late when it arrived at the bus stop? If it wasn't, was it late to arrive at the destination? What was the reason for the lateness, assuming the bus was late? The friendliness of the driver can only be determined by observing him or her. Determining whether the driver is checking whether the passenger has paid full fare is extremely difficult. This requires that they know where each passenger is going and whether they actually go to where they say they are going to go. Generally, the driver cannot enforce this easily. Each incident of a customer not paying the full fare holds the potential to disrupt the bus service. So, the efficiency and friendliness of the service can be measured using the mystery shopping observational method. This provides the necessary information at a lower cost than asking large numbers of passengers. It also measures the actual efficiency rather than the perceived efficiency of the service, which is what would be measured by the survey method. However, determining whether passengers are paying full fare is often determined using a ticket inspector who asks the passengers what they have paid and where they are going.

Question 4

Design a topic outline for a study involving in-depth interviews with teenagers about the subject of condom usage.

Answer 4

An in-depth interview with teenagers about condom usage would probably need to use interviewers who were approximately the same age, and the same sex, as the teenager being interviewed. Issues of importance to condom manufacturers (e.g., Durex) might include the following issues:

- What the condom looks like, e.g., discussions with young women regarding the female condom found that it was something of a 'turn-off' and was difficult to insert.
- How comfortable the condom is to wear and to fit.
- The features of the condom: does it affect either the males' or females' genital sensitivity? Does it contain a spermicide? How strong is the latex from which the condom is made? Is it likely to burst?

So a topic outline for a one-hour in-depth interview might include a number of different topics. In the example provided below, the conversation starts from a clinical point of view, discussing types of contraceptive method and their advantages and disadvantages. The discussion eventually considers sexual activity and its relation to love and friendship. This then sets the context for the act of love-making. It should be noted that a discussion of this type would not be entered into by everyone. It would be necessary to carefully screen the respondents to determine whether they are sufficiently open and honest to answer such questions.

1. Methods of contraception used in the past
2. Discussion of advantages and disadvantages of different methods
3. Preferred method of contraception and reason why
4. Discussion of condoms as a method of contraception specifically
5. Awareness of different brands of condom
6. Preferred brand and reason why
7. Issues related to price, packaging, distribution, advertising
8. Sexual activity (how often, when, how, where?)
9. When is it appropriate to have sex with someone?
10. Discussion of love, sex and friendship.

Chapter 5

Question 1

The first questionnaire, for London Football Club, was designed to provide the club with an insight into the opinions of local football supporters, regardless of whether they supported London Football Club or a nearby competitor club. The interviews were conducted in the high street by a trained interviewer. In order to ensure that the right sample answered the questionnaire, only those respondents who watched live matches at nearby football stadiums and were not season ticket holders were questioned (since this group was questioned separately).

(a) Critically assess the questions and the layout of the questionnaire by looking at their design.

(b) How could the questions be reworded and structured to obtain the same information?

(c) How would the questions need to be reworded if this survey was conducted by telephone?

Questionnaire 1: Personal interviews: London Football Club

Questionnaire for local population of London Football Club

Name: _____

Address: _____

_____

_____

_____

Post Code: ☐ ☐ ☐ ☐

For office use only ☐ (5)

Gender:

☐ Male ☐ Female

For office use only ☐ (5)

Occupation of Head of Household

_____

Circle Relevant Category

☐ ☐ ☐
AB C1
C2 DE

For office use only ☐ (5)

Age?
☐ Under 16
☐ 17–24
☐ 25–34
☐ 35–44
☐ 45–54
☐ 55+

Marital Status?
☐ Single
☐ Married/Living with partner
☐ Divorced/Separated
☐ Widowed

For office use only ☐ (5)

For office use only ☐ (5)

Q.1 Have you ever been to watch a match at London Football Club?

☐ Yes (PLEASE ANSWER QUESTIONS 2 TO 10)
☐ No (PLEASE ANSWER QUESTIONS 11 TO) *For office use only* ☐ (5)

271

London Football Club Enthusiasts

Q.2   When was the last time that you went to see a match at London Football Club?

☐   Within the last month
☐   Within the last six months
☐   Within the 96–97 season
☐   Within the 95–96 season
☐   Longer than two seasons ago   *For office use only*   ☐ (5)

Q.3   For how many seasons have you been coming to watch London Football Club?
(PLEASE TICK RELEVANT BOX)

☐   1   ☐   2   ☐   3
☐   4   ☐   5–9   ☐   10+   *For office use only*   ☐ (13)

Q.4   How do you travel to watch the matches at London Football Club? (YOU
MAY TICK MORE THAN ONE)

☐   Car   ☐   Foot   ☐   Bus   ☐   Tube

                                                  For office use only   ☐ (6)

Q.5   For what reason have you not purchased a season ticket? (PLEASE TICK THE
ONE ANSWER THAT MOST APPLIES TO YOU)

☐   Too expensive (PLEASE GO TO Q.14)
☐   Can't attend every home match (PLEASE GO TO Q.14)
☐   Can't afford it (PLEASE GO TO Q.15)
☐   Other _____   *For office use only*   ☐ (14)

Q.6   Would you buy a season ticket if you could get a refund for matches that you
missed?

☐   Yes   (PLEASE GO TO Q.15)
☐   No   (PLEASE GO TO Q.15)   *For office use only*   ☐ (15)

Q.7   Would you buy a season ticket if it was possible to pay for it in instalments?

☐   Yes
☐   No   *For office use only*   ☐ (16)

Q.8   Please indicate membership of the following:

☐ Riversiders   ☐ Vice Presidents   ☐ None

For office use only ☐ (17)

Q.9   Please indicate, by ticking the appropriate box, how strongly you agree or disagree with the following statements. (PLEASE START FROM TICK)

	Agree strongly	Agree slightly	Neither agree nor disagree	Disagree slightly	Disagree strongly	None	Don't know	*Office use only*
The London Football Club shop has a limited range of merchandise								_____ (31)
The merchandise sold at the shop is good value for money								_____ (32)
The merchandise sold at the shop is highly priced								_____ (33)
The merchandise at the shop is good quality								_____ (44)
I would like to sponsor match balls/players' shirts								_____ (35)
I would use the club's rooms for buffets/ weddings/functions if it was possible								_____ (36)

Q.10   How loyal a supporter are you of London Football Club? (PLEASE INDICATE GIVING A NUMBER FROM 1 TO 6 WHERE 1 IS VERY LOYAL AND 6 IS NOT AT ALL LOYAL)

VERY   NOT AT ALL

1   2   3   4   5   6

For office use only ☐ (21)

273

London Football Club and Other Football Enthusiasts

Q.11 Which teams have you ever been to see?

☐ Brentford
☐ QPR
☐ Chelsea
☐ Other London Team/s _____
☐ Other Teams _____
☐ None   *For office use only* ☐ (5)

Q.12 Where would you usually go before a football match?

_____

_____

_____

                                          For office use only ☐ (7)

Q.13 Where would you usually go after a football match?

_____

_____

_____

                                          For office use only ☐ (8)

Q.14 What pre-match facilities would you like to see available at football grounds?

_____

_____

_____

                                          For office use only ☐ (9)

Q.15 What facilities would you like to see available after a football match?

_____

_____

_____

                                          For office use only ☐ (10)

Q.16   What events, other than football, do you feel should be held at football clubs during both the closed season and non-match days?

_____

_____

_____

For office use only   ☐ (28)

Q.17   Please indicate, by ticking the appropriate box, how strongly you agree or disagree with the following statements. (PLEASE START FROM TICK)

	Agree strongly	Agree slightly	Neither agree nor disagree	Disagree slightly	Disagree strongly	Don't know	*Office use only*
Chelsea FC are a good team							____ (29)
Brentford FC are a good team							____ (29)
QPR FC are a good team							____ (29)
London Football Club are a good team							____ (29)
I only support teams that are in the Premier division							____ (29)
I only support teams that are in the first division							____ (29)
I would never support London Football Club as long as I lived							____ (29)
London Football Club play an active role in the community							____ (29)
Brentford FC play an active role in the community							____ (29)
QPR FC play an active role in the community							____ (29)
I think that football teams should play an active role in the community							____ (29)

THANK YOU FOR TAKING THE TIME TO FILL IN THIS QUESTIONNAIRE, PLEASE RETURN IT IN THE PRE-PAID ENVELOPE PROVIDED

Answer 1

This question relates to the London Football Club questionnaire.

(a) Consideration of format:
- Front page rather cluttered
- Coding of variables does not correspond to question numbers and there is no precoding of the responses
- Postcode (address) boxes are not in the relevant section
- Section labelled London Football Club Enthusiasts but this is not explained to interviewer properly in Q.1
- Section labelled London Football Club and Other Football Enthusiasts also not explained to interviewer properly in Q.1
- There are too many open questions, particularly Q.12–16
- The note at the end of the questionnaire is the type of ending required for a mailed interview yet this is a personal interview. Thus, the instruction should be to the interviewer and not the respondent.

(b) Consideration of individual questions:

Q.1—If respondent answers No they should skip to another section but proper details are not provided ('Please answer questions 11 to ?').

Q.2—This question uses different units of time.

Q.4—This question requires an 'other' category.

Q.5, Q.6—The skip instructions are erroneous.

Q.9—This question should be placed at the start of the London Football Club Enthusiasts section.

Q.10—This question needs redesigning. Most football supporters are likely to regard themselves as strong fans.

Q.11—Question needs rewording to include timeframe. 'Ever' is somewhat ambiguous here.

Q.12–16—These questions are very similar and need to be combined into a multiple fixed response question.

Q.17—Opinions of other football clubs could be collected in a simpler, less time-consuming way by asking supporters to rate or rank them.

(c) If the survey were to be conducted over the telephone it would need to be reduced significantly. Currently, it would take around 15 minutes to complete. Surveys over the telephone are usually not longer than 10 minutes. Certain questions would be very difficult to ask in their existing format including Q.9 and Q.17. The open-ended questions would also become tiresome for the average respondent. It would also be necessary to screen out ineligible respondents. In the personal interview this is done face-to-face but screening questions would need to be designed for asking over the telephone.

Question 2

The second questionnaire, for Aerospace Maintenance Company, was designed to provide the company with an insight into the extent to which the company's trade magazine advertising had impacted upon possible buyers of its services. The interviews were conducted over the telephone by a trained interviewer. Respondents in several different European countries were contacted and questioned.

(a) Critically assess the questions and the layout of the questionnaire by looking at their design.
(b) How would the fact that the sample included respondents whose native language was not English affect the design of the questions?
(c) What kind of information do you think this questionnaire would provide? Do you believe it would help the aerospace organization to determine whether its advertising really had been effective?

Questionnaire 2: Telephone interviews: Aerospace Maintenance Company

Middlesex University Business School
Questionnaire for Aerospace Maintenance Co.—Advertising effectiveness

Name: _____	INTERVIEWER—COMPLETE THIS SECTION AFTER THE INTERVIEW
Company _____	Call Length (mins.) _____
Country _____	Call Time (U.K.)
Job Title _____	☐ Morning
	☐ Afternoon
	☐ Evening
	Number of calls made prior to interview (Write in) _____

Q.1 How often do you read the following publications? (INTERVIEWER—
PLEASE READ OUT THE RESPONSE CATEGORIES FIRST FOLLOWED BY EACH
PUBLICATION)

Magazine Type	Every Issue	Frequently	Sometimes	Never
Flight				
Aircraft Technology & Maintenance				
Aircraft Economics				
Air Transport World				
Aviation Weekly				
Overhaul & Maintenance				

Q.2 Have you noticed any advertisements in the last twelve months for any of the
following companies? (PLEASE READ OUT EACH COMPANY)

Company name	Yes	No
Lufthansa Technik		
S R Technics		
Air France Industries		
British Airways Engineering		
Aerospace Maintenance Co.		
Sabena Technics		
Other (please specify) _____		

Q.3   Which of the following Aerospace Maintenance Companies do you know offer full support for the major commercial types of aircraft? (INTERVIEWER—PLEASE READ OUT AND TICK APPROPRIATE ANSWERS—read out aircraft types from card 1 if respondent has problems)

Company name	Yes	No	B737	DC10	A320	Other (WRITE IN)
Lufthansa Technik						
Aerospace Maintenance Co.						
S R Technics						
Air France Industries						
British Airways Engineering						
ARL						
Sogerma						
Sabena Technics						
Other (please specify)						
_____						

Q.4   I am now going to ask you the MAIN reason why you are using these companies. Why do you use _____? (READ OUT EACH OF THE COMPANIES MENTIONED IN Q.3 EXCLUDING ARL & SOGERMA)

Lufthansa Technik

_____

S R Technics

_____

Air France Industries

_____

British Airways Engineering

_____

279

Sabena Technics

_____

Aerospace Maintenance Co.

_____

Q.5   Which of the following attributes do you associate positively or negatively with the following suppliers? (INTERVIEWER—READ OUT THE SUPPLIER FIRST AND RECORD EACH RESPONSE—TICK IF POSITIVE AND CROSS IF NEGATIVE)

Company name	Quality	Experience	Quick turnaround time	Flexibility	Customer satisfaction	Technical enterprise	Reliability	Cost effectiveness	Customized solutions
Lufthansa Technik									
S R Technics									
Aerospace Maintenance Co.									
Air France Industries									
British Airways Engineering									
Sabena Technics									
Other (please specify)									

Q.6   Please give each company a mark out of one hundred in terms of your impression of the company's overall performance for full support and maintenance services—from 1 to 10 where 1 is very poor and 10 is very good.

Aerospace Maintenance Co.   _____
Lufthansa Technik   _____
S R Technics   _____
Air France Industries   _____
British Airways Engineering   _____
Sabena Technics   _____

THANK YOU VERY MUCH FOR YOUR TIME. ARE YOU INTERESTED IN RECEIVING A BRIEF REPORT OF THE RESULTS? (INTERVIEWER—RING RESPONSE AND TAKE ADDRESS)

YES (ASK FOR ADDRESS)

NO (CLOSE INTERVIEW—THANK RESPONDENT)

ADDRESS

_____

_____

_____

_____

_____

THANK YOU, GOODBYE

Answer 2

This question relates to the Aerospace Maintenance questionnaire.

(a) Consideration of format and layout:
Q.s 1, 3, 5 are poorly laid out and difficult to ask. Q.5 is particularly difficult to ask. The researcher is trying to ask too many questions. It would have been better to ask fewer more pertinent, clear questions.
Consideration of individual questions:
Introductory questions: what difference does it make when the call is made or how many calls are made before connection? Actually, this is useful information when planning future studies and so is used by the researchers to plan future work programmes.
Q.1—Need a category to register if the respondent has never heard of a particular publication.
Q.2—This question should be asked so that each company is considered individually. There is the potential for the respondent to only answer yes to those that they remember immediately.
Q.3—Somewhat difficult for interviewer to work out how to ask this question. Actually, the question contains two questions: one related to whether the different companies offer full support and the other question is related to which types of aircraft. This question is very confusing.
Q.4—Note to interviewer explaining that only certain companies should be read out needs to be more clearly explained.

Q.5—Very confusing question. Too much information is being asked of the respondent in one go. The instructions to the interviewer are not particularly clear. This question needs breaking down into a series of more simple questions. Q.6—Asks respondent to give a mark out of 100 then implies that the question would like a rating from 1 to 10.

(b) The fact that the survey is being conducted in numerous different countries using an international sampling frame means that one must either assume that the respondents' common language is English or translate the questionnaire for each nationality. The latter process is the most effective but it would also be very costly. For a business-to-business survey like this, where most of the respondents spoke English very well, and where the sample size was around 60 with up to 10 different languages being spoken, it is better to simply ensure that the questions asked are very easy to understand. With this questionnaire, difficulties occurred particularly with question Q.5. There was not always a good understanding of the terms used in this question despite the fact that they were areas that Aerospace Maintenance Company used in their advertising. Sometimes respondents became confused with the difference between flexibility and customized solutions, and reliability, quality, quick turnaround and technical expertise.

(c) This questionnaire would provide some useful information on awareness that the respondents had of Aerospace Maintenance Company's advertising. It would also provide some useful opinions on how respondents rated them in their core areas, e.g., customized solutions. However, it would not provide evidence that a particular advertising campaign had raised the levels of awareness. This would require a longitudinal study. Nor would it provide evidence that the respondents' ratings in particular areas had been affected by the advertising campaign. Again, this requires either a longitudinal study or a single cross-sectional study where advertising material is provided for the respondents to rate during the interview. This is not possible during a telephone interview although is possible using a personal or mailed interview. This would have been difficult with this study since the sampling frame was international.

Question 3

The third questionnaire, for a political consulting organization, was designed to provide the company with an insight into its competitors' activity in offering political campaign services such as media, research and strategic consultancy. The interviews were e-mailed and respondents were asked to return the handwritten questionnaire, which they needed to print off into hard copy, by fax.

(a) The questionnaire actually received only a very small response. Why do you think this was?

(b) Criticize and appraise the types of questions used in this example.

Questionnaire 3: E-mailed interview: Political Consultancy

Q.1   What is your main area of expertise? (*Please write in 'yes', one option only*)

Media   _____
Research/polling   _____
General   _____
Finance   _____
Other (please write in)   _____

Q.2   What is the current size of your political consulting firm? (*In terms of the number of employees, please write in 'yes'*)

1–5   _____
6–10   _____
11–15   _____
16+   _____

Q.3   How many employees do you have working SOLELY on international campaigns? (*Please write in*)

_____

Q.4   Do you have any offices abroad?

Yes/No   _____

Q.5   Please indicate where your offices are located. (*Please write in*)

_____

_____

Q.6   What are the different areas—major world regions—in which you have operated? (*Please write in 'yes'*)

Western Europe   _____
Central and Eastern Europe   _____
Commonwealth of Independent States   _____
Latin America   _____
Middle East   _____
Asia   _____
Australia/New Zealand   _____
Other (Please write in)   _____

Q.7 Please indicate in the table below, for each major world region, a maximum of THREE countries in which you have operated. The three countries which you choose should be for those countries where you had the most involvement and the names of the three countries should be written in the appropriate cell. Please also indicate in the relevant column, the actual number of campaigns you have been involved in, in each region.

Major world region	Total number of campaigns in which you have been involved	Country 1	Country 2	Country 3
EXAMPLE Western Europe	5	Britain	France	Germany
Western Europe				
Central and Eastern Europe				
CIS				
Latin America				
Middle East				
Asia				
Australasia				
Other (please write in) _____				

Q.8   Please rate the degree of adaptation necessary when using the following US political consulting techniques using a scale from 1–6 where providing an answer towards 1 means that a high degree of adaptation is necessary and providing an answer towards 6 means little adaptation is necessary. Leave blank if you have no experience of a particular technique or do not know.

Direct mail	1–6	_____
Comparative (negative) TV ads	1–6	_____
Telephone canvassing	1–6	_____
Survey-based message formulation	1–6	_____
Opposition research	1–6	_____
Fund-raising via Internet	1–6	_____
Track polling	1–6	_____
Media management	1–6	_____
Focus groups	1–6	_____
Other techniques (please write in)		_____

THANK YOU FOR ANSWERING THIS QUESTIONNAIRE.

BEST WISHES

MARKET RESEARCH CONSULTANCY ORGANIZATION

Answer 3

This question relates to the political consulting organization questionnaire.

(a) The questionnaire received a very small response because it was sent out on e-mail as a word attachment. It should probably have been sent out in e-mail format or as a request for respondents to access an on-line questionnaire placed on a particular website. We are not provided with any details of an incentive either and it is unlikely that one was offered to the political consultants. Furthermore, at least on the questionnaire document, there are no details of when to send back the questionnaire or who to contact if there are difficulties accessing the document and filling it in. These all contribute as disincentives not to fill it in. The layout is also particularly amateurish and might put off some consultants from answering it. Essentially, they might not think it worth their time to answer it, particularly as they do not appear to be getting anything out of it personally.

(b) Questionnaire design considerations include formatting and the relevance of individual questions.

Consideration of format: the format actually appears rather irregular. There are a number of open questions and the layout of the questions themselves appears amateur. Questions 7 and 8 probably contributed to the low response rate since they appear rather complicated to answer and assume a level of knowledge that the respondent may not actually have.

Consideration of individual questions: many questions are structured in such a way that the proposed answer, the answer that the respondent is asked to provide, actually looks odd in context, for instance, in Q.1, writing yes on the line.

Q.1   What is your main area of expertise? (*Please write in 'yes', one option only*)

Media _____
Research/polling _____
General _____
Finance _____
Other (please write in) _____

A better format, and the usual protocol, would have simply asked for a tick in the relevant box.

Q.2   What is the current size of your political consulting firm? (*In terms of the number of employees, please write in 'yes'*)

1–5 _____
6–10 _____
11–15 _____
16+ _____

Again, writing in yes was intended to make things easier since tick boxes cannot be easily reproduced on e-mail. However, one can question this information collection approach entirely.

Q.3—poorly formatted.

Q.5—doesn't ask how many offices the consultant has or runs.

Q.6—does not provide space for respondent to write in answer if it belongs in other column

Q.7—appears too complicated. Actually, this type of information would have been better collected by performing a quick semi-structured telephone interview and would have obtained a clearer dataset on international political consulting experience.

Q.8—Many consultants might regard this question as too difficult to answer, simply because they do not have sufficient knowledge of the different techniques mentioned. If this is the case, then it leads to respondent fatigue and can contribute to low response rates. This is likely to have occurred in this case.

Chapter 6

Question 1

The table below shows the annual sales (£ million) of desktop computers of a random sample of 140 computer showrooms of a distributor.

Annual sales of desktop computers (£m)	Number of showrooms (f)
9–13	12
14–18	28
19–23	42
24–28	35
29–33	14
34–38	9
Total	140

(i) Calculate the mean and standard deviation of the annual sales of desktop computers.

(ii) Calculate and interpret the first quartile for the annual sales of desktop computers.

(iii) Given that the third quartile of the distribution is equal to 26.8, calculate the interquartile range.

Answer 1

The table below shows the process of calculating the mean, standard deviation and quartiles for annual sales of desktop computers.

Calculation of mean, standard deviation and quartiles for sales

Annual sales (£m)	Class mark (x)	Number of outlets (f)	(fx)	x^2	fx^2	Cumulative frequency (F)
9–13	11	12	132	121	1452	12
14–18	16	28	448	256	7168	40
19–23	21	42	882	441	18522	82
24–28	26	35	910	676	23660	117
29–33	31	14	434	961	13454	131
34–38	36	9	324	1296	11664	140
Total		$\sum f = 140$	$\sum fx = 3130$		$\sum fx^2 = 75920$	

287

(i) Mean $= \bar{x} = \dfrac{\sum fx}{\sum f} = \dfrac{3130}{140} = £22.36 \approx £22$ m The average annual sales will be £22 m.

The variance is calculated by using,

$$S^2 = \frac{\sum fx^2}{\sum f} - \left(\frac{\sum fx}{\sum f}\right)^2 = \left(\frac{75920}{140}\right) - \left(\frac{3130}{140}\right)^2 = 542.2857 - 499.8354 = 42.4503$$

Then standard deviation $S = \sqrt{S^2} \Rightarrow \sqrt{42.4503} = £6.52m$

(ii) First quartile $= Q_1$ will be positioned at $\dfrac{n}{4}$

Position of $Q_1 = \dfrac{n}{4} = \dfrac{140}{4} = 35$

Therefore, the class containing the first quartile is (14–18).
Then, lower class boundary of the median class $L_1 = 13.5$
$C =$ upper class boundary $-$ lower class boundary $= 18.5 - 13.5 = 5$
$f_{Q=1} = 21$, $(\sum f)_l = 18 + 35 + 41 = 94$
Using the formula

$$Q_1 = L_1 + \frac{\left[\dfrac{n}{4} - (\sum f)_l\right]}{f_{Q_1}} \times C = 13.5 + \frac{(35 - 12)}{28} \times 5$$

$$= 13.5 + 4.11 = 17.61 = 17.6$$

Therefore, $Q_1 = £18$ m. 75% of the showrooms have annual sales of desktop computer of £18 m or less. Or 25% of the showrooms have annual sales of more than £18 m.

(iii) Interquartile range $= Q_3 - Q_1 = 26.8 - 17.6 = 9.2$
Interquartile range is £9.2 m.

Question 2

The table below shows the time spent on training during a year by male and female market research executives in the South East of England.

	Number of executives	
Time spent (minutes)	Male	Female
60	120	20
55	100	60
50	200	100
45	355	450
40	350	450
35	500	300
30	350	250
25	20	100

(i) Calculate the average time spent by male and female executives and comment on the results bringing out the advantages of using average as a measure of location in this situation.

(ii) Calculate the standard deviation for both groups.

(iii) Which group is more variable in time spent?

Answer 2

(i) Let us denote by x the time spent on training during a year by the market research executives. f_1 and f_2 are the frequencies (number of executives) of male and female respectively. Then the process of calculating average and standard deviation is given below.

Calculation of mean and standard deviation

Time spent x	Male executives f_1	Female executives f_2	f_1x	f_2x	f_1x^2	f_2x^2
60	120	20	7200	1200	864000	72000
55	100	60	5500	3300	550000	181500
50	200	100	10000	5000	2000000	250000
45	355	450	15975	20250	5671125	911250
40	350	450	14000	18000	4900000	720000
35	500	300	17500	10500	8750000	367500
30	350	250	10500	7500	3675000	225000
25	20	100	500	2500	10000	62500
$\sum x$ $=340$	$\sum f_1$ $=1995$	$\sum f_2$ $=1730$	$\sum f_1x$ $=81175$	$\sum f_2x$ $=68250$	$\sum f_1x^2$ $=3453375$	$\sum f_2x^2$ $=2789750$

The average ($\bar{x}_1$) time spent on training by male executives will be

$$\frac{\sum f_1 x}{\sum f_1} = \frac{81175}{1995} = 40.7 \text{ minutes}$$

The average ($\bar{x}_2$) time spent on training by female executives will be

$$\frac{\sum f_2 x}{\sum f_2} = \frac{68250}{1730} = 39.5 \text{ minutes}$$

(ii) The standard deviation for the time spent on training by male executives will be S_1:

$$\sqrt{\frac{\sum f_1 x^2}{\sum f_1} - \left(\frac{\sum f_1 x}{\sum f_1}\right)^2} = \sqrt{\frac{3453375}{1995} - \left(\frac{81175}{1995}\right)^2} = \sqrt{1731.02 - 1655.61}$$

$$= 8.68 \text{ minutes}$$

The standard deviation for the time spent on training by female executives will be S_2:

$$\sqrt{\frac{\sum f_2 x^2}{\sum f_2} - \left(\frac{\sum f_2 x}{\sum f_2}\right)^2} = \sqrt{\frac{2789750}{1730} - \left(\frac{68250}{1730}\right)^2} = \sqrt{1612.57 - 1556.37}$$

$$= 7.50 \text{ minutes}$$

(iii) To find which either male or female time spent on training is more variable, compare the coefficients of variation.

$$\text{Coefficient of variation for male} = \frac{S_1}{\bar{x}_1} \times 100 = \frac{8.68}{40.7} \times 100 = 21.3$$

$$\text{Coefficient of variation for female} = \frac{S_2}{\bar{x}_2} \times 100 = \frac{7.50}{39.5} \times 100 = 19.0$$

Therefore, as the coefficient of variation for male time spent is higher than that of female time spent, there is higher variation for male time spent than female.

Chapter 7

Question 1

Suggest a suitable sampling method for each of the following situations:

(a) You are a manager of company dealing in FMCG products with outlets spread across the United Kingdom. In recent months your company sales have shown a decline. To stop this decline you intend to introduce a new line in takeaway food. You wish to assess the demand for this new line and decide on its acceptability with a view to intensive nationwide advertising of the new line.

(b) You are a marketing consultant employed by a company dealing in FMCG products. You have been asked to investigate the new layout of your stores, and whether the company should adopt from a choice of three new layouts against the existing one.

Answer 1

(a) The situation requires finding the acceptability of the new line from both the existing customers and others who are likely to buy the new takeaway food. The company plans to embark on nationwide advertising campaign and as such would require the outcome of the research to give results that are reliable. Therefore, a probability method should be used. The company will have a list of the outlets split by its marketing regions, size and the turnover. Stratified random sampling is recommended, the stratification being done using marketing regions, size, and the turnover of the outlets and then choosing randomly the shoppers as they leave the outlet on selected days of the week and one weekend. For other customers (not shopping in the company outlets) a quota sample may be used. The quota is chosen on the basis of competition and at the mall whose shoppers leave as in the case of the company's own outlets.

(b) The company wishes to adopt a layout from a choice of four layouts, of which one is an existing one. This can be resolved using a experimental design approach where comparison is made on the attitudes of the customers to the four layouts and comparing the outcome of the three new ones with the existing one (which acts as a control). The choice of the customers should be made randomly and a mini test market approach would be used.

Question 2

How large a sample should you take in a product test where the intention to purchase is 30%? You would allow a margin of error of ±5% on the expected intention to purchase and have 95% confidence in your results.

Answer 2

Required estimated sample size for proportion. The sample size is estimated by using the formula

$$n = \frac{z^2.p(1-p)}{e^2}$$

where: $n =$ sample size
 $z =$ standard score for the required confidence interval, or 95% $z = 1.96$.

p = estimated proportion = 0.3
e = half of the desired margin of error = 0.05

$$n = \frac{(1.96)^2 \times (0.3)(0.7)}{(0.05)^2} \cong 323$$

Question 3

You wish to study a population with 6000 members by selecting a sample of approximately 600 from it. The aim is to achieve the greatest accuracy within limited resources. You have stratified the population into two regions, A and B, and within those regions, into two age groups, 1 and 2. The populations in the four categories are given below:

	Region A	Region B
Age group 1	$N_1 = 2000$	$N_2 = 1800$
Age group 2	$N_3 = 1000$	$N_4 = 1200$

A pilot survey has indicated the approximate amount of variation (σ_i) and cost per sampling (c_i) unit in the four categories and these are as follows:

	Region A	Region B
Age group 1	$\sigma_1 = 20$	$\sigma_2 = 18$
	$c_1 = 25p$	$c_2 = 36p$
Age group 2	$\sigma_3 = 14$	$\sigma_4 = 12$
	$c_3 = 49p$	$c_4 = 64p$

Estimate the sample size required.

Answer 3

The estimation of sample size for each stratum using optimum allocation is done using the formula below

$$n_i = n \cdot \frac{\dfrac{N_i \sigma_i}{\sqrt{c_i}}}{\sum \dfrac{N_i \sigma_i}{\sqrt{c_i}}}$$

The sample size for Region A, Groups 1 and 2 will be 279 and 70 respectively. For Region B, Groups 1 and 2 will be 188 and 63 respectively.

Calculation of sample size using optimum allocation

	Strata	N_i	σ_i	$\sqrt{c_i}$	$\dfrac{N_i\sigma_i}{\sqrt{c_i}}$	n_i
Region A	Group 1	2000	20	5	8000	279
	Group 2	1000	14	7	2000	70
Region B	Group 1	1800	18	6	5400	188
	Group 2	1200	12	8	1800	63
				Total	17200	500

Question 4

A company markets its merchandise through sales agents who operate within their respective marketing zones. It is known that the destination of 'miles travelled to customer location' in the company is normally distributed with mean = 18.2 km and standard deviation = 4.8 km.

The company plans to introduce variable travelling expenses for the agents on the basis of distance travelled and has collected information from a random sample of 400 agents of the company. The agents are divided into four country zones. It is found that the 12% are A, 18% are B, 35% are C and 25% are D. 10% are unknown.

(a) Obtain the sample size of each of the groups within the different zones.
(b) Use the sample sizes to obtain the standard error of the sample mean for each of the zones.
(c) Find the probability that the agents, on average, would travel more than 19 km within each zone.

Answer 4

(a) The sample size $n = 400$ agents.

Country zone	%	Sample size
A	12	48
B	18	72
C	35	140
D	25	100
Total	90	360

(b) $SE(\bar{x}_i) = \sqrt{\dfrac{\sigma_i^2}{n_i}}$. Assume $\sigma_i = 4.8$ km for all four social classes. Then,

Social Class	SE(Mean)
A	$\sqrt{\dfrac{(4.8)^2}{48}} = 0.693$
B	$\sqrt{\dfrac{(4.8)^2}{72}} = 0.566$
C	$\sqrt{\dfrac{(4.8)^2}{140}} = 0.406$
D	$\sqrt{\dfrac{(4.8)^2}{100}} = 0.480$

(c) To find the probability for agents on average travelling more than 19 km in each zone, using the standard error of mean (from section (b) above) we use the following formula

$$Z = \frac{\bar{x} - \mu}{\sqrt{\dfrac{\sigma_i^2}{n_i}}}$$

Given $\bar{x} = 19$ km, $\mu = 18.2$ km.

Social class	Calculated Z value	Probability
A	1.15	0.1251
B	1.41	0.0793
C	1.97	0.0244
D	1.67	0.0475

Chapter 8

Question 1

You are a market research manager of a firm with outlets across most of the United Kingdom. Your major competitor has recently introduced a new own-brand product onto the market with a nationwide launch. You notice that there is a drop in your market share. In response, you propose to introduce a similar new product with its own brand name to maintain your share of the market. To investigate the effect of the introduction of the own-brand product, you conduct a test in randomly selected outlets in four marketing regions for a period of four weeks. This provides the following results:

Marketing regions: sales (000) units of new own-brand product

	Region			
Size of the outlet	A	B	C	D
Large	145	120	65	170
Medium	135	130	45	90
Small	120	110	30	40

Conduct a test of significance at the 5% level of the association between the size of the outlet and the marketing region.

Answer 1

The sample is large $n = 1200$. The selection of the sample outlets is done randomly. What is being tested? The association of the size of the outlet and the marketing region is being tested. Therefore, a Chi-squared test needs to be used.

H_0 (Null hypothesis):   There is no association between the size of the outlet and the marketing region.

H_1 (Alternative hypothesis): There is an association between the size of the outlet and the marketing region.

α (level of significance):   0.05 (95% confidence in the outcome of the test)

Degrees of freedom: $= (r - 1)(c - 1)$ where r = number of rows = 3
$= (3 - 1)(4 - 1) = 6$ c = number of columns = 4

Decision rule: From the χ^2 distribution tables at 0.05 level with 6 degrees of freedom the critical value = 12.592

If the calculated value of χ^2 is greater than 12.592, then reject H_0; that there is no association between the size of the outlet and marketing regions at the 5% level of significance.

The table below shows the observed and expected frequencies (in brackets)

Size of the outlet	Marketing regions: sales (000) units of new brand product				Total
	A	B	C	D	
Large	145	120	65	170	500
	(166.7)	(150.0)	(58.3)	(125.0)	
Medium	135	130	45	90	400
	(133.3)	(120.0)	(46.7)	(100.0)	
Small	120	110	30	40	300
	(100.0)	(90.0)	(35.0)	(75.0)	
Total	400	360	140	300	1200

The expected frequency (E) for large outlet and region A, under the null hypothesis that there is no association between size of the outlet and the marketing region is given by:

$$\frac{\text{Marginal total A} \times \text{Marginal total large}}{\text{Grand total}}$$

$$= (400 \times 500)/1200 = 166.7.$$

$$\chi^2 = \sum \frac{(O - E)^2}{E}$$

$$= 2.82 + 6.00 + 0.76 + 16.20 + 0.02 + 0.83 + 0.06 + 1.00 + 4.00 + 4.44$$

$$+ 0.71 + 16.3$$

$$= 53.1$$

Since the calculated value of $\chi^2 = 53.1$ is greater than the value in the tables, of 12.952, we reject the null hypothesis. Therefore, there is an association between the size of the outlet and the marketing region.

Question 2

A marketing manager of a retail outlet is reviewing the results of a survey of adult women. This involved a random sample of 250 respondents and was conducted in a typical (Midlands) test area. The table below gives the cross-tabulation of the data on the working status of the respondents and the amount of money spent on washing-up liquids in a month.

Expenditure on washing-up liquid	Working full-time	Working part-time	Not working	Total
Less than £5	15	10	30	55
£5–10	25	30	35	90
Over £10	25	40	40	105
Total	65	80	105	250

Can the marketing manager infer that there is an association between working status and expenditure on washing-up liquids?

Answer 2

The sample is large $n = 250$. The selection of the sample outlets is done randomly. What is being tested? The association of the working status of respondents and the amount of money spent on washing up liquids is being tested. Therefore, a Chi-squared test should be used.

H_0 (Null hypothesis):	There is no association between the working status of respondents and the amount of money spent on washing up liquids
H_1 (Alternative hypothesis):	There is an association between the working status of respondents and the amount of money spent on washing up liquids
α (level of significance):	0.05 (95% confidence in the outcome of the test)
Degrees of freedom:	$= (r - 1)(c - 1)$ where $r =$ number of rows $= 3$ $= (3 - 1)(3 - 1) = 4$ $c =$ number of columns $= 3$
Decision rule:	From the χ^2 distribution tables at the 0.05 level with 4 degrees of freedom the critical value $= 9.488$ If the calculated value of χ^2 is greater than 9.488, then reject H_0; that there is no association between the buying pattern and marketing regions has been rejected at 5% level of significance.

The table below shows the observed and expected frequencies (in brackets)

Expenditure on washing-up liquid	Working full-time	Working part-time	Not working	Total
Less than £5	15 (14.3)	10 (17.6)	30 (23.1)	55
£5 to £10	25 (23.4)	30 (28.8)	35 (37.8)	90
Over £10	25 (27.3)	40 (33.6)	40 (44.1)	105
Total	65	80	105	250

The expected frequency (E) for expenditure less than £5 and working full-time, under the null hypothesis that there is no association between the working status of respondents and the amount of money spent on washing up liquids is given by:

$$\frac{\text{Marginal total} < £5 \times \text{Marginal total full-time}}{\text{Grand total}}$$

$$= (55 \times 65)/250 = 14.3$$

$$\chi^2 = \sum \frac{(O - E)^2}{E} = 0.03 + 3.28 + 2.06 + 0.11 + 0.05 + 0.21 + 0.19 + 1.22 + 0.38$$

$$= 7.53$$

Since the calculated value of $\chi^2 = 7.53$ is less than the value in the tables, of 9.488, we accept the null hypothesis. Therefore, there is no association between the working status of respondents and the amount of money spent on washing up liquids.

Question 3

The table below shows (1) the market share (ms) as a percentage of the total market, (2) relative price (rp) as an index with the retail price index for the industry as a base and (3) advertising share (as) as a percentage of the total advertising expenditure, for a particular company over the past 15 years.

Year	Market share % (m)	Relative price (rp)	Advertising share % (as)
1	20	100	20
2	25	100	25
3	40	95	35
4	35	95	35
5	45	80	35
6	35	90	30
7	40	85	35
8	55	80	35
9	50	85	40
10	45	85	55
11	30	105	45
12	20	110	25
13	20	95	20
14	25	100	25
15	30	95	30

(i) Calculate the rank correlation coefficient between the market share with relative price and test its significance.

(ii) Calculate the product–moment correlation coefficient between the market share and the advertising share and test its significance.

(iii) Comment on which correlation coefficient calculated in (i) and (ii) you would prefer.

Answer 3

(i) For calculating the rank correlation, as the observed values for all three variables are interval scale, you need to convert these to ranks. To calculate the rank correlation, you use the formula

$$r' = 1 - \frac{6\sum D^2}{n(n^2 - 1)}$$

The rank correlation between the market share and the relative price =

$$r' = 1 - \frac{6\sum D_1^2}{n(n^2 - 1)} = 1 - \frac{6(1033)}{15(15^2 - 1)} = 1 - \frac{6198}{3360} = 1 - 1.84 = -0.84$$

This shows a strong negative correlation between the market share and the relative price.

299

Market share (Y)	Relative price (X_1)	Advertising share (X_2)	Rank Y R_Y	Rank X_1 R_{X_1}	$D_1^2 = (R_Y - R_{X_1})^2$
20	100	20	1.5	12.0	110.25
25	100	25	4.0	12.0	64.00
40	95	35	10.5	8.5	4.00
35	95	35	8.5	8.5	0.00
45	80	35	12.5	1.5	121.00
35	90	30	8.5	6.0	6.25
40	85	35	10.5	4.0	42.25
55	80	35	15.0	1.5	182.25
50	85	40	14.0	4.0	100.00
45	85	55	12.5	4.0	72.25
30	105	45	6.5	14.0	56.25
20	110	25	1.5	15.0	182.25
25	95	20	4.0	8.5	20.25
25	100	25	4.0	12.0	64.00
30	95	30	6.5	8.5	4.00
Total					$\sum D_1^2 = 1033.00$

To test the significance of the rank correlation coefficient you conduct a t-test using the formula

$$t = r' \sqrt{\frac{n-2}{1-r'^2}}$$

The procedure for testing will be as follows:

H$_0$ (Null hypothesis): There is no relationship between the market share and the relative price.

H$_1$ (Alternative hypothesis): There is a relationship between the market share and the relative price.

(α) (level of significance): 0.05 (95% confidence in the outcome of the test)

The test statistics will be $t = r' \sqrt{\dfrac{n-2}{1-r^2}}$

Degrees of freedom: $n-2 = 15-2 = 13$ where $n =$ number of pairs of observations.

Decision rule: If the calculated value of t is less than -2.160, then reject H$_0$. That there is no relationship between the market share and the relative price, is rejected at the 5% level of significance.

$$t = -0.84 \sqrt{\frac{15-2}{1-(-0.84)^2}} = -0.84 \sqrt{\frac{13}{0.2944}} = -0.84(6.65) = -5.59$$

The null hypothesis that there is no correlation between the market share and the relative price is rejected at 5% level of significance. That is, that there is a significant correlation between the market share and the relative price.

(ii) For calculating the product–moment correlation you use the formula

$$r = \frac{n\sum xy - (\sum x)(\sum y)}{\sqrt{[n\sum x^2 - (\sum x)^2][n\sum y^2 - (\sum y)^2]}} \qquad (n = X_2 \text{ in this example})$$

Market share (Y)	Advertising share (X_2)	Y^2	X_2^2	X_2Y
20	20	400	400	400
25	25	625	625	625
40	35	1600	1225	1400
35	35	1225	1225	1225
45	35	2025	1225	1575
35	30	1225	900	1050
40	35	1600	1225	1400
55	35	3025	1225	1925
50	40	2500	1600	2000
45	55	2025	3025	2475
30	45	900	2025	1350
20	25	400	625	500
25	20	625	400	500
25	25	625	625	625
30	30	900	900	900
$\sum Y = 520$	$\sum X_2 = 490$	$\sum Y^2 = 19700$	$\sum X_2^2 = 17250$	$\sum X_2Y = 17950$

The product-moment correlation between the market share (Y) and the advertising share (X_2)

$$\frac{15(17950) - (490 \times 520)}{\sqrt{[15(17250) - (490)^2][15(19700) - (520)^2]}} = \frac{14450}{\sqrt{18650 \times 25100}}$$

$$= \frac{14450}{21635.97} = 0.668$$

This shows a positive correlation between the market share (Y) and the advertising share (X_2).

To test the significance of the product–moment correlation coefficient you conduct a t test using the formula

$$t = r\sqrt{\frac{n-2}{1-r^2}}$$

The procedure for testing will be as follows:

H$_0$ (Null hypothesis):   There is no relationship between the market share and the advertising share.

H$_1$ (Alternative hypothesis):   There is a relationship between the market share and the advertising share.

(α) (level of significance):   0.05 (95% confidence in the outcome of the test)

The test statistics will be $t = r\sqrt{\dfrac{n-2}{1-r^2}}$

Degrees of freedom: $n-2 = 15-2 = 13$ where n = number of pairs of observations.

Decision rule: If the calculated value of t is greater than 2.160, then reject H$_0$. That there is no relationship between the market share and the advertising share, is rejected at the 5% level of significance.

$$t = 0.668\sqrt{\frac{15-2}{1-(0.668)^2}} = 0.668\sqrt{\frac{13}{0.7442}} = 0.668(3.84) = 2.57$$

The null hypothesis that there is no correlation between the market share and the advertising share is rejected at the 5% level of significance. That is, that there is a significant correlation between the market share and the advertising share.

(iii) The product–moment correlation coefficient is preferred as interval scales are used in the calculations while the Spearman's rank correlation uses rank, a weaker measurement.

Chapter 9

Question 1

It is claimed that the average expenditure per adult on an overseas holiday is £450. A travel survey of 1400 such adults gives an average expenditure of £425 with a standard deviation of £80. Test at the 1% level of significance if the difference is significant.

Answer 1

Assume the sample selection of 1400 adults is random. The sample size $n = 1400$, population mean $\mu = £450$, sample mean $\bar{x} = £425$ and estimated standard deviation $\sigma = £80$. To test whether the average expenditure is different from £450, we will perform a Z-test.

H_0:	There is no difference in the average adult expenditure from £450.
H_1:	There is a difference in the average adult expenditure from £450 (two-tailed test)
α:	0.05

Test statistics: Z; critical value $Z_\alpha = 1.96$ (from Appendix II)

Decision rule: If the calculated value of $Z > Z_\alpha$ (1.96) then reject H_0, otherwise accept H_0.

$$Z = \frac{\bar{x} - \mu}{\sqrt{\dfrac{\sigma^2}{n}}} = \frac{425 - 450}{\sqrt{\dfrac{(80)^2}{1400}}} = \frac{-25}{\sqrt{\dfrac{6400}{1400}}} = \frac{-25}{2.14} = -11.68$$

Since the calculated value of Z (11.68) is greater than the critical value of 1.96, reject H_0. The average adult expenditure on holiday is different from £450 and the new (estimate of) average expenditure is now £425.

Question 2

An advertiser claims that 'eight of ten housewives cannot tell Swan margarine from butter'. A consumers group sets out to test this claim and finds that among 100 of their member selected randomly, 30 can distinguish between Swan and the butter. Would this cause you to doubt the advertiser's claim?

Answer 2

Given, advertiser's claim $p = 0.8$, $n = 100$, selection is random.
30 can distinguish, therefore 70 cannot distinguish. $q = (1 - p) = P = 1 - 03 = 0.7$

H_0:	The proportion who cannot distinguish Swan margarine from butter is not different from 0.8. $(\pi = 0.8)$
H_1:	There is a difference in the proportion who cannot distinguish Swan margarine from butter is different from 0.8 $(\pi \neq 0.8)$ (two-tailed test)
α:	0.01

Test statistics: Z; critical value $Z_{ga} = 2.58$

Decision rule: If the calculated value of $Z > Z_{\alpha}(2.58)$, then reject H_0, otherwise accept H_0.

$$Z = \frac{p - \pi}{\sqrt{\dfrac{\pi(1 - \pi)}{n}}} = \frac{0.7 - 0.8}{\sqrt{\dfrac{0.8(1 - 0.8)}{100}}} = \frac{-0.1}{\sqrt{\dfrac{0.16}{100}}} = \frac{-0.1}{0.04} = -2.50$$

Since the calculated value of Z (2.50) is smaller than the table value of 2.58, we accept the hypothesis that the proportion who cannot distinguish Swan margarine from butter is not different from 0.8. Therefore, there is no cause to doubt the advertiser's claim.

Question 3

Fast-food service companies try to devise wage plans that provide incentive and produce salaries for their managers that are competitive with corresponding positions in competing companies. A random sample of 12 unit managers for one company shows that they earn an average salary of £36750 with a standard deviation of £3100.

(a) Calculate a 95% confidence interval for the mean salary of the company's managers.

(b) Do the data suggest that the mean salary earned by the company's unit managers differ from £38500, which is the mean salary paid by a competitor firm? Use a significance level of 5%.

Answer 3

Small sample of size $n = 12$ drawn randomly.
Average salary $\bar{x} = £36750$
Estimated standard deviation $\sigma = £3100$.

(a) Confidence interval for mean salary =

$$\bar{x} \pm t_{\alpha/2} SE(\bar{x}) = 36750 \pm 2.201 \sqrt{\frac{(3100)^2}{11}}$$

$$= 36750 \pm 2.201 \sqrt{87363636.33} = 36750 \pm 2057 = £34693; \ £38807$$

(b) Given, $\mu = £38500$ and $\alpha = 0.05$
To test whether the average manager's salary differs from £38500, we will perform a t-test.

H_0:	There is no difference in the average manager's salary from £38500.
H_1:	There is no difference in the average manager's salary from £38500 (two-tailed test)

α: 0.05

Test statistic: $t_{n-1} = \dfrac{\bar{x} - \mu}{\sqrt{\dfrac{\hat{\sigma}^2}{n-1}}}$ with $n-1$ degrees of freedom.

Decision rule: If the calculated value of t is less than -2.201, then reject H_0. That there is no difference in the average manager's salary from £38500 is rejected at the 5% level of significance.

$$t_{n-1} = \dfrac{\bar{x} - \mu}{\sqrt{\dfrac{\sigma^2}{n}}} = \dfrac{36750 - 38500}{\sqrt{\dfrac{(3100)^2}{11}}} = \dfrac{-1750}{934.69} = -1.87$$

Since the calculated value of t (1.87) is less than the critical value (2.201), we accept the null hypothesis that there is no difference in the average manager's salary from £38500.

(c) The sample average salary £36750 lies within the confidence interval (£34693; £38807), indicating that the observed difference is by chance.

Question 4

A company selects nine salesmen at random and their sales figures for the previous month are recorded. Then they undergo a training course designed by a business consultant and their sales figures for the following month are recorded:

Previous month	75	90	94	85	100	90	69	70	64
Following month	77	101	93	92	105	88	73	76	68

Has the training course caused an improvement in the salesmen's ability? (You may assume that the standard deviation for the difference $= 4$.)

Answer 4

Sample is small, $n = 9$, and selected randomly. Since sales are observed for two months for the same salesmen, this will be a 'paired' t-test.

H_0: $\mu = 0$. No difference in average sales due to training.

H_0: $\mu > 0$. There is an increase in average sales due to training (one-tailed test)

α: 0.05

Test statistics: t_{n-1}; critical value $t_{n-1;\,\alpha} = 1.860$

Decision rule: If calculated $t > t_{n-1;\,\alpha}$ (1.860) then reject H_0, otherwise accept H_0.

Given $\hat{\sigma}_d = 4$, and the sample mean of the difference in sales before and after training $\bar{d} = 4.0$

$$t_8 = \frac{\bar{d}}{\sqrt{\dfrac{\hat{\sigma}_d^2}{n-1}}} = \frac{4}{\sqrt{\dfrac{(4)^2}{8}}} = \frac{4}{1.41} = 2.84$$

The calculated value of the t-statistic (2.84) is greater than the critical value (1.860), therefore, the null hypothesis that there is no increase in sales due to training is rejected. Training increases sales.

Question 5

A manufacturer of orange juice develops a new container and tests the sales of the drink in relation to its existing container in ten randomly selected shops over a period of one month. The results are shown below:

Container	Units sold in different outlets									
	A	B	C	D	E	F	G	H	I	J
Existing	36	61	60	63	57	58	61	48	54	75
New	58	58	76	63	50	54	63	64	65	87

(a) Do these results provide evidence that the existing and new containers have different mean sales?

(b) Suppose that, instead of two different groups of shops, one group of shops sold the drink in the existing container and after a month sold it in the new container. Can you now conclude that the sales are different? What is the methodological importance of the one-month gap?

Answer 5

(a) Assume the shops selected are chosen randomly. The sample sizes are small in both cases, $n = 10$. Therefore, this will be a test of two independent sample means.

H_0:	$\mu_1 - \mu_2 = 0$. There is no difference in the average sales due to two containers.
H_1:	$\mu_1 - \mu_2 \neq 0$. There is a difference in average sales due to two containers (two-tailed test)
α:	0.05

Test statistics: $t_{n_1 + n_2 - 2, \alpha}$; critical value $t_{n_1 + n_2 - 2, \alpha} = 2.101$

Decision rule: If the calculated value of $t > t_{n_1 + n_2 - 2, \alpha}$ (2.101) then reject H_0, otherwise accept H_0.

$$t = \frac{(\bar{x}_1 - \bar{x}_2) - (\mu_1 - \mu_2)}{\sqrt{\hat{\sigma}_p^2 \left(\dfrac{1}{n_1} + \dfrac{1}{n_2} \right)}}$$

$$\hat{\sigma}_p^2 = \frac{\sum (x_1 - \bar{x}_1)^2 + \sum (x_2 - \bar{x}_2)^2}{n_1 + n_2 - 2}$$

Existing (x_1)	New (x_2)	$(x_1 - \bar{x}_1)^2$	$(x_2 - \bar{x}_2)^2$	D = new−existing	$(d - \bar{d})$
36	58	453.69	33.64	−22	240.25
61	58	13.69	33.64	−3	90.25
60	76	7.29	148.84	16	90.25
63	63	32.49	0.64	0	42.25
57	50	0.09	190.44	−7	182.25
58	54	0.49	96.04	−4	110.25
61	63	13.69	0.64	2	20.25
48	64	86.49	0.04	16	90.25
54	65	10.89	1.44	11	20.25
75	87	313.29	538.24	12	30.25

Total					
$\sum x_1 = 573$	$\sum x_2 = 638$	$\sum (x_1 - \bar{x}_1)^2$	$\sum (x_2 - \bar{x}_2)^2$	$\sum d = 65$	$\sum (d - \bar{d})^2$
$\bar{x}_1 = 57.6$	$\bar{x}_2 = 63.8$	$= 932.10$	$= 1043.60$	$\bar{d} = 6.5$	$= 916.50$

$$\hat{\sigma}_p^2 = \frac{\sum (x_1 - \bar{x}_1)^2 + \sum (x_2 - \bar{x}_2)^2}{n_1 + n_2 - 2} = \frac{932.10 + 1043.60}{10 + 10 - 2} = 109.76$$

$$t = \frac{(\bar{x}_1 - \bar{x}_2) - (\mu_1 - \mu_2)}{\sqrt{\hat{\sigma}_p^2 \left(\dfrac{1}{n_1} + \dfrac{1}{n_2} \right)}} = \frac{63.8 - 57.3}{\sqrt{109.76 \left(\dfrac{1}{10} + \dfrac{1}{10} \right)}} = \frac{6.5}{4.69} = 1.39$$

$t < 2.101$, therefore accept H_0. That is, there is no difference in the average sales due to two containers.

(b) If one group of shops was used with both the containers, this will become a 'paired' t-test.

H$_0$: $\mu = 0$. There is no difference in average sales due to containers.

H$_1$: $\mu > 0$. There is an increase in average sales due to new container (one-tailed test)

α: 0.05

Test statistics: t_{n-1}; critical value $t_{n-1;\alpha} = 1.833$

Decision rule: If the calculated value of $t > t_{n-1;\alpha}$ (1.833) then reject H$_0$, otherwise accept H$_0$.

Sample mean of the difference in sales due to new and existing container $\bar{d} = 6.5$.

$$\hat{\sigma}_d^2 = \frac{1}{n-1} \sum (d - \bar{d})^2 = \frac{916.50}{9} = 101.83$$

Then,

$$t_9 = \frac{\bar{d}}{\sqrt{\dfrac{\hat{\sigma}_d^2}{n}}} = \frac{6.5}{\sqrt{\dfrac{101.83}{10}}} = \frac{6.5}{3.19} = 2.04$$

The calculated value of the t-statistic (2.04) is greater than the critical value (1.833), therefore, the null hypothesis that there is no increase in sales due to new container is rejected. The new container increases sales. In this situation the variation due to the shops is removed and the result is better than when we used two independent sets of shops.

Chapter 10

Question 1

When is international marketing research necessary?

Answer 1

International *market* research may be necessary when a company has a basic lack of understanding about a potential overseas market. This is often achieved initially using secondary data studies to provide such information as potential size of market, market structure, range and nature of competitors, and product and service ranges. Frequently, international market research is commissioned when a company is interested in entering an overseas market for the first time. International *marketing* research is often commissioned later, when a firm already has an existing position within overseas markets. In such cases, companies may commission international studies in such areas as segmentation, positioning and advertising.

Question 2

How does the environment affect the conduct of marketing research?

Answer 2

This is really a question about how different components of the environment affect the marketing research process. The marketing environment will differ in different countries. This affects the extent to which marketing research is actually valued and commissioned. It also affects the extent to which companies actively get involved in the development of the research objectives and questions associated with the study. The government and legal environments affect what kind of questions can be asked and what data can be stored electronically or otherwise. The structural and technological environments particularly affect data collection in relation to the array of interviewing methods that can be used in different countries. Finally, the socio-cultural environment can impact upon all aspects of the research process, particularly in relation to the definition of the research objectives, interviewing methods, sampling, and questionnaire design.

Question 3

Why is it difficult to achieve comparability of data across countries?

Answer 3

It is difficult to achieve comparability across countries because the environments are so different. The difficulty comes in trying to achieve equivalent data through equivalent data-collection methods. Often this is difficult because different cultures perceive concepts differently, they use products and services for different means, they communicate using different languages and different cultures often behave and consume products and services differently. This problem is usually exacerbated by a lack of easily accessible, up-to-date, relevant data. Thus, research managers often have to attempt to achieve comparability imperfectly.

Question 4

How are the differing aspects of the research process affected by differences in equivalence between countries?

Answer 4

Conceptual and functional equivalences affect the research objectives of a study. They usually also affect what questions are asked of respondents. Different language requirements influence what, and how, questions are asked. They also affect how study reports and presentations are written and interpreted. Because concepts are measured differently in different countries, questions must use units that are consistent with those used by a particular culture. Sampling equivalence and data-collection equivalence affect the process directly. Thus, which respondents are selected in different countries depends on who is the most appropriate person to question about a particular product or service, company, attitude and opinion, and behaviour. Often, respondents have different levels of accessibility in different countries in terms of how they can be contacted and communicated with. This is intrinsically interconnected with a particular country's communication and travel infrastructure.

Question 5

How should international marketing research be coordinated when a global FMCG organization like Coca-Cola wishes to determine how to customize its product for, say, the Indonesian market?

Answer 5

The example given does not necessarily change the way in which international marketing research should be coordinated. However, the fact that it is a large well-respected company such as Coca-Cola would indicate that they would wish to ensure that the process was completed professionally since there could be major repercussions on the brand's positioning if it is not. The fact that the research is also consumer would indicate that care needs to be taken to ensure that a representative sample is sought. Because the product is a standardized one such as Coca-Cola and only very limited customization of the product would take place, researchers would be well advised to pay particular attention to achieving sampling, measurement, translation, and concept and functional equivalence.

Chapter 11

Question 1

Design and send a simple e-mail questionnaire to identify the on-line shopping habits of your circle of friends and/or acquaintances.

Answer 1

In addition to asking questions that probe the on-line shopping habits of your respondents (e.g., what do they purchase, which kinds of sites do they purchase from, what types of goods and services they buy), you should also ask your respondents to provide relevant descriptions of themselves. Examples include their age and gender, their usual mode of access to the Internet, such as the PC, mobile phone, iTV, etc., and their typical pattern of on-line behaviour, including the time of day, frequency and duration of on-line visits. When designing your e-mail, remember to adopt the KISS approach ('keep it simple stupid'), and pay just as much attention to the wording of your introductory note.

Question 2

Alternative Internet access devices are appearing all the time, including: games consoles, personal digital assistants (PDAs), third-generation mobile phones, kiosks, and interactive TV. Investigate how the display and interaction technology adopted by each of these channels are likely to impact on how you design a marketing research survey aimed at identifying the on-line shopping habits of consumers.

Answer 2

There are several avenues you should consider exploring. For example, you could begin by surfing the Web, using on-line directories and search engines to identify specialist Web sites that deal with the individual technologies. What keywords would be appropriate? (*Hint*: Combine the keywords describing the individual technologies with other phrases, e.g., 'human interaction', 'usability', 'on-line shopping'.)

Question 3

Search the Web to find examples of form-based questionnaires. Draw up a list of ways in which these are similar to, and different from, conventional questionnaires, and record your own assessment of their individual strengths and weaknesses.

Answer 3

It is relatively easy to find form-based questionnaires on the Web. If you use appropriate keywords with search engines, you will find a large number of examples. (*Hint*: in addition to the more obvious keywords, such as 'questionnaire', 'Web questionnaire' or 'Web form', you might also search for one of the tags included in the Web form itself, such as 'form action='.) It is relatively easy to find examples of questionnaires as used in conventional surveys—pop into your library and look up the appendices of social survey or retailing reports. When you have found a suitable set of examples of both kinds, compare their length, layout, wording, design, etc.

Question 4

From sources available on the Web, identify the likely response rates you can expect from e-mail and Web questionnaires. How do these compare to response rates for conventional (i.e., off-line) surveys?

Answer 4

To answer this question, visit some of the professional on-line marketing research websites, many of which discuss the issue of response rates in some detail, or type relevant phrases into a search engine. (You might also read some of the publications that compare these two types of on-line survey instrument, e.g., there are several useful references at the end of the chapter by Weible and Wallace, 2001.) Bear in mind that response rates are only one aspect of the comparative performance of various kinds of on- and off-line surveys.

Question 5

Research the Web, and find out how attitudes and legislation on the control of unsolicited electronic communication varies between countries. How is this likely to affect the undertaking of on-line marketing research on an international basis?

Answer 5

In the UK, Web users can register with an e-mail preference agency not to receive unsolicited e-mails (spam). However, this is clearly not going to be very effective at blocking the large amount of spam that originates in the USA or elsewhere in the world. An interesting debate is going on within the European Union as to whether spam should be controlled by requiring Web users to 'opt-in' to e-mailing lists or whether commercial e-mailers should be permitted to use an 'opt out' approach. (Search the Web, newsgroups and discussion boards, e.g., through the groups directory on Google, for exchanges on this topic.) Are there similar international initiatives to control spam elsewhere in the world, or are voluntary codes of conduct (e.g., the ESOMAR guidelines) the main approach? Can you find any evidence of countries that have strict controls? Is there similar evidence for their success in blocking spam?

Chapter 12

These tasks will require access to some secondary sources mentioned in the chapter. These sources will certainly be available at any business school library, and are also available at many public libraries.

You work for an American company that plans to enter the UK market for heavy industrial machinery. The market leader is J.C. Bamford Excavators Ltd.

Question 1

What is J.C. Bamford's product range?

Answer 1

J.C. Bamford's product range includes:

- Tracked excavators
- Wheeled excavators
- Backhoe leaders
- Wheeled leaders

- Telescopic handlers
- Rough terrain forklifts
- Mini excavators
- Skid steer loaders
- Teletruk (telescopic forklift)
- Fastrac

Question 2

What are their primary target markets?

Answer 2

The construction industry will be a key target market for your company. The primary target markets include:

- Construction
- Mining and quarrying
- Warehousing
- Agriculture
- Forestry

Question 3

What are the key trends currently affecting the UK construction industry?

Answer 3

Here is a selection of trends organised into typical headings. Students should be able to identify a substantial list from newspaper and Internet resources. It is important to encourage students to clarify the likely impacts on the construction industry (positive and negative) rather than simply to present a list.

- (Social) Significant increases in the number of UK households, particularly single-person households
- (Social) Increasing age profile
- (Technological) Increasingly rapid introduction of new materials (e.g., lighter and easier to work with, requiring less maintenance and repair)
- (Political/economic) European monetary union
- (Environmental) Global warming and associated climatic change (likely to lead to 20% reduction in days requiring building heating and 80% increase in days requiring building cooling in the UK)
- (Environmental) Environmentalism, requiring a gradual shift towards recycled materials

Question 4

Provide a brief summary of the UK government's current plans for road building.

Answer 4

Public expenditure on road investment from 1994/5 to 2004/5 is shown in the following table, adapted from the Department of the Environment, Transport and the Regions' 10-year plan.

£billion, rounded (out-turn prices)

1994/5	1995/6	1996/7	1997/8	1998/9	1999/0	2000/1	2001/2	2002/3	2003/4	2004/5
1.5	1.3	1.1	0.9	0.8	0.7	0.9	1.0	1.1	1.2	1.2

As at 2000, the UK government's plans were for a modest expansion in road-building expenditure. Note that the above table is in out-turn prices—the real-terms' increase in expenditure is rather less. Also note that even after the modest increases expected, total investment in roads will be lower in 2004/5 than it was in 1994/5.

APPENDIX I

Selected Sources of Secondary Information

1. Business and Reference Guides

A good starting point for any secondary search is a *bibliography* or *reference guide* on your subject. Bibliographic sources are organized by key topic or subject area and list books, periodicals, articles and other published work that are available in that area. *Reference guides* generally provide detailed listings of major works, studies, publications and sources of business and marketing information. Bibliographic or access information is provided so you can then find the listed sources.

Major business and marketing reference guides, include:

1. *International Directory of Business Information Sources and Services*, 2nd edn London: Europa Publications Ltd, 1996.
2. *Directory of European Community Information Sources*, Belgium: Euroconfidential, 1994.
3. *European Business Handbook*, London: Kogan Page, 1997.
4. Foster, P. *Business Information Basics*, London: Headland Business Information, 1997.
5. *Business Information Sources*, Berkeley: University of California Press.
6. *Directory of British Associations*, Beckenham: CBD Research Ltd.
7. *Encyclopedia of Business Information Sources*, Detroit; Gale Research.
8. *The European Business Information Sourcebook*, Headland, Cleveland: Headland Press.
9. *On-Line/CD-ROM Business Sourcebook*, Headland, Cleveland: Headland Press,—European and UK business databases.
10. *European Directory of Marketing Information Sources* (biennial) and *International Directory of Marketing Information Sources*, London: Euromonitor plc.
11. *Sources of European Economic and Business Information*, 6th edn, London: Gower Publishers, 1995—a useful listing of sources of economic and statistical data.

2. Indexes and Abstracts

Indexes and abstracts are critical to the secondary information search. *Indexes* list references to often hundreds of articles and available works arranged by key word like 'cereals', by country, or by company. *Abstracts* provide not only the reference, but also a short summary of the major points raised in the article. Both indexes and abstracts are available in hard-copy books in libraries, and in electronic databases like CD-ROMs.

Among the key business and marketing indexes and abstract services are:

1. *ABI/INFORM Database*—on CD-ROM available at most libraries; provides bibliographic details and abstracts of key articles from nearly 1000 English-language journals.
2. *Predicast's Funk and Scott Index*—lists a wide range of periodicals, trade reports and articles referenced by industry. US, European and International Editions available.
3. *Business Periodicals Index*, New York: H.W. Wilson Co.—in text form and on CD-ROM as WILSONDISC; primarily American companies.
4. *Reader's Guide to Periodical Literature*, New York: H.W. Wilson Co., monthly—focus on American publications; available on CD-ROM as WILSONDISC.
5. *Social Sciences Citation Index*, Philadelphia: Institute for Scientific Information—reference to articles from hundreds of journals, newspapers and other publications; updated three times per year. The SSCI can be found on the BIDS database.
6. *Helecon*—available on CD-ROM; combined indexes from seven European databases on business and management.
7. *Index to Business Reports*—over 800 business reports published in business journals and newspapers each year.

Major On-line and CD-ROM Data Providers of Abstracts and Full-text Articles

On-line Databases help to minimize one of the major problems with secondary information, that of timeliness. While most published and CD-ROM information becomes outdated very quickly, on-line information can be updated daily. Naturally, this is more costly so on-line providers often charge very high fees for the use of their services. Users need to be efficient and experienced in searching for information on-line in order to keep the costs low.

Major on-line services provide access to hundreds of different business information databases. Some of the major on-line providers are:

1. *DIALOG* is currently the world's largest electronic data provider. The company manages 450 separate databases, including ABI/INFORM (see above) Data-monitor; FT (Financial Times) and Find/SVP, all themselves excellent sources of business and marketing information in indexed, abstract or full-text form. Access

to DIALOG's on-line services can be expensive. Searches cost £15 to £70 per hour including an annual fee.

2. *FT PROFILE* is part of the Financial Times Group. This on-line database provides full-text and abstracted business information from over 4500 sources including Economist Intelligence Unit, Euromonitor, and the Financial Times, ABI/INFORM and Mintel. Fees include a £250 registration and 40 pence per minute charge with a £50 monthly minimum usage.

3. *MAID* (Market Analysis and Information Database) contains the full text of over 40000 market research reports as well as newspaper and magazine articles and the annual reports of 4.5 million companies. MAID charges users £5950 per year for the use of its service as well as a per-minute charge.

3. Full-text Sources

Books

Books are an important source of secondary information on specific industries and business and marketing issues. Be sure to make use of the bibliographies provided in the works as a resource for further information. For a list of published books, see *Global Books in Print* on CD-ROM, available in most major libraries.

Periodicals and Journals

Academic journals such as the *Journal of Marketing, International Journal of Market Research* and *Journal of Marketing Research* often provide the most up-to-date and well-researched information on business and marketing topics. They should be one of the first sources you consult in the secondary search.

Commercial Business Periodicals

For general marketing intelligence, recent economic trends, competitor information and new ideas, the commercial business press is essential reading. *The Economist, Business Week, Fortune, Marketing,* and *Advertising Age* are just some examples. As noted above, previous articles from these publications can be found in indexed or abstracted databases such as ABI/Inform.

Articles in commercial business periodicals do not usually provide references to their sources or represent primary research. They may also be biased towards a point of view or political orientation so treat them as a basic source of information that requires further investigation.

Newspapers

The Financial Times is the major business newspaper in the United Kingdom as is the *Wall Street Journal* in the United States. Other important newspapers include *The Sunday Times, The Times, The Guardian, The Daily Telegraph, The Observer,* and *The New York Times.* Backdated articles can be found in full-text or abstracted form in key CD-ROM databases like ABI/Inform. While an excellent source of current economic trends, new or proposed legislation,and company information, newspaper articles do not always provide the full story behind an event and do not provide references. You should try to look for the original source of information behind the story before using it in your research.

4. Market and Industry Research Studies

For competitive information, company directories and guides contain information on company size, subsidiaries, brand names, financials, locations, market share, products, and other marketing topics. For example, the annual *Kelly's Business Directory* has information on 82000 companies listed in its database and *FT Extel*, part of the Financial Times Group, provides financial and marketing information on companies around the world.

Major providers of market and industry research reports and studies include:

1. *Findex: The World Wide Directory of Market Research Reports, Studies and Surveys*, London: Euromonitor, annual—10600 citations from US and non-US research publishers arranged by 12 general industry classes.
2. *Market Research: A Guide to British Library Collections*, London: The British Library Business Information Service.
3. *Market Research Europe*, London: Euromonitor, annual—trends, forecasts, size and performance of consumer products in Euorpe.
4. *Frost and Sullivan Research Reports Abstracts*.
5. *Market Research Society's Yearbook*, London: Market Research Society.
6. *Corporate Intelligence Group* publishes a variety of research and market reports such as 'Retail Rankings' and 'Europe's Top Retailers'.
7. *Taylor Nelson AGB (TNAGB)* publishes a range of reports on consumer markets such as food, chemists, etc.
8. Other organizations that publish market research reports include: Arbitron, Datamonitor, Economist Intelligence Unit, Find/SVP, and ICC Keynote Reports.
9. *Key Note Market Research Reports*, London: ICC—industry and market sector reports with background, trends, prospects, and major companies. Available in most university libraries.
10. *Market Intelligence*, London: Mintel Information Group—Mintel produces detailed research reports on key market sectors such as FMCG, consumer durables, leisure and retailing. They also do special subject reports each year (e.g., 'The gardening market') and detailed financial reports on major companies. Mintel reports are available on CD-ROM in most university libraries.
11. *Economist Intelligence Unit*, publications—market reports by sector such as the automotive sector.

12. *Euromonitor Reports*—market reports for Europe and international such as the *European Marketing Data and Statistics* (1997); *Market Research: Great Britain*; *Market Research: Europe*; and *Market Research: International*.
13. *Organization for Economic Co-operation and Development* (OECD)—publishes economic and market reports on member countries.
14. *Industrial Performance Analysis: A Financial Analysis of UK Industry and Commerce*, Hampton: ICC Group, Ltd—financial analysis of 27 major UK industries.

5. Government Publications

Key publications produced by the Office of National Statistics (ONS), http://www.statistics.gov.uk, are:

1. *Annual Abstract of Statistics*, a regularly updated listing of key statistics on such sectors as housing, population, manufacturing and services.
2. *Monthly Digest of Statistics*—monthly edition of the above.
3. *Economic Trends*—monthly review of key economic indicators for the UK economy, plus one article per month on selected international economic indicators.
4. *Social Trends*—key social trends in the UK and changing expenditure patterns.
5. *Regional Trends*—major economic and industrial trends across the UK.
6. *Business Monitor*—information on trends and performance in key UK industries.

Details for statistics from the US census bureau (particularly on the North American Industrial Classification System—NAICS) can be found at: http://www.census.gov

6. Trade Associations, Professional Bodies, and Trade Journals

Lists of trade associations, trade journals, and professional organisations are available in:

1. *Current British Directories*—all British industry, trade and professional directories.
2. *Business Organisations, Agencies, and Publications Directory*, Detroit: Gale Research Co.—20000 business and trade organizations, professional agencies, government agencies and publications.
3. *World Directory of Trade and Business Associations*, London: Euromonitor—3500 institutions.
4. *Advertisers Annual*, East Grinstead: Reed Information Services—a listing of key trade journals.
5. *British Rates and Data Guide (BRAD)*—a list of all key magazines and trade publications with detailed information on publication dates, target markets, and costs to advertise in.
6. *The Chartered Institute of Marketing*, Moor Hall, Cookham, Berkshire.
7. *Association of Chambers of Commerce*, London.

7. Company Directories, Guides and Information

Among the most regularly consulted sources of information on companies and competitors are:

1. *Kelly's Business Directory*, East Grinstead: Reed Information Services—82000 companies listed in this database.
2. *KOMPASS Register*, East Grinstead: Reed Information Sources—more detailed information on over 44000 companies.
3. *Major UK Companies*, London: Financial Times, annual.
4. *Key British Enterprises* and *Europe's Major Companies Directory*, London: Euromonitor, annual.
5. *The World's Major Companies Directory*, London: Euromonitor.
6. *Who Owns Whom*, (annual) High Wycombe: Dun and Bradstreet International, Ltd—guide to the ever-changing ownership of companies and brands.
7. *Dun and Bradstreet Registers*, High Wycombe: Dun and Bradstreet International, Ltd—30 volumes with detailed company information.
8. *FAME*—financial information database on over 100000 UK private and public companies. Available on CD-ROM in most university libraries.
9. *FT Extel*—part of the FT Group; provides financial and marketing information on companies around the world.
10. *Standard and Poor's Register of Corporations*—a key American service.
11. *Key Business Ratios*, High Wycombe: Dun and Bradstreet International, Ltd, 1997 —a guide to British business performance.

8. International Markets

A first step in your search for information on markets and consumers abroad is the *Department of Trade and Industry (DTI) Export Library* located at:

Export Market Information Centre (EMIC)
Kingsgate House, 66–74 Victoria Street
London SWE1 6SW
UK
Telephone: 0207-215-5445

Other published or electronic sources of international business information include:

1. *Europa World Yearbook*, London: Europa Publications—a two-volume overview of economic, political and social trends in most countries.
2. *Eurostat—Your Partner for European Statistics: A Guide* by the Statistical Office of the European Communities—a guide showing where to get detailed statistical information on EU countries and *Eurostat Yearbook 1997: A Statistical Eye on Europe (1986–1996)*, Luxembourg: Office of Official Publications for the European Community, 1997. *European Official Statistics: A Guide to Databases—*

listing 100 databases with detailed economic and social information on EU and affiliated countries.

3. *European Marketing Data*, London: Euromonitor, annual—includes data on consumer expenditure, population trends as well as forecasts and other statistical coverage for European countries and markets.
4. *International Marketing Data and Statistics*, London: Euromonitor, annual.
5. *Moody's International Manual*, New York: Moody's Investors Service—an annual guide with updates giving financial and business data on major corporations in 100 countries.
6. *Overseas Trade Statistics of the UK*—an ONS publication.
7. *World Economic Outlook*, Washington, DC: International Monetary Fund (biannual).
8. *World Economic Factbook*, London: Euromonitor, annual—summaries of key economic indicators, political situations and risk factors for most countries.
9. *OECD Economic Summaries*, Paris: OECD Publications, annual—country studies.
10. *FT Country Surveys*, London: FT Publishers—booklets of market information on most countries.

9. Information on the Environment

For information on economic trends, industry legislation, and general business statistics, consult the following government information sources:

Economies

1. *Economic Trends*—Office of National Statistics (ONS)—monthly review of economic situation (see above)
2. *European Trends*—ONS publication
3. *Retail Business*—ONS publication
4. *OECD Economic Outlook*, Paris: OECD Publications
5. *Bank of England Economic Survey*
6. *Barclays Bank Economic Surveys*

Legislation

The following CD-ROMs are available in most university libraries.

1. *EC Infodisk*—a CD-ROM containing the official bibliographic database of the European Community, including implemented, proposed, and draft legislation.
2. *Eurolaw*—a CD-ROM containing the full text of European Union legislation and briefings on UK implementation prepared by the Department of Trade and Industry (DTI).

Statistical Data

In addition to economic and industry statistics provided by the ONS, two comprehensive sources of statistics are:

1. *World Marketing Data and Statistics*, London: Euromonitor—updated every six months; includes data on retailing, advertising, consumer markets, households, etc. With the CD-ROM version, you can customize data for your particular research purpose.
2. *Predicasts Forecasts*, Predicasts International—short- to long-range statistics on various products and industries.

10. Information on Consumers and Consumer Markets

Information on target markets and consumer buying patterns can be found in:

1. *ACORN* (A Classification of Residential Neighbourhoods)—provides consumption indices and patterns by type of neighbourhood in the UK.
2. *CACI/Instant Demographics*—various publications.
3. *Family Spending Survey*—ONS Publication.
4. General *Household Survey*—ONS publication.
5. *Social Trends*—ONS publication.
6. *Consumer Europe* and *Consumer International*, London: Euromonitor, biannual— gives volume and value market size data for over 230 consumer products across 55 countries with forecasts to the year 2000; CD-ROM version.
7. *A to Z of UK Marketing Data; A to Z of UK Brands, A to Z of UK Retailing*, London: Euromonitor—marketing pocket books with quick references for all types of consumer goods, brands and retailers across the UK.
8. *Marketing in Europe*, London: Corporate Intelligence on Retailing—reports on consumer products sectors (e.g., processed foods); provides prospects and forecasts for consumer spending; and selected market surveys (e.g., tea in France).

11. Libraries and Information Services

Below is a list of key private and public business libraries and information services.

University

City Business Library (0207–683–8215)
London Business School Information Library (0207–723–3404)
Manchester Business School Library (0161–275–6333)

Government

Office of National Statistics—see above for address and phone
British Library Business Information Service (0207-412-7457/7454)
Export Market Information Centre (EMIC)—see above for address and phone

Associations and Professional Bodies

Chartered Institute of Marketing, Moor Hall, Cookham, Berks, SL6 9QH, http://www.cim.co.uk

Confederation of British Industry, Centre Point, 103 New Oxford Street, London WC1A 1DU, http://www.cbi.org.uk

Market Research Society, 15 Northburgh Street, London, EC1V 0JR, http://www.mrs.org.uk

The Construction Industry Research and Information Association (CIRIA), 6 Storey's Gate, London SW1P 3AU, http://www.ciria.org.uk

The Construction Industry Council, 26 Store Street, London WC1E 7BT, http://www.cic.org.uk/

The Chartered Institute of Purchasing and Supply, Easton House, Easton on the Hill, Stamford, Lincolnshire, http://www.cips.org/

Information Services

Euromonitor Research (0207–251–8024)
FT Business Research Centre (0207–873–3000)

Appendix II

Statistical Tables

Standard normal distribution table

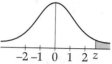

z	0	1	2	3	4	5	6	7	8	9
3.0	.0013	.0013	.0013	.0012	.0012	.0011	.0011	.0011	.0010	.0010
2.9	.0019	.0018	.0018	.0017	.0016	.0016	.0015	.0015	.0014	.0014
2.8	.0026	.0025	.0024	.0023	.0023	.0022	.0021	.0021	.0020	.0019
2.7	.0035	.0034	.0033	.0032	.0031	.0030	.0029	.0028	.0027	.0026
2.6	.0047	.0045	.0044	.0043	.0041	.0040	.0039	.0038	.0037	.0036
2.5	.0062	.0060	.0059	.0057	.0055	.0054	.0052	.0051	.0049	.0048
2.4	.0082	.0080	.0078	.0075	.0073	.0071	.0069	.0068	.0066	.0064
2.3	.0107	.0104	.0102	.0099	.0096	.0094	.0091	.0089	.0087	.0084
2.2	.0139	.0136	.0132	.0129	.0125	.0122	.0119	.0116	.0113	.0110
2.1	.0179	.0174	.0170	.0166	.0162	.0158	.0154	.0150	.0146	.0143
2.0	.0228	.0222	.0217	.0212	.0207	.0202	.0197	.0192	.0188	.0183
1.9	.0287	.0281	.0274	.0268	.0262	.0256	.0250	.0244	.0239	.0233
1.8	.0359	.0351	.0344	.0336	.0329	.0322	.0314	.0307	.0301	.0294
1.7	.0446	.0436	.0427	.0418	.0409	.0401	.0392	.0384	.0375	.0367
1.6	.0548	.0537	.0526	.0516	.0505	.0495	.0485	.0475	.0465	.0455
1.5	.0668	.0655	.0643	.0630	.0618	.0606	.0594	.0582	.0571	.0559
1.4	.0808	.0793	.0778	.0764	.0749	.0735	.0721	.0708	.0694	.0681
1.3	.0968	.0951	.0934	.0918	.0901	.0885	.0869	.0853	.0838	.0823
1.2	.1151	.1131	.1112	.1093	.1075	.1056	.1038	.1020	.1003	.0985
1.1	.1357	.1335	.1314	.1292	.1271	.1251	.1230	.1210	.1190	.1170
1.0	.1587	.1562	.1539	.1515	.1492	.1469	.1446	.1423	.1401	.1379
0.9	.1841	.1814	.1788	.1762	.1736	.1711	.1685	.1660	.1635	.1611
0.8	.2119	.2090	.2061	.2033	.2005	.1977	.1949	.1922	.1894	.1867
0.7	.2420	.2389	.2358	.2327	.2296	.2266	.2236	.2206	.2177	.2148
0.6	.2743	.2709	.2676	.2643	.2611	.2578	.2546	.2514	.2483	.2451
0.5	.3085	.3050	.3015	.2981	.2946	.2912	.2877	.2843	.2810	.2776
0.4	.3446	.3409	.3372	.3336	.3300	.3264	.3228	.3192	.3156	.3121
0.3	.3821	.3783	.3745	.3707	.3669	.3632	.3594	.3557	.3520	.3483
0.2	.4207	.4168	.4129	.4090	.4052	.4013	.3974	.3936	.3897	.3859
0.1	.4602	.4562	.4522	.4483	.4443	.4404	.4364	.4325	.4286	.4247
0.0	.5000	.4960	.4920	.4880	.4840	.4801	.4761	.4721	.4681	.4641

Source: *Introductory Statistics* by Prem Mann, Copyright © 2001 John Wiley & Sons, Inc. This material is used by permission of John Wiley & Sons, Inc.

The *t* distribution table

The entries in this table give the critical values of *t* for the specified number of degrees of freedom and areas in the right tail

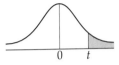

df	Area in the right tail under the *t* distribution curve					
	0.10	0.05	0.025	0.01	0.005	0.001
1	3.078	6.314	12.706	31.821	63.657	318.309
2	1.886	2.920	4.303	6.965	9.925	22.327
3	1.638	2.353	3.182	4.541	5.841	10.215
4	1.533	2.132	2.776	3.747	4.604	7.173
5	1.476	2.015	2.571	3.365	4.032	5.893
6	1.440	1.943	2.447	3.143	3.707	5.208
7	1.415	1.895	2.365	2.998	3.499	4.785
8	1.397	1.860	2.306	2.896	3.355	4.501
9	1.383	1.833	2.262	2.821	3.250	4.297
10	1.372	1.812	2.228	2.764	3.169	4.144
11	1.363	1.796	2.201	2.718	3.106	4.025
12	1.356	1.782	2.179	2.681	3.055	3.930
13	1.350	1.771	2.160	2.650	3.012	3.852
14	1.345	1.761	2.145	2.624	2.977	3.787
15	1.341	1.753	2.131	2.602	2.947	3.733
16	1.337	1.746	2.120	2.583	2.921	3.686
17	1.333	1.740	2.110	2.567	2.898	3.646
18	1.330	1.734	2.101	2.552	2.878	3.610
19	1.328	1.729	2.093	2.539	2.861	3.579
20	1.325	1.725	2.086	2.528	2.845	3.552
21	1.323	1.721	2.080	2.518	2.831	3.527
22	1.321	1.717	2.074	2.508	2.819	3.505
23	1.319	1.714	2.069	2.500	2.807	3.485
24	1.318	1.711	2.064	2.492	2.797	3.467
25	1.316	1.708	2.060	2.485	2.787	3.450
26	1.315	1.706	2.056	2.479	2.779	3.435
27	1.314	1.703	2.052	2.473	2.771	3.421
28	1.313	1.701	2.048	2.467	2.763	3.408
29	1.311	1.699	2.045	2.462	2.756	3.396
30	1.310	1.697	2.042	2.457	2.750	3.385
31	1.309	1.696	2.040	2.453	2.744	3.375
32	1.309	1.694	2.037	2.449	2.738	3.365
33	1.308	1.692	2.035	2.445	2.733	3.356
34	1.307	1.691	2.032	2.441	2.728	3.348
35	1.306	1.690	2.030	2.438	2.724	3.340
36	1.306	1.688	2.028	2.434	2.719	3.333
37	1.305	1.687	2.026	2.431	2.715	3.326

Chi-square distribution table

The entries in this table give the critical values of χ^2 for the specified number of degrees of freedom and areas in the right tail

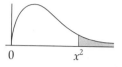

Area in the right tail under the Chi-square distribution curve

df	0.995	0.990	0.975	0.950	0.900	0.100	0.050	0.025	0.010	0.005
1	0.000	0.000	0.001	0.004	0.016	2.706	3.841	5.024	6.635	7.879
2	0.010	0.020	0.051	0.103	0.211	4.605	5.991	7.378	9.210	10.597
3	0.072	0.115	0.216	0.352	0.584	6.251	7.815	9.348	11.345	12.838
4	0.207	0.297	0.484	0.711	1.064	7.779	9.488	11.143	13.277	14.860
5	0.412	0.554	0.831	1.145	1.610	9.236	11.070	12.833	15.086	16.750
6	0.676	0.872	1.237	1.635	2.204	10.645	12.592	14.449	16.812	18.548
7	0.989	1.239	1.690	2.167	2.833	12.017	14.067	16.013	18.475	20.278
8	1.344	1.646	2.180	2.733	3.490	13.362	15.507	17.535	20.090	21.955
9	1.735	2.088	2.700	3.325	4.168	14.684	16.919	19.023	21.666	23.589
10	2.156	2.558	3.247	3.940	4.865	15.987	18.307	20.483	23.209	25.188
11	2.603	3.053	3.816	4.575	5.578	17.275	19.675	21.920	24.725	26.757
12	3.074	3.571	4.404	5.226	6.304	18.549	21.026	23.337	26.217	28.300
13	3.565	4.107	5.009	5.892	7.042	19.812	22.362	24.736	27.688	29.819
14	4.075	4.660	5.629	6.571	7.790	21.064	23.685	26.119	29.141	31.319
15	4.601	5.229	6.262	7.261	8.547	22.307	24.996	27.488	30.578	32.801
16	5.142	5.812	6.908	7.962	9.312	23.542	26.296	28.845	32.000	34.267
17	5.697	6.408	7.564	8.672	10.085	24.769	27.587	30.191	33.409	35.718
18	6.265	7.015	8.231	9.390	10.865	25.989	28.869	31.526	34.805	37.156
19	6.844	7.633	8.907	10.117	11.651	27.204	30.144	32.852	36.191	38.582
20	7.434	8.260	9.591	10.851	12.443	28.412	31.410	34.170	37.566	39.997
21	8.034	8.897	10.283	11.591	13.240	29.615	32.671	35.479	38.932	41.401
22	8.643	9.542	10.982	12.338	14.041	30.813	33.924	36.781	40.289	42.796
23	9.260	10.196	11.689	13.091	14.848	32.007	35.172	38.076	41.638	44.181
24	9.886	10.856	12.401	13.848	15.659	33.196	36.415	39.364	42.980	45.559
25	10.520	11.524	13.120	14.611	16.473	34.382	37.652	40.646	44.314	46.928
26	11.160	12.198	13.844	15.379	17.292	35.563	38.885	41.923	45.642	48.290
27	11.808	12.879	14.573	16.151	18.114	36.741	40.113	43.195	46.963	49.645
28	12.461	13.565	15.308	16.928	18.939	37.916	41.337	44.461	48.278	50.993
29	13.121	14.256	16.047	17.708	19.768	39.087	42.557	45.722	49.588	52.336
30	13.787	14.953	16.791	18.493	20.599	40.256	43.773	46.979	50.892	53.672
40	20.707	22.164	24.433	26.509	29.051	51.805	55.758	59.342	63.691	66.766
50	27.991	29.707	32.357	34.764	37.689	63.167	67.505	71.420	76.154	79.490
60	35.534	37.485	40.482	43.188	46.459	74.397	79.082	83.298	88.379	91.952
70	43.275	45.442	48.758	51.739	55.329	85.527	90.531	95.023	100.425	104.215
80	51.172	53.540	57.153	60.391	64.278	96.578	101.879	106.629	112.329	116.321
90	59.196	61.754	65.647	69.126	73.291	107.565	113.145	118.136	124.116	128.299
100	67.328	70.065	74.222	77.929	82.358	118.498	124.342	129.561	135.807	140.169

Glossary

Accuracy—the degree to which a measure conforms to the truth or a standard.

Adequacy—a measure by which the researcher determines whether data is sufficient to answer the company's information needs.

After-market—sales of component parts for use in maintaining, repairing or upgrading equipment that is already in use, e.g., the sale of replacement tyres to a vehicle owner.

Alternate hypothesis—a positive statement indicating belief in the nature and level of possible difference between the estimate and the parameter.

American Marketing Association—the association of marketing practitioners and academicians in the USA that publishes journals and organizes conferences for the dissemination of marketing knowledge.

AMSO—Association of Market Survey Organizations.

Analytical bias—A source of bias arising when the technique used to analyse the data is not sufficiently appropriate.

AQR—Association of Qualitative Researchers.

Association—measure of the degree to which two or more variables interrelate. Usually refers to nominal measurements.

Attitudes—mental states used by individuals to structure the way they perceive their environment and to guide the way in which they respond.

Backhoe loader—a heavy-duty industrial digger. The backhoe loader is often known as a 'JCB' in the United Kingdom because JC Bamford Excavators Ltd manufactures the market-leading product.

Back-translation—a method of translation that initially uses a translator fluent in the foreign language into which the research method is being translated and then uses a translator whose native language was the original language to translate back again.

BARB—Broadcast Audience Research Board.

BMRA—British Market Research Association.

Browsing—visiting and reading a particular Web document or website.

CAPI—computer-assisted personal interviewing—a method of data collection using a hand-held personal computer designed to reduce the time required for data input and analysis.

Case analysis—a method of conducting research whereby data is collected on individual companies, industries or situations.

CASI—computer-assisted self-administered interviewing—a method of data collection where the respondents themselves read the questions on the screen and enter the answers. No interviewer is required as the interviewing program guides the respondent through the questionnaire.

CATI—computer-assisted telephone interviewing—a method of data collection using a computerized telephone system, often using random digit dialling, designed to reduce the time required for data input and analysis.

Causal design—a research design used specifically to investigate the relational link between two or more variables by manipulating the independent variable(s) to see their effect upon the dependent variable(s).

CAWI—computer-assisted Web interviewing—a method of data collection using the Internet to obtain responses.

Census—a survey where every respondent in the population is investigated.

Chat room—a service on the Internet, which enables people to exchange (usually) text messages with others in real time—i.e., when all are on-line at the same time.

Chi-square analysis—a test to determine the association between two categorical (nominal) variables.

Chi-square automatic interaction detector (CHAID)—a technique for finding interactions in a sample by using nominally scaled independent variables to find sub-groups that differ with respect to a dependent variable by analysing the group differences using chi-square.

Chi-square test—a test for determining the association between categorical (nominal) variables.

Closed questions—a method of questioning where a choice of answers is specified and the respondents are asked to select among them.

Cluster analysis—a statistical technique for segmenting heterogeneous groups into homogeneous groups using a variety of different measurements.

Coding—the assignation of values to responses to survey instruments.

Coefficient of variation—a value without units which measures the variation of the mean in relation to the standard deviation, usually expressed as a percentage.

Comparative test—a test determining the differences relating to two or more estimates.

Completeness—the depth and breadth of the data in relation to the research question.

Completion technique—a projective method that requires the respondent to complete sentences or stories to provide insights into their hidden motivations, feelings or attitudes.

Conceptual equivalence—the extent to which interpretation of behaviour, or objects, is similar across countries.

Confidence—a measure of the degree of reliability associated with an estimate.

Confirmatory test—a test designed to determine whether a hypothesis confirms the researcher's prior expectations (for example, confirming that advertising increases sales).

Constant sum scale—a scale in which the respondent must allocate a fixed number of points among items to reflect the relative preferences for each item.

Construct validity—a method of determining the validity of the data involving the measurement of the degree of correlation with similar and dissimilar variables.

Consumer profile—a study designed to determine specific characteristics of a consumer group. Usually incorporates socio-economic and demographic data.

Content analysis—a technique used to study qualitative data by breaking it into meaningful categories.

Content validity—the use of the researcher's subjective judgement to determine whether an instrument is really measuring what it is supposed to measure. Also referred to as face validity.

Contingency table—a table illustrating the observed values of two nominal variables to show the relationship between them.

Control sample method—a method that involves recruiting people from a reputable sampling frame, so that the sample results are generalizable.

Convenient sample—a method of non-probability sampling selected using the judgement and convenience of the interviewer.

Correlation coefficient—a number between ±1 that reflects the degree to which two variables have a linear relationship.

Critical value—the value of the test statistic used for deciding the significance of the sample statistic thereby determining whether to accept or reject the null hypothesis.

Cross-tabulation—the determination of frequency distribution for two or more sub-groups.

Customer relationship management (CRM)—a group of management techniques which position the relationship between a customer and the supplier to the satisfaction of both.

Data—unassimilated facts or measurements.

Data analysis—the procedure used to investigate the information collected.

Database—an organized store of data, usually within a computer.

Data-collection equivalence—the degree to which data collected is similar to that collected in other countries.

Data-collection instrument—the means by which information is collected.

Decision rule—a rule that allows the researcher to determine whether or not to accept or reject the null hypothesis.

De-duplication—the procedure used to take out information, often from a sampling frame, which is already present. Arises where respondents belong to more than one membership list, for example.

Degrees of freedom—the number of independent variables.

Derived demand—where the demand for goods and services is based on the contribution that those goods and services can make to the production of other goods and services for sale to businesses or consumers, that demand can be said to be derived.

Descriptive design—a technique which provides a summary of the data collected when the hypotheses are confirmatory in nature.

Desk research—the procedures used to collect primary data.

Dichotomous questions—questions that require choosing between two alternative answers, e.g., yes/no, male/female.

Direct demand—where the demand for goods and services is for consumption for personal satisfaction, that demand is said to be direct.

Direct questioning—a form of questioning where the aims of the question asked are clear to the respondent.

Discriminant analysis—a statistical technique for developing a set of independent variables which classify people or objects into one or more groups. Often used in positioning studies.

Distribution list—list of people to whom e-mail messages are sent in bulk.

Door-to-door interviewing—a form of interviewing method where the interviewer questions the respondent in-home.

Double-barrelled questions—when one question incorporates more than one request for information and requires more than one choice of answer because the question is improperly constructed. For example, 'how often do you purchase *and* use Product X?'

Double sampling—when an element is sampled more than once to provide more information about specific elements of particular importance.

DRTV—direct response television—a form of advertising campaign where the organization's contact details are provided to encourage members of the audience to purchase goods and services directly from the company.

Duplication—when information is repeated more than once.

E-mail—digital text message that is exchanged between individuals over the Internet.

E-mail address—a destination on the Internet to which individual e-mail messages may be sent.

Equivalence—the degree of similarity between two or more objects.

ERNIE—Electronic Random Number Indicating Equipment.

ESOMAR—European Society for Opinion and Marketing Research, founded in 1948.

Expected value—the value obtained by multiplying each consequence occurring by the probability of its occurrence.

Experience survey—a type of survey used to gain insights from professional people in a specific industry.

Experimentation—research procedures used to determine the relationship between independent and dependent variables.

Exploratory design—a technique which generates ideas when the hypotheses are vague or ill-defined.

Exploratory test—a test of significance, used when there is no prior knowledge of what is expected, which is designed to confirm whether the observed data indicate a difference from that expected.

External reliability—In order to determine how reliable the data is, researchers might conduct the same research over two or more time periods to determine the consistency of the data.

External sources—a marketing data source found outside the organization. These include syndicated research reports, external marketing research agency reports, government reports and statistics, publications, and other library sources.

Extranet—an extended form of an Intranet, which provides access to selected external partners.

Face validity—the use of the researcher's subjective judgement to determine whether an instrument is really measuring what it is supposed to measure. Also referred to as content validity.

File transfer—the exchange of files between computers connected to the Internet.

Fixed nodes—a term used to denote the codes used in NUDIST computer software application for coding information during qualitative analysis. Fixed nodes are differentiated from free nodes because the researcher has determined that there is a relationship between two or more free nodes.

Focus group—a group discussion on a series of topics introduced by the moderator where the group members are encouraged to express their own views on each topic and to elaborate or react to each other's views.

Free nodes—a term used to denote the codes used in NUDIST computer software application for coding information during qualitative analysis. Free nodes are data groupings coded without connection to other data groupings.

Frequencies—a measure of how often a particular measurement is repeated.

Frequency distribution—a report of the number of responses that question has received.

F-**statistic**—a statistic used in the analysis of variance (ANOVA) test for differences between groups.

Functional equivalence—functional equivalence relates to whether a concept has the same function in different countries.

Funnel technique—where the discussion is conducted initially at the broadest possible level and slowly narrowed down. In this method, the interviewer has a list of general points that need to be covered.

Generalizability—extent to which patterns in the data in the sample portray patterns in the population.

Graphic scale—a continuous scale that uses pictorial images to portray specific points along the continuum. An example might include simple pictures of a face depicting different moods of the respondent, i.e., happiness to unhappiness.

Group discussions—when 8–12 people are grouped together to discuss specific issues related to the research problem for between 1–3 hours. Also called a focus group.

Group dynamics—the interrelationships between respondents and the moderator, the respondents themselves, the moderator and the respondents and the respondents and the moderator during a focus group constitute group dynamics.

Grouped data—raw data classified into different classes.

Hidden issue questioning—when indirect questions are asked of the respondents and the researchers' information requirements are not immediately obvious to the respondent.

HTML—hypertext mark-up language—used to create hypertext documents for use on the World Wide Web.

Hypothesis—a statement that the researcher is making about characteristics of the population of interest.

Hypothesis testing—a procedure used to determine whether the null hypothesis should be accepted or not, based by comparing the sample statistic with the population parameter.

IMRA—Industrial Marketing Research Association.

Inability error—where the respondent cannot answer a specific question either because they cannot understand it or because they are inhibited in answering the question, inability error arises.

In-depth interview—a qualitative research method designed to explore the hidden feelings, values and motivations of the respondents using a face-to-face interview with the researcher.

Indirect questioning—with this form of questioning, the respondent tends to be asked about other people's behaviour or opinions of how other people might respond under certain circumstances.

Industrial market—a market for goods and services composed of industrial firms and government agencies rather than individual consumers.

In-house research—where research is conducted within the organization, probably by their own marketing research manager and team, rather than sub-contracting the whole of the research project to an agency.

Instrument clusters—the automotive industry term for the collection of indicators that provide the driver with important information, including the speedometer, the tachometer and the temperature gauge.

Internal reliability—where responses are divided into subsets and those sets are tested independently. The sets of results are then correlated to see whether they match.

Internal sources—a marketing data source found within the organization. These include customer profiles, sales and accounting records.

International environment—this comprises marketing, government, legal, economic, structural, technological and socio-cultural environments.

Internet—a global interconnected network of computers and computer networks connected by publicly accessible communication systems.

Interquartile range—a range between the first and third quartiles. It provides an illustration of the spread of the data; 50% of the values within a dataset will lie in this range.

Interval estimate—the estimation of the interval in which an unknown population characteristic is judged to lie, for a given level of confidence.

Interval scale—an ordered scale in which the difference between the measurements is a meaningful quantity that does not involve a true zero point.

Interviewing methods—includes mail, personal and telephone forms of questioning and their computer-assisted derivatives CAPI, CASI, CAWI, and CATI.

Intranet—an internal or private form of the Internet, usually restricted to members of a particular organization.

ISIC—International Standard Industrial Classification of the United Nations.

ISP—Internet service provider—the company that provides access to the Internet for individuals or organizations.

iTV—interactive television—a television system, mainly offered by cable companies, that allows users to purchase products and services, read content and play games.

Judgemental sampling—a non-probability sampling method in which an expert uses judgement to identify representative samples.

Laddering—a method used whereby questioning proceeds from product characteristics to user characteristics.

Likert scale—a scale developed by Rensis Likert in which the subject must indicate the degree of agreement or disagreement with a variety of statements related to the attitude object and which are then summed over all statements to provide a total score.

Mail interviewing—a form of questioning where the instrument used to collect the data is a questionnaire is delivered through the postal service.

Mail survey—the mailing of questionnaires and their return through the postal service by designated respondents.

Mall intercept interview—where respondents are interviewed within a shopping precinct or in a town centre.

Management problem—a statement outlining the situation faced by the company that requires further investigation.

Management problem definition—a process of understanding the causes and predicting the consequences of problems or processes when exploring the size and nature of opportunities.

Market potential—the possible share of the market that can reasonably be attained by a particular organization within a particular market.

Market research question—the statement(s) of specific information required for progress toward achievement of the marketing research purpose.

Market Research Society—UK-based professional association for market researchers.

Market segmentation—the development and pursuit of marketing programmes directed at sub-groups or segments of the population that the organization could possibly serve.

Marketing information systems—a system incorporating *ad hoc* and continuous market and marketing research surveys with secondary data and internal data sources for the purpose of marketing decision making.

Marketing research—the specification, gathering, analysing, and interpretation of information that links the organization with its environment.

Mean—the number obtained by summing all observations in a set and dividing by the number of observations.

Measurement—the assignment of numbers by rules to observations in order to reflect quantities of properties.

Measurement equivalence—deals with the methods and procedures used by the researcher to collect and categorize essential data and information from different sources. Particularly important in international marketing research.

Measurement error—error that occurs due to variations between the information sought by the researcher and the information generated by a particular procedure employed by the researcher.

Measures of dispersion—includes widely used measures such as standard deviation, variance, range, semi-interquartile range and interquartile range.

Measures of location—includes widely used measures such as mean, mode, median.

Median—a measure of location which splits the data into two equal halves, is not affected by extremes, and represents the middle value of a dataset.

Mode—a measure of location that represents the most frequently occurring measurement.

Moderated e-mail group—involves a moderator posting questions by e-mail to a small group of respondents, collating and summarizing their answers, and sending these to the group for comment. The process is repeated several times.

Moderator's outline—a list of topics to be addressed by the moderator in conducting a focus group.

Monadic test—a test for a single sample comparing the sample statistics with the population parameter.

MRO—market research organization.

Multichotomous questions—a question where there are more than two choices of answer but where a single response is required from the respondent.

Multi-dimensional scaling—set of techniques for developing perceptual maps.

Multiple fixed-response questions—a question where there are more than two choices of answer but where more than one response may be chosen by the respondent.

Mystery shopping—this form of research is usually aimed at determining the standard of customer service received by a customer. It allows organizations to measure the service performance of their own (or other's organizations') staff.

NACE (Nomenclatures par Activités Economiques)—the European Union's equivalent of ISIC.

NAICS—North American Industrial Classification System.

Netizen—someone who frequents the Internet.

Newsgroup—an Internet-based discussion group relating to a particular topic of interest. Participants write text that is read by other members of the public who have access to the newsgroup.

Nielson Retail Index—an index based on a retail-store audit conducted by AC Nielson for four major groups of stores: grocery products, drugs, mass merchandisers and alcoholic beverages.

Nominal—a measurement that assigns only an identification or label to a set of objects.

Non-parametric statistics—a branch of statistics dealing with the analysis of nominal and ordinal measurements.

Non-probability sample—a sample selected where the probability of selection of individual respondents is not known.

Non-probability sampling—any sampling method where the probability of selection of the population elements' inclusion is unknown.

Non-response error—error that occurs due to non-participation of some eligible respondents in the study. This could be due to unwillingness or inability of the respondents to participate in the study, or the inability of the interviewer to contact the respondents.

Normal distribution—a bell-shaped distribution of measurements or estimates providing probabilities of chance occurrences, usually used in hypothesis testing for large samples.

NUDIST (Non-Numerical Unstructured Data Indexing Searching and Theorizing)—a computer software application used to investigate the nature of qualitative data.

Null hypothesis—a negative statement indicating the belief in the nature and level of possible difference between the estimate and the parameter.

Observational studies—a study where behaviours of interest are recorded. Examples include mystery shopping and mass transit studies.

Obsolescence—where data is considered to be out of date, and therefore of little or no use to the existing research question.

Off-line—not on-line.

Omnibus survey—a regularly scheduled personal interview survey comprising questions from several set platforms.

One-tailed test—a test of significance where the expected difference is uni-directional, e.g., sales training increases sales, or sales training decreases sales, but not both.

On-line—when a user is connected to the Internet (or some other interactive communication medium) they are said to be on-line.

Open questions—questions where the choice of response(s) is left to the individual.

Open to all method—involves collecting data where the sample is not specified. Usually referred to in Internet marketing research.

Optimum allocation—a method used to select sample size based on population size, population variance and unit cost of conducting investigation.

Ordinal—a measurement that ranks a set of objects.

Original equipment manufacturer (OEM)—companies that buy components to incorporate them into new products that will then be sold to users, e.g., Dell is an original equipment manufacturer in the personal computer industry and Ford is an original equipment manufacturer in the automotive industry. Often shortened to OEM.

Paired test—a test based on using the same respondents in two different situations to measure the relative differences.

Panel studies—a study which uses information collected from a fixed group of respondents (panel) over a period of time.

Parallel translation—where a research instrument, usually a questionnaire, is translated using teams of translators fluent in at least two languages until a final version is agreed upon.

Parameter—a value associated with the population.

Parametric statistics—a branch of statistics dealing with the analysis of interval and ratio measurements.

Participant observation—when the researcher monitors public chat and discussion groups in which they are taking part.

Pearson's product moment correlation—a coefficient of relationship between two metric variables.

Perceptual map—a spatial representation of the perceived relationships among objects in a set, where objects could be brands, products or services.

Personal interview—face-to-face interview where the respondent is questioned by the interviewer.

Pictorial construction—a projective technique used whereby respondents are asked to draw pictures or complete partly drawn pictures to uncover underlying motivations, opinions and attitudes.

Pilot study—an exploratory study conducted prior to a descriptive study, which allows relatively unstructured data collection procedures to be used.

Pop-up questionnaire—a small window that appears while visiting a website asking the visitor questions.

Positioning—a marketing term used to denote customers or consumers' perceptions of a product, service or company *vis-à-vis* their competitors.

Predictive validity—is used to determine the extent to which a variable measures a phenomenon by comparison with a proxy measure.

Primary data—data that is collected for the first time and has been specifically collected and assembled for the current research problem.

Primary research—a technique used to collect primary data.

Probability sampling—any sampling method where the probability of any population elements' inclusion is known and is greater than zero.

Projective techniques—a set of presentation methods of ambiguous, unstructured objects, activities or persons for which a respondent is asked to give interpretation and find meaning. The more ambiguous the stimulus, the more the respondent has to project him- or herself into the task, thereby revealing hidden feelings, values and needs; examples are word association, role-playing, pictorial construction and completion tests.

Proportional allocation—a method used whereby the sample is proportionately divided into sub-samples based on population size.

Qualitative research—a form of exploratory research involving small samples and non-structured data-collection procedures, usually conducted to identify hypotheses for later testing in quantitative research. The most popular examples include in-depth interviews, focus groups and projective techniques.

Quantitative research—research designed to elicit responses to predetermined, standardized questions from a large number of respondents involving the statistical analysis of the responses.

Questioning error—error arising when the interviewer reads out a question wrongly or perhaps stresses a section of a sentence in a way that connotes a meaning that the researcher did not intend.

Quota sample—a non-probability sampling method that is constrained to include a minimum from each specified sub-group (strata) in the population.

Random error—measurement error due to changing aspects of the respondent or measurement situation.

Range—a measure of the degree of dispersion of the data.

Ranking scales—a scale in which the respondent is required to order, in increasing or decreasing order of importance, a set of objectives with regard to a set of common criteria, on a discrete scale.

Rating scales—a scale in which the respondent is required to rate, often by allocating points to illustrate increasing or decreasing order of importance, to a set of common criteria, on a continuous scale.

Ratio scales—a measurement that has a true meaningful zero point allowing for the specification of absolute magnitudes of objects.

Recording error—error that occurs due to improper recording of respondents' answers.

Relevance—a criterion used to judge whether a marketing research study acts to support strategic and tactical planning activities.

Reliability—the extent to which the data generated would be replicated in a repeat study, i.e., the random error component of a measurement instrument.

Representativeness—the degree to which particular characteristics of the sample elements replicate those same characteristics of the population elements. It is usually enhanced by using quota sampling and stratified sampling procedures.

Research brief—a formal document prepared by the client organization and submitted to the MRO (or marketing research department when conducted in-company). It outlines the management problem.

Research design—encompasses determining how the different components (i.e., sampling, research objectives, interviewing method, data analysis, question(-naire) design, and research type and methods) of a research project should interrelate.

Research process—the process followed in providing relevant information designed to solve a management problem involving different stages comprising problem definition, data collection, data analysis and interpretation, and report preparation and presentation.

Research proposal—a formal document prepared by the MRO (or marketing research department when research is conducted in-company) and submitted to the potential client to outline the procedures that will be used to collect the necessary information.

Retail audits—panel data collected for retailers providing market and competitor information.

Role-playing—a projective technique where the respondent is asked to assume the role of another person, in order to provide the researcher with an understanding of their underlying motivations, opinions and attitudes.

Sample—a subset of elements from a population.

Sample estimates—a sample value corresponding to a parameter used in hypothesis testing.

Sampling equivalence—deals with the question of identifying and operationalizing two comparable populations and selecting samples that are representative of other populations and that are comparable across countries.

Sampling error—error associated with the method of sample selection.

Sampling frame—a listing of population members that is used to create a sample. Examples include membership lists, telephone directories and industry directories.

Sampling unit—any type of element that makes up a sample such as people, shops and products.

Scatter diagram—a two-dimensional plot of two variables.

Search engine—a system that allows Internet users to search for clickable links to websites of their interests.

Secondary data—data that has been previously collected for a purpose other than the current research situation.

Secondary research—a technique used to collect secondary data. The process is often referred to as desk research.

Segmentation study—a study used to divide heterogeneous markets into homogeneous sub-groups along specific customer/consumer and/or product-related characteristics.

Semantic differential scale—a scale in which the respondent is asked to rate each attitude object in turn on a five- or seven-point rating scale bounded at each end by bipolar objectives or phrases.

Semi-structured interview—a type of in-depth interview in which the interview attempts to cover a specific list of topics or sub-areas.

Sequential sampling—a sampling method in which an initial modest sample is taken and analysed, following which, based on the results, a decision is made regarding the necessity of conducting further sampling and analysis. This continues until sufficient data are collected. Examples include tracking polls.

Short-listing—a procedure used by an organization when commissioning research to select a small group of MROs, which are then used for final selection.

Significance level—the probability of obtaining the evidence that the null hypothesis was true.

Simple random sampling—a sampling method in which each population member has an equal chance of being selected.

Snowball sampling—a judgemental sampling method in which each respondent is asked to identify one or more of the sample members.

Spam—unsolicited e-mail (hence spammer and spamming).

Spearman's rank correlation—a coefficient of relationship between two ordinal variables.

Split-half reliability—a procedure used to indicate the reliability of the data collected by determining the consistency between two sets of data from one sample.

SPSS (Statistical Package for the Social Sciences)—a computer software application extensively used for the analysis of quantitative data.

Standard deviation—the square root of the variance. It is a measure of the degree of dispersion of the data.

Standard error of estimate—the square root of the variance of the sample estimate. It indicates the degree of sampling error.

Standard industrial classification (SIC)—a uniform numbering system developed by the government for classifying industrial establishments according to their economic activities.

Standardization—the procedure associated with transforming a measurement such that it has zero mean and unit variance for easy comparison of values.

Statistic—a value associated with a sample.

Strata—a specified sub-group. Often referred to specifically in sampling, e.g., stratified sampling and quota sampling.

Stratified random sampling—a sampling method that uses pertinent characteristics to design homogeneous sub-groups from which a representative sample is drawn.

Street interview—a method of data collection where respondents are selected for interview in the street.

Student's *t*-distribution—a distribution for a sample selected randomly with a sample size of less than 30.

Subjective sample—a sample drawn using the interviewer or researcher's judgement.

Superego—a term originally coined by Sigmund Freud to denote the ethical component of an individual's personality. This is often termed conscience.

Surfing—visiting a sequence or collection of Web documents and/or sites.

Survey method—a method of data collection, such as a telephone or personal interview, a mail survey or any combination thereof.

Symbolic analysis—a technique used where the symbolic meaning of products or services is determined by asking respondents what they would do if they could no longer use that particular product or service.

Syndicated data—information collected from published studies designed and conducted by firms such as AC Nielsen.

Syndicated research—ongoing studies that are conducted continuously or regularly on a number of different topics or for a number of different firms and then sold back to the firms for use in decision making.

Telephone interviewing—a method of data collection that uses the telephone as the primary data-collection instrument.

Telnet—an Internet service that enables people to log on to remote computers.

Test-retest method—a method of data analysis which allows the researcher to determine external reliability by collecting data from the same sample over time.

Test statistic—sample value used in hypothesis testing, which when compared with the critical value allows the researcher to decide whether to reject the null hypothesis.

Text unit—the smallest denomination of text that is used by computer software applications in qualitative analysis.

Thematic Apperception Test (TAT)—a projective technique where respondents are asked to comment on, or construct a story about, pictorial images.

Tracking studies—on-going surveys, to identify changes in consumer/customer characteristics whereby data is analysed by comparing data over time, usually from different sets of respondents.

Transcript—a verbatim report of an interview or focus group.

Translation equivalence—the degree to which the meaning in one language is represented in another in translation.

t-**test**—a test of difference used for small randomly selected samples with a sample size of less than 30.

Two-tailed test—a test of significance where the expected difference is bi-directional, e.g., sales training increases **or** decreases sales, but not sales training decreases sales, or sales training increases sales.

Type I error—error associated with rejecting a true hypothesis, usually denoted by α.

Type II error—error associated with accepting a false hypothesis, usually denoted by β.

URL—uniform resource locator—the 'address' on the Internet where a Web document may be found.

Usenet—an Internet service that hosts discussion groups ('newsgroups').

User forum—location on the Internet where visitors can exchange messages and views.

Validity—the ability of a measurement instrument to describe the phenomenon it is attempting to measure.

Variance—a measure of dispersion based on the degree to which elements of a sample or population differ from the average value.

Verbal rating scale—allows respondents to express their degree of favourability with a particular concept.

VOIP (Voice-over-Internet-Protocol)—the set of protocols that allow users to communicate voice data over the Internet at a very low cost.

Web—the World Wide Web (or WWW)—the network of interconnected documents hosted globally by the Internet.

Web document—a document containing text, graphics and/or sound (i.e., multi-media) and embedded links to other documents.

Web form—a set of interactive elements in a Web document that enables a visitor to enter and submit information to the website.

Website—a collection of Web documents hosted on a particular computer connected to the Internet.

Word association—a projective technique where respondents are asked to think of words that they commonly associate with products, services, or companies in order to uncover their underlying motivations, opinions and attitudes.

Yates' correction—a correction applied to discrete observations when the actual distribution is continuous.

Z-test—a test of difference used for large randomly selected samples with a sample size of 30 or more.

Index